Japan as a Low-Crime Nation

Japan as a Low-Crime Nation

Dag Leonardsen
Lillehammer University College, Norway

First published 2004 by
PALGRAVE MACMILLAN
Houndmills, Basingstoke, Hampshire RG21 6XS and
175 Fifth Avenue, New York, N.Y. 10010
Companies and representatives throughout the world

PALGRAVE MACMILLAN is the global academic imprint of the Palgrave
Macmillan division of St. Martin's Press, LLC and of Palgrave Macmillan Ltd.
Macmillan® is a registered trademark in the United States, United Kingdom
and other countries. Palgrave is a registered trademark in the European
Union and other countries.

ISBN 1–4039–4111–4 hardback

This book is printed on paper suitable for recycling and made from fully
managed and sustained forest sources.

A catalogue record for this book is available from the British Library.

Library of Congress Cataloging-in-Publication Data
Leonardsen, Dag.
    Japan as a low-crime nation / by Dag Leonardsen.
        p.   cm.
    Includes bibliographical references and index.
    ISBN 1–4039–4111–4
    1. Crime—Japan. 2. Crime—Sociological aspects—Japan. 3. Social
values—Japan. 4. Japan—Social conditions—1945– I. Title.

HV7113.5.L46 2004
364.952—dc22   2004042840

10   9   8   7   6   5   4   3   2   1
13   12   11   10   09   08   07   06   05   04

To Maja

Contents

List of Figures and Tables

Figures

Tables

Preface

In February, 1998 I visited the Japanese town of Nagano (360,000 inhabitants), to watch the XV Olympic Winter Games. Towards the end of the Games I interviewed the police about the impact on crime of such a big event. I was surprised to hear that two days before the closing ceremony only two people had been arrested (one Norwegian and one Swedish: both were journalists). With the exception of these minor episodes due to the consumption of too much sake (Japanese wine) by the Nordic journalists, the police had not disclosed any serious infringements. Despite the huge influx of people, and 14 days of heavy partying, this extraordinary situation had apparently not been exploited for criminal purposes (according to the police). My own impression confirmed the police report. At least from a tourist's point of view, the streets felt very safe.

I had the same impression from the other Japanese towns I visited. What I had read in my tourist guidebook,[1] and what I continually was told by people, matched closely my own observations. Walking the streets of Tokyo at midnight I was never worried about crime. And, being a very absent-minded person, I experienced that my camera, my bag, and a jacket that I had at different times left behind me, were shortly afterwards brought back to me.

My story does not end here. My first meeting with Japan should not only be told with words of *absence*. The absence of street crimes should be supplemented with a positive story of the *presence* of friendliness and hospitality.[2] From the very minute I landed at Narita Airport in Tokyo I was taken care of in a most friendly way. Not only my hosts, but also people in general were much more obliging and helpful than I have experienced in any Western country. Whenever I found myself hesitating at a street corner, unsure where to go, I was immediately supported and guided by friendly members of the public. Travelling back to Norway, I experienced a minor cultural shock on changing (in Amsterdam) from Japan Airlines to a Western company. When I had checked in with Japan Airlines for my return flight I had been lucky to avoid any queuing. Nevertheless, I was met with a friendly smile and a comment about 'sorry to keep you waiting'! In other words: absence of street crime seemed to go in tandem with the presence of a general friendliness.

For a sociologist, experiences like this are a bit surprising. They do not match with our textbook view of the world! Big cities (like Tokyo) and social turbulence (like the Olympics in Nagano) should be synonymous with high crime rates. If there are any nomothetic relationships documented in the social sciences, the link between urbanization, rapid social change, and crime is one of them. Also, an urban lifestyle should be synonymous with a blasé, reserved, aloof, sophisticated, unconcerned, cold and rational way of behaving. Naturally, my curiosity was triggered by my Japanese experience. If my observations were valid, how could it be that a modernized and urbanized country like Japan had managed to avoid some of the devils of modernization?

Back in Norway I noticed with surprise that I started scrutinizing *my own behaviour* in Japan. This was also a new experience. Staying in Japan for only a relatively short time (altogether four visits, each lasting some two weeks) had made me wonder about the qualities of Japanese culture. Even more important, my visits had given me a mirror to place against my own culture and in which to study my own way of behaving. As I started reading my first books about Japan, I became more and more embarrassed about my own behaviour during my stay. As a matter of fact, I had a feeling of *shame*. During my stay I had obviously lacked sensitivity, lacked alertness, been too talkative, too direct and inquisitive in my behaviour. I had used my mouth much more than my eyes and ears, I had been too much in search of rational and logical answers instead of being perceptive of ambiguous observations and formulations. Back in Norway my superego turned on me and invited a new interest in the sociological tradition called symbolic interactionism. How had my own 'presentation of the self in everyday life' been during my stay in Japan? Had I mis-managed my identity? Had I been able to reach behind the front stage of Japan? Had I been able to interpret the *meaning* of the many performative aspects of Japanese culture? Had I played my own role on the Japanese stage as a humble stranger, or had I (unconsciously) given myself a prominent role? The answer was obvious. On my first night, I had not paid much attention to the personal cards I received. I had put them carelessly into my pocket instead of having a special case for cards. In Japan one does not put the signifier of a human being into a dirty pocket! I had also helped myself to the drinks that were served instead of waiting until somebody cared for me. At the official tea ceremony to which I was invited, I was unable to read the subtle meaning of this performance and, consequently, made some mistakes. And during my two-hour ride with my colleague, I probably talked much more than 50 per cent of the time. Fortunately, I brought my hosts some presents from Norway. But too late I discovered that the wrapping of my presents was more important than the content. Just handing over an unwrapped bottle of Norwegian Aqua Vita represented another breach of Japanese etiquette.

Let me end this masochistic scrutiny of my own performance in Japan (which could have been extended considerably) and return to a more analytical perspective. If my observations concerning little crime in Japan are valid – how should this phenomenon be interpreted? And if my description of Japanese society as a kind of 'belly communicating culture' could be defended – are there any links between this observation and the apparently low crime rates in this country? To the extent that Japan might be described as a *'defensive shame culture'* – are there any links between such a cultural characteristic and little crime? These questions are the main challenges I try to address in this book. It is a book about crime and (Japanese) culture. Nonetheless, this topic should be of interest in a broader perspective.

For more than 40 years Western scholars as well as politicians have discussed policies to prevent crime. Apparently, crime rates have increased in proportion to the accumulating criminological knowledge and in proportion to the policies of deterrence. The more the social sciences can teach us about causes of social and individual malfunctioning, the worse the figures of misery depicting human existence seem to have become. It has even been argued that the study of crime has contributed to a debilitating social response to crime, rather than the opposite. From this, it is tempting to conclude that, until now, the criminological stock of knowledge has either not been applied/applicable, or – worse – it has been quite simply wrong and – consequently – dysfunctional! The confidence that the social sciences will one day come up with some kind of remedial social engineering knowledge seems to be vanishing. However, the case of Japan might hide the missing link in the criminological stock of knowledge. It might be that crime prevention is not so much a question of policies of social engineering, but more a question of a holistic cultural analysis. For some years 'Asian values' have been the focus of economic and organizational studies. The Japanese economic wonder (until 1990!) has been explained with reference to specific cultural characteristics in this society. Should the same perspective be applied to the question of crime prevention? This is the main underlying question behind my interest in Japan, Japanese crime and Japanese culture. Could Japan teach Western societies a lesson on curbing crime?

The work presented in this book was prepared while I took my sabbatical in 2000–2001. During that year I had the chance to do my research and to teach at the Institute of Criminology, Victoria University, New Zealand. I would like to express my gratitude to my own institution, Lillehammer

University College, for giving me this chance to do my research and for economic support. Next, I appreciate the chance I was given by Allison Morris and John Pratt to stay at the Institute of Criminology, Victoria University. Most of the chapters in this book were presented to my students at the 'honours course'. Discussion with students and teachers at the Institute of Criminology provided important feedback and further stimulation in my work. I express special gratitude to Willem deLint, not only for being a very patient and stimulating commentator, but also for helping me translating my 'Englichian' (a strange combination of English and Norwegian) into a readable manuscript. His contribution to this book is invaluable. I am very grateful to Reece Walters and Trevor Bradley at the Institute of Criminology for challenging me both professionally and as a soccer player.

Japan has appeared to me to be a very friendly country and this is not least due to the hospitality shown by two Japanese colleagues: Hirsohi Komuku and Kazunori Matsumura. During my four stays in Japan they have on each occasion assisted me in the most obliging way, and my daughter, Maja, is proud of knowing that 'she has a home in Japan'. Without the assistance of these two gentlemen and their gentle wives I would probably have been lost. Monica Nakamura deserves the same thanksgiving. She has been invaluable to me, both as a host and as a source of information. When De Mente writes about Japanese people that 'they routinely go beyond expectations in their efforts to help visitors enjoy their country', these people I have mentioned can stand as typical representatives of this friendliness. Fujimoto Tetsuya has been very kind in permitting the re-print of two of his graphs from his book *Crime Problems in Japan* (Chuo University Press, Tokyo, 1994). Also, I would like to express my gratitude to Takeshi Koyanagi, Deputy Director at the Research and Training Institute, the Ministry of Justice, for permission to reproduce figures from the White Paper on Crime. Kunihiko Sakai, Toru Miura, Kei Someda and Tomoko Akane, all employed by the United Nations Asia and Far East Institute for the Prevention of Crime and the Treatment of Offenders were very helpful during my stay at the Institute. Together with Hirsohi Tsutomi and Yoko Hosoi they have been very supportive of my search for data and knowledge of Japanese society.

During my work on this project I have received travel and project grants from the Norwegian Non-Fiction Writers and Translators Association (NFF) and a travel grant from the Scandinavia–Japan Sasakawa Foundation. This made it possible to travel both to New Zealand and to Japan, and I am very grateful for this support. I have also received travel grants and economic support from my own college.

To me, Japan has represented an extraordinary experience. I have never had the opportunity not only of learning so much about a specific culture, but also of learning even more about my *own* culture. People need mirrors to see themselves. I do hope this book will function as such a mirror for all my readers.

Dag Leonardsen
January 2004

Part I

Theoretical and Methodological Clarifications

1
The Western Welfare Paradox. Or: Why is Japan an Interesting Case?

The negative case of Japan

Textbooks on methodology tell us to pay extra attention to reports that seem to contradict established knowledge (the so-called negative cases). These are the cases that can give us interesting new knowledge. In criminological research Japan has for a long time been regarded as such a 'negative case'. In the period 1950–90, while most Western countries[1] experienced an increase in crime, Japan's registered crime decreased or stabilised (see Chapter 2). In 1989 Japan experienced 1.3 robberies per 100,000 population compared with 48.6 for West Germany, 65.8 for Britain, and 233.0 for the US. Regarding murder, the figures show 1.1 per 100,000 in Japan, 3.9 for West Germany, 9.1 for Britain, and 8.7 for the US (Japan Government). In this book I intend to answer the following question: If the figures concerning registered crime are valid (and in this book *I restrict myself to the mentioned period*), why is it that Japan deviates from the general tendency in the West?[2]

It is 'established knowledge' that increasing crime[3] is positively associated with rapid social change and urbanization. Empirical studies of the urbanization process in the 1920s and from the 1960–80s have largely confirmed this hypothesis of classical sociology. However, Japan, having experienced an extremely rapid urbanization process since the early 1950s, does not fit in. Consequently, the negative case of Japan might be an interesting lesson on the crime problem. What is it about Japanese society that (apparently) makes it deviate from the general pattern?

The Western welfare paradox

> It is in many ways a paradox that, in welfare societies with a high standard of living and almost full employment, we have to spend more and more money on welfare expenditures. I think this situation appears especially paradoxical for the elder generation from the working-class movement who thought that the abolishment of mass poverty, better living conditions and better educational and working life conditions would make much of the social policy superfluous. However, it was not that simple (Norwegian Minister of Health and Social Security in 1969, in Leonardsen, 1993, p. 61).

It is important to begin the study of the negative case of Japan by locating it in broad context. Indeed, as I hope to show, the answer to the problem depends on allowing for the examination of social, economic and cultural indicators. To begin, the study of crime in Japan might be contextualized within the debate on what I call the '*Western Welfare Paradox*'. Since this represents my primary motivation for finding Japan to be an especially interesting case, let me explain a bit further.

The fruits of modernity are of two kinds. We can readily see that modernity has ushered in widespread access to material goods, physical well-being, social welfare and quality of life indicators. The list of blessings is extensive and well known. On the other hand, modernity has also given us 'damaged fruits'. We find extensive unemployment and poverty in the midst of affluence. Accompanying elaborate systems of social welfare and extensive interventionist programmes we find increasing rates of divorce, suicide, abuse, drug addiction and crime.[4] The Western Welfare Paradox, or what has also been called 'the sociology of worry', is about the unexpected, negative social impacts of progress. It is about co-variation between social problems and money spent on solving them.

In the period between the mid-1960s and the early 1990s, it appears that an increase in both private affluence as well as public welfare was mirrored by a decrease in important indexes of social integration. According to Fukuyama and other 'worried social scientists', Western societies experienced manifold social problems and seriously deteriorating social conditions. This period was marked by crime and social disorder, spiralling divorce figures, out-of-wedlock childbearing, and the decline of fertility and kinship as a social institution. Even more troubling, the more the Western welfare states invested in preventive programmes to avoid different types of social problems, the more problems they seemed to experience. After at least three decades with an actively preventive governmental policy, we are witnessing what Offe (1984) has labelled 'the crisis of crisis management'. Western democracies, continually striving to realize individual rights and liberties, have sought Rousseau, but have found Hobbes (to use Dahrendorf's (1985) expression). Discussing Great Britain, Hutton (1995) maintains that we are experiencing 'an increase in anxiety, dread of the future and communal breakdown. The impact is nearly universal' (p. 197). Fukuyama (1995) puts it this way: 'At the "end of history" there is a widespread acknowledgement that in post-industrial societies further improvement cannot be achieved through ambitious social engineering. We no longer have realistic hopes that we can create "the great society" through large government programs' (p. 4). As a result, 'trust and confidence in institutions [has gone] into a deep, forty-year decline' (Fukuyama, 2000, p. 4–5).

Jock Young (1999) talks ironically about the many varieties of panacea that have been on offer to solve the crime problem: zero-tolerance, neighbourhood watch, CCTV, nutritional supplements, treatment of offender dyslexia or even psychodrama. 'Take your pick, the fashions come and go' (p. 130), Young declares. Unfortunately, they all suffer from two fallacies. One is what Young calls 'the cosmetic fallacy' which conceives of crime as a superficial problem that can be dealt with without any profound changes in society at large. The other is the fallacy that regards the social world as a simple structure in which crimes, suicides, etc. can be related to narrowly delineated changes in other parts of the structure. However, these approaches will not have a chance to tackle the root causes of crime. Gradually, the state seems to have abdicated as a guarantor of law and order.[5]

Although these reports are missing nuances, this reading of events is a backdrop against which Japanese society appears to be an interesting negative case. In Japan, rapid social change has taken place without (at least apparently so) some of the 'social ills' registered in Western countries (especially crime, drug addiction and divorce). And this is so even if Japanese social spending in 1990 amounted to only the average OECD level of the 1960s (12–14 per cent; see Esping-Andersen, 1997, Gould, 1993, p. 12). This challenges the viewpoint that the public sector, via informed interventionist programmes, is a prerequisite to avoid modern social problems. And it triggers a question about the role of cultural and moral values in preventing social disintegration.

For governments following more robust social democratic practices the experience of the 'welfare paradox' has been especially acute. Adopting a Keynesian economic philosophy after the Second World War, they expected that government intervention would at least prevent the worst expectations of discontent and mal-adaptation associated with non-egalitarian society. A re-distributive economic policy together with a welfare security system was expected to create the necessary foundation for both economic development and social harmony. When this turned out to be too optimistic, those governments developed an extensive repertoire of planning instruments that made it possible to target their measures in a more direct way. With the support of an expanding profession of social scientists, governments (not only social democratic!) embarked on a huge variety of 'preventive programmes', be it within the domain of physical planning, health, education, family, drugs or crime. The implicit working idea for this was the presumption that the 'soft' social sciences (like social psychology, sociology and political science) could attain what the economists had attained from the mid-1930s. If the economists had been able to bring back harmony to the economy, why not expect the same contribution from the new experts on social integration? This was the basic presumption in the social engineering project. The Norwegian Prime Minister Trygve Bratteli (Leonardsen, 1981) gave a good illustration of this way of thinking when he claimed:

> Along with the comprehensive social change and innovation in society we also have to direct our efforts towards the science about the human being and its environment, about the health of the body and the mind, about contact and life together, about the society of human beings and their history. In every way we shall accept the help that can be offered from science (p. 18).

Unfortunately, the results did not match the intentions. The social sciences appeared to be unable to bring forward Keynesian solutions for the socio-cultural system. There seemed to be no 'social equivalents' to the economic interventionist programmes. Even though public administrations in Western countries were supplied with a wide range of social science expertise, they did not come up with instrumental knowledge that demonstrated any significant effect on the developing social problems. As a result, the stage was set for the postmodern tableau: denial of 'the power of reason' and the acknowledgement that there is no 'refuge from scepticism' (Taylor-Gooby, 1997, p. 177).

The failure of sociology?

Perhaps the failure of the take-up of social scientific solutions in policy solutions can partly be explained by the ambivalent status of social science disciplines themselves in the context of late-modern anxieties. The impotence at the *political–administrative level* reflected a corresponding impotence at the *professional, social science* level. To take sociology as an illustration, in 'The Death of the Sociology of Deviance' Bendle (1999) argues that a number of recent works suggest that the sociology of deviance and criminology, and sociology in general, have entered into a state of crisis. This crisis, he argues, is broad in scope: one has not succeeded in developing theories that illuminate relevant problems, and one has not been able to suggest relevant policy responses. Consequently, the traditional forms of state interventionism have become discredited as the central strategy in confronting crime and social deviance. The social sciences have not been able to deliver the goods that would empower confused and hesitating governments. Whatever knowledge these sciences possess, has been of little help in implementing adequate preventive measures.[6] Instead, neo-liberalism has made a strong impact, both within the social sciences and within the public management thinking (cf. the increasing abandonment of the 'social' as a viable category and the idea of the decentred state).

Braithwaite (1989) has taken the argument one step further. Not only has crime increased in most Western countries despite a strong commitment to policies and programmes designed to reduce crime, but what Braithwaite regards as even worse is that criminology itself might be regarded as a *cause* of crime. He suggests that, 'the professionalization of the study of crime is part of a wider societal movement which has tended further to debilitate the social response to crime, rather than strengthen it' (p. 5). Even though I think Braithwaite is exaggerating his point, his argument shows to what extent (some) criminologists have given up the belief in the role as purveyors of professional social engineering knowledge. For those who believed we still lived in the era of Enlightenment, and for those who believed that human rationality would bring humanity forward in a never-ending social progress, this was a depressing message. The 'soft' social sciences (contrary to economy) seem to have little to offer the intelligent administration of society, and what little they can offer might even have a negative effect, making bad worse. Illich *et al.* (1977) expressed this very eloquently in a book with the telling title *Disabling professions*.

The end of the state?

This unexpected and frustrating situation at the end of the twentieth century inspired a vast amount of 'what went wrong' literature.[7] The sociology of worry seemed to be fertile soil for the production of a continuous crop of depressing stories about social disruption and social impotence. More than one hundred years after Durkheim wrote on this topic, his concept of 'anomie' received new interest. Hutton (1995) gives this brief characterisation of the situation: 'Not merely the economy but society has been "marketised" with an increase in anxiety, dread of the future and communal breakdown. The impact is nearly universal' (p. 197). Jordan (1996), addressing the development of the new poverty in the West, expresses the same worry over social integration in these societies when he declares that, 'there is urgent concern to find a new cement for society' (p. 21). In a more popular way the general climate was summed up in the last edition in the twentieth century of the German journal *Die Zeit* (51/1999): '3.000 Jahre nach Moses, 2.000 Jahre nach Jesus: Wo ist die Moral?'

This general feeling of dissolution and lack of norms is most often linked to people's experience of crime and the fear of being victimized. There is little doubt that the crime problem, both as a matter of objective 'fact',[8] but even more powerfully as a matter of subjectively experienced *fear*, is increasingly a mental preoccupation among ordinary citizens (see Adler, 1983; Dahrendorf, 1985; Garland, 1996; Currie, 1989; Skolnick, 1995).[9] During the 1980s crime in many Western societies was increasingly regarded as a 'natural phenomenon', something one had to live with and adapt to. Not disregarding the important debate concerning the extent to which registered crime rates really mirror 'objective reality', Garland (1996) puts it convincingly:

> Despite the fact that crime has an uneven social distribution, and that high risk victimization is very much a pocketed, concentrated phenomenon, crime is widely experienced as a prominent fact of modern life. For most people, crime is no longer an aberration or an unexpected, abnormal event. Instead, the threat of crime has become a routine part of modern consciousness, an every day risk to be assessed and managed in much the same way that we deal with road traffic – another modern danger which has been routinized and 'normalized' over time. High rates of crime have gradually become a standard background feature of our lives – a taken for granted element of late modernity. Advertisements that tell us that 'a car

theft occurs every minute' make the point quite well – crime forms part of our daily environment, as constant and unremitting as time itself (p. 446).

While Western countries entered the postwar period in 1945 with a broad optimism and strong belief in progress and knowledge-based rationality, the atmosphere was dramatically different 30–40 years later. The welfare state was no longer seen as the omnipotent power that was able to solve all types of problems. And the social sciences had not been able to support the socio-cultural system in the same way as Keynes and other economists had supported the economic system a few decades earlier. On the contrary, much of the literature focused on a broad variety of 'crises': fiscal, ecological, social; one even talked about a legitimation crisis (Habermas, 1976). If state planning still had any relevance, it was at best to avoid 'dysfunctions' rather than to attain 'the good society'. After years with climbing crime indexes and escalating economic costs,[10] governmental ambitions were gradually and radically lowered. Talking about 'the crisis of penal modernism' Garland (1996) describes the situation in this way:

> Modest improvements at the margin, the better management of risks and resources, reduction of the fear of crime, reduction of criminal justice expenditure and greater support for crime's victims, have become the less than heroic policy objectives which increasingly replace the idea of winning a 'war against crime' (p. 448).

According to this author we are now witnessing the end of 'one of the foundational myths of modern societies: namely, the myth that the sovereign state is capable of providing security, law and order, and crime control within its territorial boundaries' (p. 448). Young (1999) supports this sad statement by describing the precautions against crime as a ghastly Maginot Line of colossal cost and minimal effectiveness. The situation could hardly have swung more from the optimism dominating after the Second World War. An appropriate way of describing this development could be 'from state omnipotence to state impotence'. However, we have to add that state impotence should not be understood as synonymous with state disappearance. According to the neo-Foucaultian tradition the modern Western state has not evaporated; it has only developed new forms of social control at a distance; a control that might even be more extensive than before (see Garland, 1996).

Right and left reactions

Loss of confidence in (social) *scientific* solutions and loss of confidence in *political-administrative* interventions invited other solutions. Within the academic world the stage was set for a return to a more individualistic and moralistic way of explaining social problems. Once again there was a market for 'voluntaristic' approaches in the social sciences (rational choice, economic man models, managerialism). Geertz's old slogan of 'bringing people back in' once again became relevant, even though the meaning and the context in which it appeared was very different. The new focus on the individual was not least visible within criminology. Fattah (cited in Bendle, 1999) has summed up the situation in this way:

> Within two centuries criminology seems to have gone a full circle. It moved from the voluntaristic notions propagated by the philosophers and legal scholars of the Classical School to the hard determinism espoused and defended by the Italian Positivist School, followed by the soft determinism characteristic of psychological and sociological criminology, only to come back to the notion of rational choice and of the reasoning criminal (p. 5).

From the 1970s there emerged (at least in the US), what Currie (1989) calls 'the conservative revolution in criminology' that had a major impact on how one should approach the crime problem. The social sciences, with their causal and therefore deterministic way of understanding crime, were dethroned. But also, there was no longer to be any market for 'social programmes' that might help prevent crime. Instead, the criminal act came to be regarded as an expression of a 'rational choice' and had to be responded to accordingly. The logical answer was to invite more deterrence and more incapacitation.

Politically, neo-liberal and neo-conservative agendas took hold. There was increasing popularity for politicians who were 'tough on crime' and who insisted that the expense of crime properly belonged not to society but the wrongdoer. Leaders furthered the 'moral economy' and the individual's 'freedom to choose' (cf. Friedman and Friedman, 1980). Thatcher (with the nickname 'The Iron Lady') and Reagan gave a voice to the many who believed that the state should do less but do it firmly.

The ideology of 'The New Right' (see Levitas (ed.), 1986, Bosanquet, 1984), with the accompanying economic policy labelled 'Monetarism', was celebrated as the winner in this situation of confusion and public impotence. As Levitas (1986) almost deterministically expressed it, 'monetarism became the international policy to which all governments committed to an open world economy felt obliged to subscribe' (p. 34). However, it would be wrong to describe the ideological climate as 'mono-ideological'. If we restrict ourselves to the social dimension, four political reactions could be identified:[11]

The social democratic reaction

Even though the 'new' social democracy (cf. Giddens (1998), *The Third Way: the renewal of social democracy*) acknowledged the limits to state power, and even though social democrats worked for a more liberalized economy, they still carried on with an ideology of social engineering. The idea of improved international planning (EU, WTO, IMF) within a liberalised free trade economy was a part of this recipe.

The neo-liberal/neo-conservative reaction

Most clearly demonstrated in England, New Zealand and the US, this tradition could be characterized by the slogan 'blaming the victim'. Both Thatcher and Reagan presented their political programme with a strong moralistic pathos. By restoring the idea of a rational choice for everybody, the message was for the public sector to keep hands off, and for the citizens to take responsibility for their own lives. Public intervention was replaced with moral campaigns.

The communitarian reaction

The communitarians represent a blend of both the left and right. A strong appeal to moral obligations and individual responsibility was combined with a call for a more collectivistic society. The self-interest embedded in the idea of an economic man had to be supplemented with a restoration of a common purpose and a sense of membership in the community. After the rights revolution, there has been a (nostalgic) call to reinvigorate group life.

The leftist reaction

The political left was declared 'dead' shortly after the fall of the Wall. The end of the Soviet imperium represented the final nail in the Marxist coffin. Nevertheless, based on Marxist inspired scholars one can argue that what was left of this tradition argued along a perspective of value or rationality conflicts when explaining the great disruption. A society cannot attain both social stability (in the socio-cultural system) and social change (in the economic system) at the same time. These are value conflicts and have to be addressed as exactly that. Consequently, there is no scientific solution to the modern welfare problems, only political. In this perspective the limits of state power were less related to insufficient measures, and more related to inherent value conflicts.

The leftist reaction, focusing on value conflicts, has until recently been closest to my own understanding of the Western Welfare Paradox.[12] However, I have to admit that this perspective is one that the case of Japan seems most readily to prove false. As I will show later, Japan is a society which apparently has succeeded in upholding a capitalist market economy with a set of traditionalistic values. It seems to have succeeded in undergoing a rapid modernization process, and yet has low levels of drug abuse and crime. If this turns out to be the case, I do not hesitate to call it 'remarkable'. However, it is first necessary to delve more deeply into the question of value conflicts.

Value conflicts between economy and society

Following authors like Polanyi (1944), Lockwood (1964), George and Wilding (1978), and Currie (1998), I have preferred to read the Western Welfare Paradox as an expression of a value-, or rather a rationality-conflict between the economic (production) and the socio-cultural (re-production) system.[13] Societies that try to base their *economic* system on one set of values will automatically have problems with realizing corresponding opposite values. I have outlined the contradictions between the basic value system in a (liberalistic based) economic system and a (solidarity based) socio-cultural system in table 1.1.[14] The characteristics are meant to be illustrative, and should not be regarded as reciprocal excluding categories.

Table 1.1 Basic values in the (liberalistic) economic and (solidaristic) socio-cultural system

Economic system	Socio-cultural system
Competition	Co-operation
Individualism	Collectivism
Egoism	Altruism
Efficiency	Time
Change	Stability
Individual maximization	Social obligation
Unpredictability	Predictability
Insecurity	Security
Independence	Belonging

Starting with this ideal type of basic values that has to be addressed within each system, it appears obvious that no government, no matter how interventionist it might be, can be fully successful in both spheres. Compromises have to be made, which means that the more one of the systems presents something like an imperative demand, the more the other system will have to suffer.

For example, unfettered competition is a basic principle in a free market economy. According to liberal ideology a well-functioning economy repels most kinds of manipulation with this principle. However, a basic prerequisite for an integrated socio-cultural system is the opposite of a competitive 'all against all' philosophy. In the family as well as in school we try to teach the younger generations to co-operate rather than to compete (even if that might have changed somewhat in the school system recent years). In the market place (as an ideal type) we operate more or less atomized, but in real life there are of course modifications on this point. As members of the socio-cultural system we are invited to dispose of more collectivistic values. Thus, an egoistic attitude is consistent with our participation in the market competition, while a more altruistic attitude is expected in our interaction with family members and friends.

And, if we follow down our list of values in the economic and the socio-cultural system, we see more value conflicts. No doubt, efficiency is of increasing importance to survive in the market system. However, the situation is quite the reverse in the socio-cultural system. Time for our children, partners and friends, quality time, and time just to *be*, is the basic condition for social harmony in the reproductive sphere. To the extent that continuous change is essential for a well-functioning market economy, social stability is comparably important in the socio-cultural system. Furthermore, one can like Hirsch (1976) argue that there is a 'conflict between traditional morality, with its stress on duty and social obligation and individual maximization of consumption as a goal in itself' (p. 72). Most people need a certain degree of predictability in their lives. As Berger and Luckmann (1972) have shown, human beings very rapidly institutionalize their activities. This helps us reduce the complexity and unpredictability in an everyday world that otherwise would appear rather chaotic. On the other hand, life in the economic system has become more and more unpredictable. Booms and busts seem to be an integral part of life in the market place, and this tendency has definitely increased as the globalization process has increased. Another aspect of this syndrome is the search for security. Western welfare states represent an institutionalized expression of how we have tried to 'protect' life within the socio-cultural system. The broad variety of social benefits illustrates a continuous search for ways to inoculate against insecurity. Today this development has gone so far that one can register opposing tendencies: political critique of paternalism, and a new 'quest for excitement in unexciting societies', as expressed by Elias and Dunning (1986). Both in their everyday lives, and also at the institutional level, people try to protect themselves against insecurity. Finally, to satisfy economic demands for flexibility, it is important to secure independence from networks that can retard social change, while the opposite condition – belonging – is basic for human satisfaction. (All of this will be elaborated further in Chapter 3.)

The main message from this brief overview is to stress that no governmental planning, no crime preventive programme, etc. can abolish the inherent contradictions in the sets of values that underpin Western political systems. It would appear that the state cannot realize contradictory rationalities at the same time. We are confronted with a kind of zero-sum game: what is given priority in one system will suffer in the other. This would also appear to answer our question regarding the apparent failure of social engineering: it is the impossible task of realising *excluding rationalities*. If priority is given to values like individualism, competition, and rapid change in the economic system, one will not be able to attain the *opposite* values (collectivism, solidarity, and, by implication, little crime) in the socio-cultural system.[15] What we have now seen however, is that under neo-liberal values, the economic system more and more invades or colonizes the socio-cultural systems. Values that are important to safeguarding social integration have been losing out.

And then there is Japan. At first glance, Japan seems to challenge the assumption that there is an antagonistic opposition between the value foundation of the economic and the socio-cultural system. Perhaps there *is* a chance that we might answer like Winnie the Pooh, when asked if he wanted milk or honey: 'Yes, please; both!' Might there be a chance that we can have both rapid social change *and* little crime? Maybe a turbulent society is compatible with moral integration. Was Adam Smith right when he supposed that one could counteract the egoistic motivation of the market by way of 'moral sentiments'? Was Adler (1983) striking the nail on the head when she explained low crime rates in Japan by way of 'time-honoured traditional codes of social behaviour'? Or to put it this way: will a sociological analysis of Japanese society give us some clues to understand if, and then how, one set of (altruistic?) values may counteract another set of (egoistic?) values? If this is so, we must address the next logical question: does the Japanese 'crime wonder' come at an acceptable

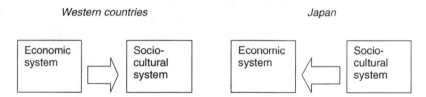

Figure 1.1   The connection between the economic and the socio-cultural system in Western capitalistic countries and in Japan

price? Is Braithwaite's (1989) communitaristic-inspired plea for the Japanese shame culture giving us the complete story?

In short, the topic I address is this: instead of the usual assertion that the socio-cultural system is characterized by *adaptation* and a *lag* in relation to the economic system, does Japan represent a case where the relationship and the dependency go the opposite way (Figure 1.1)? Is there any sense in the argument that 'Asian values' and Asian principles of social organization infiltrate the whole society in ways that even abolish the rationality of the market logic? Is the Japanese crime pattern proof that economistic and materialistic claims have to surrender when confronted with Confucian and Buddhist norms and values? Does Japan show us that culture (see Chapter 4) and social organization can determine economy? Is Japan an optimistic case for those voluntarists who argue that normative values can take precedence over economic values? Or to link this to a Marxist vocabulary, does Japan represent a case where the 'superstructure' determines the 'base'? The answer to this question will be elaborated in the following chapters. In this introduction I limit myself to a brief summary of how some Western scholars (who argue that 'Asian values' (in general) and Japanese culture (in particular) create a different 'ideological hegemony' than in the Western countries) have answered these questions.

Have socio-economic values gained the upper hand in Japanese society?

In many respects Japan can be described as a capitalist society.[16] However, little is explained – and understood – by such labelling. What more can be said? First, it is important to make a clear distinction regarding what has been written on this topic *before* and *after* the burst of the bubble economy in the early 1990s. As McGregor (1996) points out, from that time 'all the things that the Japanese had seen as their postwar strengths – from a uniform education system to lifetime employment and an elite bureaucracy – were being reviled in the media as rigidities that were bringing the country to ruin' (p. 26). Before that time many scholars underlined the uniqueness of Japanese capitalism, even to the point of describing Japan (and East Asian capitalism in general) as a 'second case'. 'That is, East Asia has generated a new type, or model, of industrial capitalism' (Berger, 1987, p. 140). The basic element that makes for the uniqueness is definitely the Confucian value system. This literature can be summarized as follows:

In Japan, socio-cultural, Confucian values have not been a (losing) competitor with the economic system, they have rather been fundamentally incorporated, contributing to the success of the Japanese model.

According to Dore (1987, 1986),[17] the Japanese have never really caught up with Adam Smith (who, as I will show later, was far more open to 'moral sentiments' than we used to think). On the contrary, they have managed to develop a common purpose and social solidarity as their starting point for running their economy. Based on Confucian principles, the main idea has been to put the general interest in front of the individual interest, and in that way Japanese society has succeeded in integrating and engaging people into a shared national enterprise. Dore (1986) describes the way the Japanese think like this:

> They don't believe in the invisible hand. They believe – like Mao unleashing the Cultural Revolution and all other good Confucianists – that you cannot get a decent moral society, not even an efficient society, simply out of the mechanisms of the market powered by the motivational fuel of self-interest, however clever, or even divinely inspired, those mechanisms may be. The morality has got to come from the hearts, the wills and motives, of the individuals in it. The butcher and the brewer have got to be benevolent. They need to have a conscience about the quality of the meat and the beer they supply. They need to care (p. 1).

To Dore these characteristics make Japanese economy different from Western economy. Individualism and egoism are the touchstones in Western countries, and these qualities penetrate into the socio-cultural system. Even among friends and within the family you will see the footprints of the egoistic market rationality. Basic rules, like 'honesty is the best policy', are legitimated by a kind of functionalistic self-interest: this is what pays! In Western countries it is the basic prerequisites in the economic system that determine the premises for social development. In Japanese society, on the other hand, the economy is based on more holistic principles, where trust relationships and altruistic attitudes to a far larger extent are fundamental.

With this foundation, Japan is understood by many as a unique blend of a deliberate interventionist policy and a capitalist market economy. In his much disputed *Japan as no. 1* Vogel championed the Japanese model in a rather panegyric way. Even though Vogel (1979) himself argues that he puts a stronger focus on organizational structures, policy programmes and conscious planning than on traditional values to explain the Japanese success, the cultural element underlies most of his arguments. 'Japan's success derives not from a carefully enunciated ideology but from a strong commitment to what George Lodge calls communitarian values and from the determination and imaginative efforts of group participants at all levels to maintain their cohesiveness' (p. 129).

Hofstede and Bond (1988) also link the surge in Asia's (including Japan's) economy until the early 1990s to the tenets of Confucius. The cultural inheritance of this philosophy has constituted a competitive advantage for Japanese economy. In Confucianism there exists no final Truth. Whatever knowledge human beings attain it should be regarded as partial, and one truth should not exclude its opposite (cf. the Indian proverb: 'the opposite of one truth is another truth'). Western Judean/ Christian culture, on the other hand, has been in search of the one and overarching Truth and the correct answer to things. This was probably an asset during the Industrial Revolution, leading to the discovery of the laws of nature. However, 'by the middle of the twentieth century, the Western concern for truth gradually ceased to be an asset and turned instead into a liability. Science may benefit from analytical thinking, but management and government are based on the art of synthesis' (*op. cit.*, p. 20). The secret behind the Japanese success is (according to these authors) to be found in the Japanese pragmatism (what is true or who is right is not so important as what works), and 'Confucian dyna-mism' (which deals with a society's search for virtue). Furthermore, an important focus is to give priority to the collective best. One main challenge in modern society is how to co-ordinate different individuals and different thinking patterns toward a common goal. Pragmatism and collectivism are the important ideas to attain this. In a modern economy it is important to succeed in co-ordinating the efforts of more or less atomized individuals towards one common goal. The empirical data in the research of Bond and Hofstede indicate that Japan has had a strategic advantage in this regard. If this is correct it shows how an individualistic and 'truth seeking' Western culture is less competitive than its Asian contrast.

Triandis (1987, 1994), Streeck (referred in Olofsson, 1999), and Smith (1983) also find the roots of Japanese economic success in socio-cultural factors, including its other-directedness, collectivism, and emphasis on duty over rights. Triandis sees Japan as unique in demonstrating the privilege of culture over economy. One of the ways in which this uniqueness is revealed is in the language. Referring to Kitayama, Triandis reports how the Japanese language has many more interpersonal emotional terms than English. English has many words expressing self-focused emotions, while Japanese has a large vocabulary for other-focused emotions. Comparing American and Japanese culture it has also been noticed that Americans attribute success to their own ability, while Japanese will rather point to the help they receive from others. Economic considerations are only one of many calculations informing people's way of behaving. Streeck also shows that Japan illustrates the case for the social preconditions for economic growth. Normative regulations coupled with strong institutions that regulate economic processes are necessary to attain effective economic performance. Economic success cannot in the long run be attained without an institutional framework and normative regulations that are socio-culturally founded. These preconditions have been present in Japan. Smith uses the area of industrial relations to argue for the uniqueness of Japanese capitalism. The Japanese government has much stronger restrictions as to what can be done in times of economic downturn. Rather than firing people the government will contribute to heavily subsidizing firms that are in trouble. 'This hardly disintegrated policy clearly reveals a sensible assessment of the high psychological and social costs, not to mention the political danger, of allowing unemployment to rise sharply in times of economic decline. It is apparent that government and business share the view that the employment practice in question is a major key to industrial and social harmony' (Smith, 1983, p. 119).

Finally, Fukuyama (1995, 2000) (writing *after* the breakdown of the Asian economy) underlines much of the same perspectives as Dore. In his celebrated book *Trust* he elaborates the fundamental differences between Asian/Confucian and Western/Judeo-Christian values. While the former tradition sets forth its moral imperatives as duties rather than rights, and stresses the view that human beings are socially embedded (filial piety, benevolence), the latter focuses on individual rights and adds that these rights belong to isolated, self-sufficient individuals. The difference between the two cultures is fundamental and has major implications on how the economy is run. In Fukuyama's (2000) perspective Japan (and Korea) have (so far) resisted the great social disruption exactly because of 'the power of culture to shape economic choices' (p. 135). Consequently, Japanese society has adapted to modernization in a very different way from what characterizes Western countries.

In sum, Japan (and other East Asian capitalist countries) has, according to these authors, largely succeeded in avoiding the individuating and alienating effects of modernization. In the West, modernity has come to mean the freeing of the individual from the constraints of traditional groupings, be it kinship, village, caste or ethnicity. In Japan, however, Confucian values, stressing groupism and hierarchy, have to a large extent 'survived', not only in the socio-cultural system, but also in the economic system. According to Berger (1987) 'there is widespread agreement to the effect that East Asia in general and Japan in particular are characterised by strong communal solidarities and, consequently, by resistance to Western-style individuation' (p. 168).[18]

What we see from this literature is the opposite of the Western liberal ideology. The message is that the economy should not be disentangled from a broader cultural and social setting. Both from a purely moral standpoint, and also from a narrower economistic point of view the invisible hand of the market should not be left to itself. What Western economists define as 'rigidities' for the free and effective expansion of the economy should according to this perspective be defined alternatively. The so-called rigidities should be regarded as a necessary frame for establishing a common purpose where people feel they are engaged in a shared national enterprise, and where they are seen and taken care of within a broader context. Rigidities should be regarded as an

> attempt by societies which are rapidly modernizing and experiencing fast social change to hold on to something of their traditional cultures, their traditional patterns of thought and behavior – in particular, to find a future which is wholly modern but which does not lead to inner-city decay, drug use, high rates of illegitimacy, unemployment, welfare dependency or the other social pathologies associated with the downside of contemporary Western societies (Sheridan, 1999, quoted in the *Japan Times* 9th May 2000)

This strong emphasis on socio-cultural values does not necessarily mean that the model (Fig. 1.1) based on Western experiences in which the socio-cultural system is dependent on the economic system, is totally wrong. Both Berger and Fukuyama appear to project that the East

Asian societies will sooner or later face some of the current problems of Western societies. However, what the 'Asian exceptionalism' *does* show is that 'culture is a dynamic force that is constantly being remade, if not by governments, then by the interactions of thousands of decentralized individuals who make up a society' (Fukuyama, 2000, p. 138). This is definitely not to say that 'culture' can easily be transplanted or invented at will (I will return to this in Chapter 5). We must also add at this point that we have not discussed the ideological content of the Asian Values. There is of course a lot that could be said at this point, in relation to democracy, to power relations (in general), and to gender relations (in particular). I will come back to this later. It is also important to mention that what the authors above celebrate as civilizing hallmarks in Japanese society, others – especially since the early 1990s – will describe as naïve and utopian voluntarism. McGregor (1996) is contemptuous of the Japanese distinctive brand of 'victimless capitalism' (p. 36), while Katz (1998) argues that 'those who would sacrifice efficiency for job security will eventually end up with neither' (p. 58). Lincoln (1998) criticizes Japan's financial mess by describing it as a kind of inverted Darwinian economy run by the principle of the survival of the weakest.

Obviously it is not possible to give a definitive response to the questions of how and to what extent economic principles can be overruled by 'culture'. One could argue that the burst of the Japanese bubble economy in the early 1990s is proof that Marx was right: the market economy, with its nomothetic imperatives, will – at least in the long run – subjugate the value foundation in the socio-cultural system. Such a conclusion, I will argue, would be premature and simplistic. But I will set aside what triggered the economic crisis in Asia. What I will examine is how Japanese society, during a period of some 45 years, seemingly combined a unique blend of capitalist market economy with a social and cultural system that in many ways put firm claims and restrictions on the 'free' economy. In the same period the official crime rate in Japan decreased or stabilized. The question that concerns us here is: are there causal connections between these two observations?

Organization of this book

I will examine this question through the following logical structure.

In Chapter 2 I will clarify what I (in this analysis) include in defining crime. I present a discussion on the tricky methodological question *how can we compare crime between countries and cultures*? Is it 'really true' that Japan deserves credit for being a nation with little crime? Only by narrowing our definition of crime, excluding crimes in the private sphere and white-collar crime, is it possible to approach our main subject. The intention with this chapter is to comment on all those highly-relevant methodological objections that are naturally invited when this type of macro-sociological analysis is undertaken. I also comment on a competing hypothesis concerning little crime in Japan, namely whether it is simply due to economic variables. What role does little unemployment and economic equality play in explaining Japanese uniqueness? What kind of economic and social embeddedness does Japanese society offers its members?

Given this wide frame for discussing my subject, it seems useful to prepare my discussion on crime in Japan by presenting some main sociological perspectives on social integration and social change, and this is done in Chapter 3. How is crime in modern (Western) societies interpreted within the sociological tradition? Approaching an answer to this question should be of relevance when addressing the social and cultural structure of Japanese society. Since criminologists seem to have linked crime in modern societies to urbanization and rapid social change, it is important to specify in more detail what exactly this means. Japanese society is modernized and urbanized as well, so we have to go deeper into this subject. Consequently, we need a closer presentation of the sociology of social integration/disintegration.

In Chapter 4 I present Japanese society along five dimensions: Japan is described a) as a society with a high degree of value consistency and unity concerning main aims; b) as a social-conservative and group-based society; c) as an other-directed, relational and contextual society; d) as a hierarchical and patriarchal society; and e) as a defensive shame society. All these characteristics are linked to the sociological presentation in Chapter 3 and are used as intakes to understand why Japanese society appears to have less crime than its Western comparisons.

Finally, Chapter 5 brings together the main topics presented in this introductory chapter. Having, I hope, reached a closer understanding of how and why Japan diverges from Western societies concerning crime, I ask what kind of mirror (if any) Japan might represent to Western societies? Is it possible to address the 'Western Welfare Paradox' in a new way after having studied Japanese society? Does Japan really represent a falsification of my supposition until now, namely that crime problems in the West basically have to be addressed as a question of value conflicts? Or to put it this way: does the key to fighting crime problems in the West lie in the political or in the professional sphere?

2
Is Japan Really a Low-Crime Nation?

If we tried to compare the number of cars in Japan with the number of cars in the US we would probably find fairly reliable statistics in this field. Maybe we would have some minor problems concerning differences as to what is defined as a 'car' in the two cultures, and maybe differences in registering cars would make our comparisons a little bit uncertain. Nevertheless, cars are physical and identifiable objects that are officially registered. Consequently, it should be fairly easy to determine the density of cars in those two countries, and we could properly talk about 'facts' in this connection.

The problem of objective fact is more complicated, to say the least, if we want to compare crime rates. Everybody knows that most types of statistics lie. Crime statistics lie even more. This means that the assertion of little crime in Japan cannot be taken as a given fact, but is something that has to be discussed. *Is* Japan really a low-crime nation?

Let me make this statement very clear at the outset: there is no 'correct' answer to this question. Even though I will argue that Japan for a long period after the Second World War should be described as unique for showing little crime, it would be presumptuous to give the impression that this is an unequivocal fact comparable to a statement such as that Japan is a 'high density' society with respect to car volume. Crime is not a physical object (like the car) but a social construction. Consequently, we have to comment on how crime is constructed in Japan and how we can relate and compare this to Western countries. Furthermore, it is important to specify and delimit our concept of crime.

There are good reasons to ask the fundamental question: is it really possible to compare the same social phenomenon (for example, crime) between different countries? There are also good reasons to ask what we mean when we talk about 'the same social phenomenon'. The first of these questions has continuously been discussed among criminologists and statisticians. In 1946 the International Penal and Penitentiary Commission and the International Statistical Institute jointly declared that 'a material comparison of national criminal statistics [has] been judged impossible from the beginning because of the diversity of penal law and of the statistical–technical methods of the various countries' (Vetere and Newman, referred in Wilkins, 1980, p. 23). Since then, this pessimistic conclusion has been repeated many times. In a critical article Watts (1996b) defines it as a 'puzzle' why criminologists wish to explain something that is not 'real' (talking about crime), and declares that the crime rate is nothing but a statistical artefact. To Watts, it makes things even worse if one tries to explain differences *between* this society and that. Numbers give the impression of exactness, but the empirical reality behind the numbers is very hard to determine, within one country and even more so between countries. Nevertheless, international agencies and scholars in criminology engage in the business of comparing crime rates. Which leaves us in a quandary if we wish to assess whether there is anything like a scientific foundation for including Japan in the group of what Adler (1983) defined as *Nations not obsessed with crime*.

The second question above (what do we mean when we talk about 'the same social phenomenon') touches upon *why* it is so complicated to compare crime between nations. Wilkins (1980) makes an analogy to elucidate this problem for us. 'The classification of "murder" is like the idea of a "shopping basket" – it will have different contents in different parts of the world and at different times. To add together the number of murders is like adding together the number of shopping baskets found in different countries without reference to the contents'! (p. 25). These short illustrations should tell us that we obviously have to go a bit deeper into some of the tricky problems related to comparing crime between nations. I will make two comments; one concerning the social construction of crime, and one concerning the social construction of crime statistics.

A theoretical comment on comparative analysis: On emic and etic concepts and the social construction of crime

If we – as an illustration – start with the concept of 'democracy', we might ask if Japan really is a democracy. We could do that by comparing one or two Western countries. We could go on to ask which is the most democratic, Japan or one of these Western countries? Would there be any major problems related to making such a comparison?

To answer if, or to what extent, Japan is a democracy, we have to use our language consisting of words designating phenomenon. To discuss democracy we first of all need to have a clear comprehension of concepts like 'individual' and 'individual rights'. But as Hsu and Hamaguchi argue (see Befu, 1989, p. 334), in Japan an analysis of any social phenomenon must start with relations between persons, not with individuals. The idea of individual rights is fundamental for liberal Western countries, and the model of a democratic society takes this as its starting point. This is not so in Japan. Individual rights are not superior but secondary to the collective best in this culture. Consequently, it will represent an ethno-centric bias if we apply a Western standard as our frame of reference. In the West the good society is based on a kind of inductive perspective: first, we have to determine and safeguard the 'necessities' at the individual level, and then, as a result, we will reach the best for the whole society. A main thesis in classical liberal economy argues that everybody, as a collective unit, will be better off if each person pursues her/his individual self-interest. The same argument is applied in the political sphere. A free and open society should take the individual as its starting point, and the focus is on protecting the individual against 'external' forces, be it the state or other citizens. In Japan the basic model of thinking is reversed. First priority is given to collective interests, while the individual has to subordinate him/herself to society. This fundamental difference between the two cultures shows that a discussion of democracy has to qualify what is meant by the individual interest.

This is not the place to discuss strengths and weaknesses in these two models. However, the illustration should make us aware of some inherent general problems in cross-cultural analysis. It is easy to forget that we all wear glasses coloured by cultural filters. The concept of the individual is not just an abstract 'nomen' which, without any further clarification, can be applied in an objective, scientific way in any culture. As I will reiterate in Chapter 4, Japanese language does not even use the term 'individual'. How, then, can we use 'individual rights' as our starting point for a discussion of democracy?

Within an anthropological frame of reference one would define the term 'individual rights' as an *emic* concept, meaning a concept that is 'specific and peculiar to a particular culture, and meaningful only to its members' (Sugimoto, 1997, p. 20). Concepts that are more universally applicable, transcending national and ethnic boundaries, are called *etic*. These terms are derived from linguistics where phon*etics* refers to universal sounds found in languages all over the world, while phon*emics* refers to sounds peculiar to a given language. This distinction has subsequently been brought over from linguistics to the social sciences and made us aware of the danger of ethnocentrism. During the last 10–20 years it has become more and more apparent that Western social sciences have undertaken comparative studies where they have apparently used etic concepts, but where it could be argued that their concepts are emic, based on a Western cultural model.[1]

In other words: if we want to compare democracy between cultures, if we want to compare religiousness in different countries; *or* if we want to compare crime, we have to include a reflection on our basic analytical tools. 'God' and 'Heaven' are not very useful concepts in a Buddhistic culture. Since the *context* of meaning is different in West and East, the *meaning* of the concepts will also be different.[2]

The above discussion does not necessarily lead to a resigned conclusion that all concepts are so unique that they make sense only in their own cultural setting. Some *emicists*, like Goldschmidt, argue in this way: 'Cross cultural comparisons of institutions is essentially a false enterprise, for we are comparing incomparables' (referred to in Hofstede, 1998, p. 18). Campbell (in Triandis, 1994) comes to the same conclusion, arguing that the comparison of any two cultures (instead of *many* cultures) is essentially useless. I am more of an *eticist*, but I am sensitive to the dangers and limits of any cross-cultural study.[3] As Befu (1989) underlines, neither the etic nor the emic approach is foolproof. In all contexts man is an evaluating animal. In this evaluation she/he will easily make 'mistakes'. None of the methodological techniques within the social sciences gives us the ultimate 'truth' about the empirical world. Imperfections are always built in, not only in a strictly technical sense, but also because of a relational argument. Answers to socio-cultural questions are 'true' only in relation to a given frame of reference. Both our language and our methodological techniques will limit the completeness of our research results. Such a comprehension should not lead us into a postmodernistic agnosticism but should rather alert us to specify our discussions. The first step in such a specification is to make a general warning concerning our conceptual tools. Our language does not mirror 'reality' in a neutral way, but it constructs the outer world in a given way. As much as 'heaven' denominates widely different phenomena in the West and the East, so does 'crime'. Those who compare crime figures in the West with crime figures in Japan without much further consideration run the risk of 'comparing apples with oranges' (to use an expression from Hofstede, 1998). Consequently, it should be safe to conclude that crime is a typical emic concept. Or is it?

In one way we might, as a matter of fact, argue that crime is an *etic* concept. A universal way of delimiting crime is to define it as 'an action prohibited by law'. An important aspect of the majority of criminal actions is that they are committed by persons who *know* the actions are illegal. It is that the awareness that an action is deviant that makes it possible to define crime in a universal way (and which, according to Braithwaite (1989) brings new hope for the search for a universal criminological theory). However, this way of defining crime does not make the *content* of this concept universal. If we define any device with four wheels to be a car, then we certainly have determined this device in a universal way. But that does not mean that we cross-culturally will have the same material reality included in our definitional determination. On the contrary, we will most probably mix together oranges and apples, cars and trams. This, of course, also goes for our discussion of crime. Accordingly, we have to conclude that crime is an emic concept. Let me illustrate in more detail what this means in our case.

In general I support Ben-Yehuda (1992) when he argues that, 'processes of devianization and criminalization take place within cultures, and must be interpreted by taking into account the very nature of these cultures. Developing a sociological interpretation of devianization and criminalization thus necessitates adopting a broader view of cultures and social systems' (pp. 74–5). According to this view, crime is a relative phenomenon, both in regard to time and space. Ideological hegemony and different aspects of political power (e.g. moral entrepreneurs) will decide which symbolic universes will have the power of definition and then the power to criminalize certain actions. It is especially important to underline this perspective if we talk about 'sin crimes': actions like homosexuality, prostitution, abortion, pornography, drugs and alcohol abuse, and gambling. At different times and in different cultures social movements and political actors have tried to legitimize their concepts of morality and deviance by criminalizing certain actions. This constructionist perspective is well known within criminological theory and should make us very alert when it comes to comparing crime between nations and cultures. As mentioned above, this reminder is particularly important to keep in mind when we are talking about regulations of sexual or drug-related behaviour. But even if we try to compare as universally condemned an action such as homicide, we will run into problems concerning conceptual content. Neapolitan (1999) gives us a good illustration. Homicides reported in the *International Crime Statistics* (published by the International Criminal Police Organisation) do not allow for two important biases. First, some nations include attempted murders in their statistical data while others do not. A closer scrutiny concerning the implications of this tells us that figures between different countries are easily misread. Next, there seems to be quite a bit of under-reporting from many developing countries while, on the other hand, developing nations sometimes report rates that are too high. Nations also vary in the way they distinguish between 'homicide' and 'death by other violence'. Some nations will define that death will have to occur within 24 hours after a violent action is committed, while other nations have other time limits.

What is the relevance of these methodological problems for the study of Japan? Let me continue my argumentation by sticking to homicide as an illustration, since most people will regard this as an unequivocal and universal action. Intuitively one would think that homicide *has* to be an etic concept. The two following illustrations should alert our critical senses. *Japan Times* (16.11.00) refers to a mother who killed one of her daughters and tried to kill the other one as well. She had also been convicted of killing another daughter in 1995. This earlier killing was part of an unsuccessful bid at what is called *muri shinju* (killing a loved one and then committing suicide), so the woman was given a suspended sentence. The mother tried to kill herself, but failed. So in this case this 'murder' was defined as *muri shinju* which is something different. White (1987) refers to a comparable case, where a Japanese woman, abandoned by her husband, tried to drown herself and her two children. Only the mother survived, but she was acquitted of murder since, according to Japanese beliefs, a child is part of her mother and cannot survive without her. Consequently, the mother's action (called *oyako shinju*=parent–child suicide) was seen, not as murder, but rather as an honourable act! It is probable that cultural interpretations like this will contribute to mislead us if we compare homicide numbers in Japan with those in Western countries.[4]

From these illustrations and from what I referred to earlier we have to recognise that even homicide to a large extent is a social construction. Different cultures apply different schemes of interpretation and, consequently, apply different categorizations when actions are sorted out in the criminal process. When deaths from internal conflicts are defined as murders, countries like Rwanda could report more than 12,000 homicides in 1994 (Neapolitan, 1999). For other cultures, registration of abortion as homicide will of course have a huge impact on the crime statistics.

I mentioned that cultural differences concerning the definition of crime is of special relevance regarding 'moral crimes'. The traditional philosophy of law in Japan is based on a principle that defines crime as narrowly as possible. If there is a chance that one can avoid the process of criminalization the formal structure of justice gives wide discretional authority. The invocation of the criminal justice mechanism is avoided much more often in Japan than in Western countries. This is especially apparent when it comes to crimes against morality. According to Westermann and Burfeind (1991) the concept of morality and crimes against morality has been one constant in Japanese consideration of crime. Japanese morality is based on influence from Shintoism, Buddhism and Confucianism, and all of these traditions convey a perspective on the purpose of the law where legislating morality is alien. The result is that

> a large number of acts, particularly those involving sexual crimes and crimes against family, fall outside the bounds of criminality in Japan . . . Homosexuality, incest, and sodomy are not punishable. The crime of adultery was abolished after the war . . . Abortion is punishable under the Penal Code, but Eugenic Protection Law promulgated after the war legalized [it] within broad limits . . . Maintenance of houses of prostitution was prohibited in 1957, but the act of prostitution itself is not treated as a crime . . . Obscene literature is not strictly controlled . . . The scope of criminal law as actually applied is even more limited (Hirano, quoted from *op. cit.*, p. 64).

Even though it would be wrong to describe Japan as unique concerning the above-mentioned cases, there are good reasons to be aware of cultural diversities leading to main differences in criminalization.

What this means is that the Japanese – both as formal and informal controllers ('re-actors') as well as 'actors' (i.e. 'criminals' in this connection) – will try to find peaceful and non-formalized ways of solving conflicts, and they will avoid condemning an action without seeing it in a more holistic perspective. If they can make people regret/apologize for an indecent action, very often a crime will be excused.

This basic orientation is mirrored in the extent to which deviant actions are actually criminalized. Many forms of behaviour defined as criminal in Western societies are not criminalized in Japan, or, eventually, are rather defined as something else. According to Henshall (1999) 'acts that in the west would be considered criminal are often seen in Japan as an indication of a mental problem. It has more than 300,000 people in its thousand or so mental institutions, more than the number of those in prison' (p. 104). In the US the picture is reversed. This reminds us to be very careful when we try to make a comparative analysis at a high aggregate level. 'Crime' will easily become too wide a concept to give valid and comparable data between countries. There will have to be a great deal of specification before we can draw any conclusions.

In summary, it is important to be aware that 'crime' (except in the Braithwaite way of defining this concept) is an emic concept. Even though we all might accept the general statement of crime as a social construction, we easily forget the implications of this in more concrete comparative analysis. As I have pointed out above, not only does the broad variety of 'moral crimes' make comparisons between cultures challenging, but also comparing homicide invites some particular problems because even such a fatal action appears to be a social construction. From this one might wonder if we are forced to conclude in the pessimistic way I noted above – that comparing crime rates between countries is an impossible puzzle. I will not deny or try to hide that there are some valid reasons for such a conclusion. However, *problems* are not synonymous with *impossibilities*. First of all, we have to recognise a certain degree of uncertainty in our analysis and conclusions. Next, we have to accept a more probabilistic and relational approach in our research. We should always try to express how things are *in relation to* a frame of reference, and we should also avoid under-communicating uncertainties in our data and perspectives. But, most important, we have to support our conclusion with more than statistical data.

The social construction of crime statistics

Different legal definitions of offences are but one of the problems we face when doing cross-cultural crime analysis. Once an action is agreed upon to be a crime and then included in the penal code system, new filtering processes start. Textbooks in criminology used to make a distinction between 'discovery', 'reporting', 'recording', and 'clearing up' of criminal actions (see for example Coleman and Moynikan, 1996, p. 32). Variations in law enforcement practices open up different forms of selectivity in all of these phases. In this study of Japan, where I focus on crimes committed, this selection process is primarily of importance in relation to the first two of these phases, namely the detection and reporting of crimes. Two factors will determine the number of crimes that will be reported: the police themselves and the general audience. Let me start with a comment on the role of the Japanese citizens in the criminal system.

Japanese culture has a strong belief in informal control, in seeking consensus between people, and in compromising and apologizing rather than in confrontation and the use of formal law as a solution. Seeking harmony is the most important value in human interaction and, consequently, people will avoid conflicts. They will rather try to find pragmatic solutions than just solutions, which in turn means that, 'many matters which in Western nations are dealt with within the framework of the regular machinery of law are left in Japan to work themselves out outside this machinery' (Tanaka, 1976, p. 254). The consciousness of law of the Japanese people is very different from what we find in the West and, until recently, this has meant that people do not tend to dispute in terms of rights and obligations. Settlement of conflicts without promoting their own interests is of supreme importance. Although this 'tradition' has biggest impact in civil cases it will also influence the amount of criminal cases reported. Haley (1998) focuses on one specific aspect of this polite and other-directed Japanese culture – the fundamental importance of apology and repentance – as the main explanation of the low Japanese crime rates. Haley argues that 'those accused of an offence who confess, display remorse, co-operate with the authorities, and compensate or otherwise reach an accommodation with their victims stand a reasonable chance of being released without further official action' (p. 852). This applies even for offenders who have committed rather serious crimes. It seems reasonable to conclude from this a certain under-reporting of crime in Japan compared to Western countries. Furthermore, with a Confucian legacy consisting of principles of honesty, uprightness, integrity and obligation, and a Buddhistic legacy advocating the importance of mental and moral purity, some 80–90 per cent of Japanese perpetrators will confess immediately. Also, the Japanese have different ideas from Western people concerning human nature and the idea of 'evil'. In Japan, human nature is naturally good and to be trusted, and no evil is inherent in man's soul (see Benedict, 1967, p. 134). The Japanese do not isolate and focus the single act (for example a crime) in itself, but regard it in relation to certain circumstances. I will return to this type of 'contextual ethics' in Chapter 4, but at this point I would like to underline the methodological implications of this: fewer criminal cases will end up in the statistics.

Next, let me then turn to the agents of formal social control and remark briefly on discretional judgements in the Japanese criminal system.

While Western countries have equal treatment of equal cases as a basic premise for their systems of justice, in Japan both the police and the prosecuting authorities have much wider powers of discretion. If a conflict/crime (usually the minor ones, but not only those) can be resolved on the spot in an amicable way this will be done. Both in cases of crimes without victims (where, unfortunately, it seems that violence against women in the private sphere must be included), and in cases where the offender shows signs of 'sincere regret', the police will often avoid further prosecution. Vogel (1979) argues that crimes without victims are dealt with in a very permissive way (at least unless the acts disturb or endanger others). Henshall (1999) points to the fact that if an offender signs a statement expressing contrition (except for the most serious crimes) she/he will be given a second chance. If it is in general correct that only 15 per cent of all crimes ever become fully known (see Dahrendorf, 1985, p. 16), it is obvious that varying priorities will have a huge influence on the final crime statistics. It has been argued that only about half of all victims report a crime to the police (Anleu, 1999). In cases of sexual assault only 25 per cent of victims report the incident (while the figures are 94 per cent in cases of theft of motor vehicle). In other words, we should not only talk about the social construction of crime, but also the social construction of crime statistics (Pfohl, 1994). The reporting of graffiti crimes in Norway and Japan gives a good illustration of how crime figures might play us a trick.

According to Høigård (1997) charges for graffiti in Oslo increased from 19 cases in 1990 to 1,491 in 1994. This, of course, gave the impression of a serious aggravation in this field, and it was easy to conclude that things had got out of control. People reading the crime figures at face value would naturally conclude that the criminal climate had worsened in the Norwegian capital. However, in discussing this development, Høigård shows how the establishment of a special office within the underground railway company that co-operated closely with the police led to these changes. In addition, the police had changed their way of registration during this period. A person who previously would have one charge that might cover up to 24 incidents of graffiti a night would, in 1994, have 24 charges! (For a parallel example, see Watts, 1996b, Kyvsgaard, 1991, and Olaussen, 1996a, 1996b). Compare this with the following report in *Mainichi Daily News* 7 December 2000: Over the previous six months graffiti had been sprayed repeatedly over pillars outside the Osaka theatre. The police had taken into custody on separate incidents four teenagers. While all of them were found guilty they all escaped charges by apologizing for their actions. The newspaper reported that only if a targeted retailer pressed charges against a vandal would the police make an arrest.

This example should make us aware of how easily we might misread a situation if we judge public crime figures at face value. I do not think that graffiti is nearly as big a problem in Japan as in many Western countries. Nevertheless, 'the real situation' is probably less different in these two cultures then we would interpret from the public figures. When tagging increases by 88 per cent during five years primarily due to a change in police policy we have a strong indication of the importance of statistical fallacies.

The fact that Japanese police probably report less crime detected than police in many Western countries, indicates more underreporting of crimes in Japan. This is probably so. However, we should also add that other characteristics in the work of the Japanese police point in the opposite direction. Relations are much closer (though not necessarily more confident) between citizens and the police in this country than we find in the West.[5] Smith (1983) reports that 'it is today the assumption of the vast majority of Japanese that police and public alike are on the same side in the unremitting effort to maintain order and to minimize the dangers encountered by ordinary people in the conduct of their daily lives' (p. 125). A point to which I will return is that Japanese neighbourhoods are organized in 'voluntary' citizen groups that are supposed to co-operate closely with the police.[6] (To what extent this is voluntary could be disputed.[7]) Since crime is regarded as a community phenomenon, 'it is essentially defined by, detected by, prosecuted by, and determined by community involvement' (Clifford, 1976, p. 97). Compared to the situation in many Western countries one would expect from this that the citizens in Japan would report much more crime.[8]

The high degree of procedural discretion in Japan continues in the rest of the justice system. J. Haley (1998) presents the following summary of the criminal procedure:

> The three most critical institutional features of Japan's criminal justice system are thus: the authority given to the police not to report minor offences (bizai shobun) in cases where they deem it appropriate (Code of Criminal Procedure, art. 246); the authority of prosecutors to suspend prosecution where warranted by the nature and circumstances of the crime and the offender's attitude (Code of Criminal Procedure, art. 248); and the court's broad authority to suspend execution of sentences (Criminal Code, art. 25) (p. 852).

At all levels in the criminal justice system the potential for discretionary judgements is more extensive than in the West. The Japanese strongly believe that appropriate remedies are often found outside the formal justice system, and in 1990 over 70 per cent of criminal cases were not sent to the prosecutor. No less then 30 per cent of all charges will never be taken to court in Japan[9] (see Thornton and Endo, 1992, p. 32, Kühne,

1994, p. 189) and, once a case is taken to court, there is much opportunity for case suspension. According to Article 248 of the Code of Criminal Procedure these are the criteria for suspension:

> Where it is found unnecessary to prosecute because of the character, age and situation in life of the criminal, the gravity of the offence, the circumstances under which the offence was committed, and the circumstances which follow the commission of the offence, a public prosecution need not be instituted (quoted from Tanaka, 1976).[10]

Again, this alerts us to be very careful when comparing crime statistics between countries.[11] This is especially so if we refer to prosecuted cases. It is well known that the value of a crime rate for index purposes decreases as the distance from the crime itself in terms of procedure increases. Crimes known to the police give us a more valid basis for comparative analysis than cases cleared, and it is these types of data that are of interest for my analysis. The reason why I refer to this peeling off of cases in the criminal court process is mainly to illustrate the general 'modus operandi' of the Japanese criminal justice system.

From what I have said so far it should be obvious that a constructivist perspective is especially relevant in cross-cultural analysis of crime. Both crime and crime statistics are obviously a result of negotiating processes, and these processes have spatial and temporal peculiarities. Different actions are defined in different ways at different times and in different places. Accordingly, even with a strong awareness on a variety of methodological problems we must admit that the chances for misreading figures are legion.

As a first step to simplifying my discussion of Japan as a low-crime nation let me comment briefly on two types of crime that I will exclude from my final analysis, but which – if included – would complicate the picture of Japan as essentially a low-crime nation. The first is the question of violence in the private sphere; the other is the question of white-collar crime.

Crime in the private sphere – how big is the iceberg?

In Japan, as in the West, a huge proportion of violent crime is committed within *the private sphere*. A very tiny percentage of violence against women, violence against the elderly (especially parents), or violence against children ends up in the crime statistics. It is next to impossible to compare the 'real' situation between Japan and Western countries in this regard. However, we should keep in mind that Japan is a culture based on hierarchical relations (man–woman, adult–child), with asymmetrical power relations between them. Submission to authority, obedience, and adaptation are treasured values, and these values do not necessarily contribute to the prevention of domestic violence. Buddhism, Shintoism, and Confucianism are all based on a principle that makes the man superior to the female (with the geisha as the prototypical tamed womanhood). Scattered data also indicate that Japan has a serious challenge in this regard. Henshall (1999) reports that wife-beating was until very recently publicly admitted and even seen as a macho thing to do. As an illustration he refers to former Prime Minister Sato Eisako who admitted having beaten his wife regularly. Henshall goes on to report that 'the daughter of another former prime minister, Tanaka Kakuei, has publicly stated that her father beat her and that he even urged her husband to do so too "if it makes you feel more like a man"' (p. 39). Sugimoto (1997) refers to a survey from 1992 where 78 per cent of Japanese women revealed that they had experienced violence from their husbands. In a survey from 1989, 49 per cent of married men were reported to have beaten their wives, and violence from the husband is the second most important reason why women want a divorce. Another factor in this is the lack of women's shelters. In 1993 *Japan Times* reported on a survey that found only 171 out of almost 1,000 female respondents (out of 4,675 questionnaires distributed) reported no violence against them, and more than half said that they were frequently beaten and/ or sexually assaulted. Hardly any of them had reported the incidents to the police (reported in Henshall, 1999, pp. 191–2). *Japan Times* (20 December 2000) reports that one out of twenty women has received death threats from her husband, and Henshall (1999) maintains that wife-beating still continues 'on a widespread and frequently horrific scale (requiring hospital treatment for a third of all respondents)' (p. 39). Jolivet (1993) presents a frightening picture of isolation and frustration among stay-at-home wives. Her data from the 'baby help line' shows that there are obvious links between an increasing isolation among home-staying women, a feeling of desperation and, as a result, violence against children.

Based on what scarce and highly uncertain data we have concerning domestic violence (both from Western societies and from Japan) there is little support for defining Japan as a low-crime society. Even if Finch (2001) refers to a comparative study where the overall levels of violence between husbands and wives seems to be lower in Japan than in the US, this only contributes to my pragmatic conclusion: crime in the private sphere will be excluded from my analysis.

White collar crime – extensive but impossible to validate and compare

Also excluded is the substantial area of *white-collar crime*. Here, too, the reasoning is similar: we have very little knowledge about this topic in Japan (which, of course, is an interesting fact in itself). Even if we did have valid data on this topic we really would have a hard time comparing like with like. If the distinction between emic and etic concepts ever should have any relevance it would be in relation to white-collar crime. Let me just mention one illustration. During the long period of one-party rule in Japan after the Second World War 'a collusive system of exploiting the public by massive corruption evolved' (McCormack, 1996, p. 33). In Japan there has for many years been no open competition for contracts when big construction work has been undertaken. Rather, the Ministry of Construction allocates contracts to firms that belong to officially recognized cartels, and collusion, price fixing, and bribery have (according to McCormack) long characterized this industry. What McCormack reports on here is not a coincidental and atypical incident, but a structurally built-in system with authoritative acceptance. When construction costs are four times as high in Japan as in Germany, and nine times as high in Japan as in the US, this is mainly due to a structure of collusive corruption. From a Western perspective this system comes close to a regular criminal culture, and in Japan quite a few of these cases have been prosecuted during the last 20 years. However, Japanese culture is a typical 'gift culture', and it is not always easy to define the borderline between cultural tradition and criminal violation. According to McCormack between 0.5 and 1 per cent of all public works contracts in 1993/94 has been dedicated as gifts to politicians. But this system of 'lubrication' has to be understood in a broader cultural context. Japanese people give and receive gifts on very many different occasions and money gifts often function as a sincere expression of warm feelings. (For example in weddings, it is common to use money gifts as an expression of devotion.) According to McGregor (1996, p. 80) cash is a means of communication, and money gifts in Japan often express something spiritual and sacred. Contrary to what we are used to in the West, money is a symbol of a pure heart from the donor, and to refuse it would cause an embarrassing situation. What all this means is that we are facing insurmountable obstacles if we try to determine the amount of bribery in Japan, and it follows that it would be next to impossible to compare this in a meaningful way with Western countries. In this area we really are facing the problem of emic and etic concepts![12]

The involvement of the *yakuza* (mafia groups) in the established business world provides another illustration of a peculiar Japanese form of white-collar crime. Since the early 1970s organized criminals have involved themselves as corporate fixers and as land-sharks or land-hike specialists, which has led to the coining of a new term, *keizai yakuza*, or economic gangsters. In the first instance, members of the yakuza (in this connection called *sōkaiya* or general meeting specialists) acquire shares, and then they legitimately attend the annual general meetings in the companies. Here they can either represent some external interests, and then force the company to make decisions in their interest, or, alternatively, they can represent the company itself and then silence potentially critical share holders. A *sōkaiya* is like a hyena that harasses companies and in some cases blackmails them. According to Kaplan and Dubro (1987) most major companies have hired yakuza members to ensure that no troublesome questions are asked at the general meetings (and consequently, these meetings will typically only last less than half an hour!). Again, in traditional Western language this type of activity would rightly be designated as intimidation or as extortion, and would consequently be subsumed as a serious criminal action. Also in Japan, the operation of the *sōkaiya* is illegal. In 1982 a commercial law was passed making it illegal to pay money to a *sōkaiya*. However, this activity continues to thrive and famous companies have featured in scandals involving huge payments to organized criminals (see Henshall, 1999, p. 201).

Land-sharking refers to the role of the yakuza as extortionists against landowners who refuse to sell their plots or against tenants who refuse to move out of apartments. Since the late 1980s there has been an increasing demand for real estate among corporations, which has resulted in a strong pressure for trading premises. To speed up this process companies have hired yakuza members (called *jiageya*). Their job has been to persuade, intimidate, or force people to sell their land (often at a give-away price). Van Wolferen (1989) reports that several cases of arson have been traced to *jiageya*, and this phenomenon has reached the headlines in the media.

Loan-sharking refers to lending money at exorbitant interest rates. Several crime syndicates affiliated with major Japanese gangster organizations are operating networks of underground loan shark services. According to *Japan Times* (26 January 2003) 'there are thought to be several thousand underground loan sharks in Tokyo alone'. The police suspect that more than 1,000 of them are believed to work under the umbrella of crime syndicates. The profits from illegal lending activities represent a major source of funds for the crime syndicates. It is not unusual for lenders to charge more than 100 times the legal daily limit of 0.08 per cent in interest.

No doubt, this activity is clearly criminal, and it is linked to powerful economic interests in society. Like most other white-collar crime this is a type of crime that disturbs the general peace and order in society only to a very little extent. As a matter of fact, the activity of the *jiageya* has been described as protecting public interests against opportunistic criminals, and this is a story that seems to have been accepted by the general audience (Henshall, 1999, p. 70).

When Japan is presented as a low-crime society among criminological scholars the above-mentioned types of criminal activity are rarely mentioned. Even though the social damage produced by white-collar crime is widely known, there has been little focus on more or less 'cultivated' white-collar crimes when discussing the uniqueness of the Japanese crime pattern. Because of this omission it is very important to make the following statement explicit: there is little reason to define Japan as a nation 'not obsessed with crime' (as Adler, 1983, does) if we include the broad variety of economic white-collar crime. Today there is hardly any empirical evidence to prove one way or the other in this regard. Even though one could argue (as has been done) that communitarian shame cultures (like Japan) are particularly effective in suppressing white-collar crime (so much honour to lose), there is another side to the story. As Braithwaite (1989) comments, communitarianism is a two-edged sword. In some regards such cultures might function in a crime preventive way because of shame mechanisms. In other regards, however, the same cultural elements might be mobilized to sustain white-collar criminal subcultures. Braithwaite uses Japan (and Switzerland) precisely as illustration of this. Consequently, I conclude that there is little reason to expect less white-collar crime in Japan than in most Western countries. However, since it is impossible to come to a more precise conclusion on this topic I also choose to drop white-collar crime from the rest of my discussion of crime in Japan.

With all these serious critical remarks on the correctness of describing Japan as a low-crime nation, how, then, can I still embark on an analysis on this topic? I have two answers: first, the sum effect of different (though not all independent of each other) sources indicate the validity of this conclusion, and, second, because of the way I delimit my discussion of period and types of crimes. Let me explain this a bit further.

What do statistics tell us?

First of all, I am focusing on *the period 1950–90* in my analysis. The reason for this delimitation is simple: this is the period when crime *increased* in the West but *decreased, stabilized*, or only slightly increased in Japan. Since the end of the 1980s some new tendencies have been emerging. In 1985 Japanese criminologists reported a new rise in crime in Japan, and this happened for the first time in almost four decades (a slight increase had been registered already since 1973, but this was mainly due to an increase in minor theft, especially shop-lifting. Violent offences continued the downward trend). Approximately at the same time Western countries to a varying extent registered stagnation or a turn around trend in their crime rates. My interest in this analysis lies in understanding Japan as a 'negative case', that is, as a country that diverges from the typical or 'normal' pattern in most other modernised countries. Even though Japan today still has essentially lower crime rates than most Western countries, things seem to have been changing since the burst of the bubble economy in the early 1990s. In the West there are indices of opposite trends. Since my interest is on prerequisites for creating social integration in a society, I will restrict my analysis to the mentioned period.

In the period immediately after the Second World War (1945–48) crime in Japan increased in much the same way as it did in another war-losing country in the West, namely in Germany (see Schneider, 1992, Dahrendorf, 1985). Japan (like Germany) was characterized by a classical anomic situation during these years, with a weakened central authority and with chaos concerning legitimate norms (Leonardsen, in print). (As an illustration, Dahrendorf prefers to replace the word 'steal' with the word 'take' to characterize people who these days acquired things that did not belong to them, since 'stealing' seemed to have lost its meaning.) In addition Japan experienced a steep increase in the amount of street children in these years (estimated at 124,000 in 1948), not least due to the many orphans as a result of the war (EAMM, 1996).

For my analysis it is very important to notice this development of crime just after the War. Since I, in my interpretation of the unique Japanese crime rates, will focus the *cultural* dimension as a very important explaining 'variable', it is interesting to register that 'culture' (which supposedly was the same in 1945 as in 1955) did not hinder the negative development in these years.

However, in a most remarkable way, crime figures (in general) soon started to fall, and for almost four decades crime decreased or (roughly)

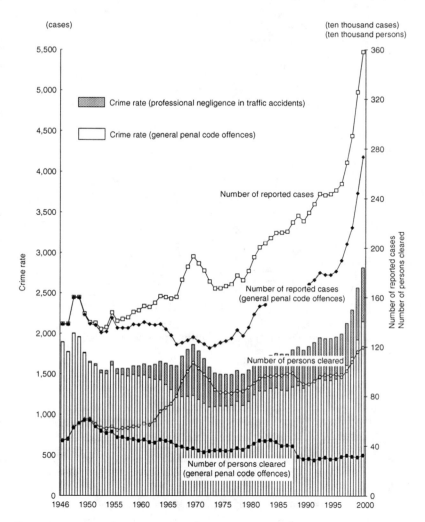

Figure 2.1 Trends in number of reported cases, number of persons cleared, and crime rate for penal code offences in Japan (1946–2000)
Source: Ministry of Justice. Research and training institute: White paper on crime 2001, p. 4.

stabilized in Japan. In Western countries the situation was quite the opposite, at least since the 1960s. Figure 2.1 presents some basic information on crime in Japan 1946–2000. (The period 1990–2000 will not be commented on in this book. For a discussion on the changes since the early 1990s, see Leonardsen, in print.)

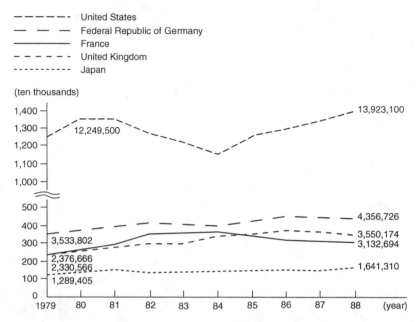

Figure 2.2   Trends in the total number of major crimes reported to the police 1979–88, for different countries
Source: Fujimoto, 1994, p. 4.

If these figures are compared to a sample of Western countries we will soon register Japan to be a unique case. Fujimoto (1994) gives us comparative data for the years 1979 to 1988 for the United States, the United Kingdom, the Federal Republic of Germany, and the Republic of France. (See Figure 2.2. See also Westermann and Burfeind, 1991, Thornton and Endo, 1992, White Paper on Crime, 1998, 1999.)

As discussed earlier in this chapter, the exact meaning of a specific crime will vary from country to country. As we have seen, we cannot compare even the most serious crimes of all – homicide – between countries without serious reservations. However, we should also add to what I have written above that a lot has been done at the international level to make national statistics comparable (see Adler, 1983, p. 3). With the cautions mentioned earlier we can look at the figures for homicide 1986–88 for our five nations in Table 2.1.

Westermann and Burfeind (1991, based on a study by Kalish) have compared the two 'extremes' (Japan and the US) for one year (1984) and looked into different types of crime. Here is their summary conclusion:

Table 2.1 Number of homicide cases reported, crime rate and clearance rate 1986–88, for different countries

Year/Item	US	UK	FRG	France	Japan
1986					
Homicide Cases Reported	20,613	2,160	2,728	2,413	1,744
Crime Rate	8.6	4.3	4.5	4.4	1.4
Clearance Rate	70.2	76.7	93.9	89.4	96.4
1987					
Homicide	20,100	2,764	2,651	2,286	1,645
Crime Rate	8.3	5.5	4.3	4.1	1.3
Clearance Rate	70.0	81.5	94.0	93.0	97.6
1988					
Homicide Case Reported	20,680	3,722	2,543	2,567	1,476
Crime Rate	8.4	7.4	4.2	4.6	1.2
Clearance Rate	70.0	81.5	94.4	83.1	96.6

Source: Fujimoto, 1994, p. 7.

There were over five times as many homicides per person in the United States in 1984 as there were in Japan – a rate of 1.5 per 100,000 in Japan compared to a rate of 7.9 in the United States.

Rape was committed twenty-two times more frequently in the United States in 1984 than it was in Japan – 35.7 per 100,000 in the United States, 1.8 per 100,000 in Japan.

In 1984 the rate for armed robbery in the United States was 114 times the rate for that crime in Japan – 205.4 per 100,000 in the United States, 1.8 per 100,000 in Japan (p. 3).

Let me finally supply these figures with the number of larceny offences for our five nations (1988). The rate in the United States was 5,027 per 100,000, in the United Kingdom it was 5,373, Germany had 4,336 per 100,000, France had 3,479, while the Japanese figures were 1,158 per 100,000.

Even though I have underlined the extraordinary uncertainties connected to crime statistics, the referred figures are thought-provoking. We should of course not jump to any easy conclusion from these figures, but – very modestly – I would argue that together with some other indicators this points in the direction of supporting the assertion of Japan as a low-crime nation.

What do criminological scholars tell us?

A simple way of supporting the assertion that Japan is a low-crime nation would be to refer to all those criminological researchers who have supported this conclusion. There really is a broad agreement among scholars on this topic, and one might argue that broad unanimity in the interpretation of the crime statistics in itself is a strong indication of trustworthiness. Most criminologists are aware of dangers connected with comparing statistical data between nations, but still they all conclude that Japan really has a unique crime record.

In the book *Nations not obsessed with crime* Adler (1983) picks out Japan as one among ten countries in this category. Adler is supported in this conclusion by a lot of researchers who have studied the case of Japan. Without going into a detailed and boring documentation of this unanimous conclusion let me refer to the following list of scholars who define Japan as a low-crime nation: Clifford (1976, 1980), Christiansen (1974), Westermann and Burfeind (1991), Vogel (1979), Parker (1987), Miyazawa (1992), Braithwaite (1989), Becker (1988), Ito (1998), Ladbrook (1988), Haley (1998), Shikita and Tsuchia (1992), Schneider (1992), Kühne (1994), Hechter and Kanazawa (1993), Crawford (1998), Yoshida (2000), MacFarlane (1995), and Fujimoto (1994). Haley (1998) even goes as far as to argue that 'no contrast between Japan and the United States could be greater than Japan's postwar success and the United States' failure to reduce crime and its awesome social and material costs. Japan today has the lowest rates of crime of any industrial state' (p. 843). Even though few of the mentioned authors have undertaken in-depth critical analysis of existing data, one could be inclined to lean to the thesis that sometimes quantity becomes quality! No one scholar has seriously refuted the uniqueness of the crime situation in Japan, even though Kersten (1993) reminds us that street youth, *bosozuko* (hot-rodder groups, and the yakuza) represent a significant and visible problem in Japan. Also, Steinhoff (1993) reports that some smaller body of research has recently produced 'studies that call into question the basic assumption that Japan's low crime rates are produced by benign, neighborhood-level criminal justice institutions operating in a culturally supportive environment' (p. 828). However, although arguments have been put forward that dispute to what extent different 'cultural variables' are most relevant to explain the case of Japan, this does not disturb the general picture of concord among criminologists in describing Japan as a low-crime society. This concord is of course not a proof in itself, but it definitely gives a strong indication that the Japanese uniqueness is more than an illusion.

The researchers I have referred to above have all based their analysis on data at a general level. Methodology textbooks tell us that intensive *case studies* will represent important supplements to this type of documentation. Do we have such information from Japan? To the best of my knowledge Thornton and Endo (1992) have published the only *case study* focusing on crime from fairly recent years.[13] In their book *Preventing crime in America and Japan – A comparative study* they have undertaken a study of two cities: Salem in Oregon (107,000 inhabitants) and Kawagoe in Japan (272,000 inhabitants). These researchers collected material during a period of 48 months. They based their research on participant observation, in-depth interviews, and co-operation with city officials and employees, police officers, educators, students, family court judges, civilian attendees at neighbourhood meetings, youth counsellors, mental health professionals, crime prevention trainers, public and private welfare agencies, parole and probation officers, youth corrections personnel, and volunteers in different areas. In their final evaluation of total crime in the two cities they concluded that 'a horrific picture' emerged. Computed on a per-population basis, they reported 37.8 times as many crimes committed against persons in Salem as in Kawagoe (for the year 1986). There were 25.7 times as many property crimes in the US city as in the Japanese one. In short, this case study supports the general picture where crime rates in the United States by far exceed those in Japan. Thornton and Endo make only two reservations to this conclusion: Japanese crime rates for organized crime and juvenile offences approach those of the United States.

Bestor (1989) comments only briefly on crime in his study of *Neighborhood Tokyo*. However, in this in-depth presentation of the institutional bases of an urban neighbourhood he gives a very interesting report that deserves to be cited in full:

One obvious reason for the chokai's [neighbourhood association, DL] low level of activity in this domain is that, like most of Tokyo, Miyamoto-chō is almost crime free. The only crime of any consequence that occurred in the neighborhood during my two years of fieldwork was an arson case, a fire in the teachers' office at the local junior high school that was apparently set by a disgruntled student. The arson shocked the neighborhood and was the subject of gossip and speculation for days, but for residents it was only indirectly a neighborhood matter. Although the school stands in the center of Miyamoto-chō next to the Shintō shrine, residents did not see the crime as a smirch on Miyamoto-chō's reputation, nor did the crime and fire prevention divisions redouble their efforts in the fire's aftermath. To the extent that local opinion assessed blame for the incident, people held the school responsible: the school's night watchman for failing to prevent the arson, and the school's principal for allowing so bad a situation to develop that one of his students could even consider, let alone carry out, such an act. The principal was transferred to another school at the end of the term, and local residents agreed that his career – abruptly and irreversibly – would go no further (p. 129).

This report is suggestive not only because of the observation of little crime in a large city like Tokyo, but also for the reactions the referred incident called forth. As I will repeat in later chapters, it has been argued that Japan has little crime because its citizens 'police themselves'. This small glimpse into one of Tokyo's neighbourhoods supports such a perspective.

Available *victimization studies* support the conclusion of Japan as a low-crime nation. According to MacFarlane (1995) there have been a number of victimization studies in Japan, and they seem to confirm that the official figures are more than a statistical illusion. However, research on the *fear* of crime in Japan shows (as in Western studies) that fear levels are far higher than actual crime rates. A survey from 1988 revealed that 54.3 per cent of the respondents were afraid of burglary, 34.7 per cent of robbery, and 17.3 per cent of assault or threat, while the possibility of victimization was only 0.9 per cent, 0.0 per cent and 0.7 per cent, respectively (Ito, 1993, p. 387).

Let me finally refer to a different way of arguing for the likelihood of a Japanese uniqueness concerning crime. This perspective does not focus on structural elements in Japanese society but rather on the Japanese way of socializing people. Studies of *Japanese immigrants abroad* indicate that even outside the national borders Japanese citizens behave in a much more law-abiding way than their native co-habitants. Haynes (referred to in Thornton and Endo, 1992, p. 24) writes about the Japanese children in the Japanese colony in Seattle in the pre-war period. His interesting argument is that these children had a very low delinquency rate, though their families were as poor as the people in surrounding areas, whose children had rather high delinquency rates. To Matsushita this case illustrates the role of morality in Japanese socialization. Shame, duty, loyalty, and respect for human relationships are the three most important social standards that can explain Japanese conformity to established rules and norms. Thornton and Endo (1992) support this way of arguing by referring to how Japanese immigrant parents were successful in transmitting their Japanese value orientation to their Oregon-born children. Their starting point was the simple fact that Japanese Americans, be it those who arrived to the US and the Hawaiian Islands in the early 1900s, or immigrants of today, rarely ever violated the law. How could this be explained? Their data, based on interviews with these immigrants, revealed a common pattern. It was the importance of qualities like duty, honour, respect for elders and a strong sense of self-discipline that characterised the upbringing of these children. What these studies tell us is that Japanese immigrants (and not only the first generation!) are carriers of a culture that in a unique way galvanizes against crime. Of course a lot could be said about the soundness of these social standards, but this is a topic I will return to later.

What does popular information on Japan tell us?

Another way of approaching the question of Japan as a low-crime nation is to refer to 'popular opinion'. As we have seen above, statistical comparisons entail many difficulties, so perhaps a more commonsense approach might give an indication of some value? What would that be? I think the judgements given in serious tourist information books give us an interesting testimony. Shelley[14] (1993) report in his book *Japan – Culture Shock* that Japan is one of the safest countries in the world where people can walk anywhere alone after dark. Davies and Jansz (1990) report in their book called *Women Travel* that 'sexual harassment and violence are relatively rare (at least on the streets) and, even wandering around at night, you're unlikely to feel personally threatened' (p.267). De Mente[15] (1992), another author who writes in the popular manner about Japan, has published an insightful *Guide to Appreciating and Experiencing the Real Japan*. This is what De Mente writes under the heading 'The Sense of Safety':

> One of the great advantages of travelling on your own in Japan, either by yourself or with a friend or friends, is that you do not have to worry about personal security. Japan is one of the safest countries in the world. Incidents of public violence, muggings, purse-snatching, and the like are very, very rare. Women (and children) of all nationalities come and go as they please in Japan, day or night, in what could be described as the most disreputable parts of cities, without fearing for their safety. Of course one should exercise sensible caution just to avoid becoming the victim of some rare incident, but there is a great feeling of relief and comfort in the sure knowledge that you do not have to be constantly on guard against a threat of violence (pp. 66–7).

Although some researchers might argue that these popular sources are of little value as scientific documentation, I will dispute this viewpoint of two reasons. These sources are talking about crime only in relation to *public safety*. This means that safety in the private sphere is excluded and so is the huge topic of white-collar crime. It is hard to disregard unanimity among well-informed authors writing in the field of tourist information. I have problems seeing how this type of essential information to travellers could be printed again and again if this was only a vague or disputed characteristic of a society. At least if we exclude (as I do) cases of traffic violence (criminal or not) I regard the evaluations given in these tourist books as one (among many) interesting indications of Japan being a low-crime nation. Let me in this regard also refer back to what I reported in Chapter 1. Both my own experience from the turbulent Olympic City of Nagano during the Games, as well as my experience of travelling with my own daughter in Tokyo, support this conclusion.

Defining the field: narrowing the concept of crime

From what I have written above it should be clear that I am not going to argue in this report that Japan is a low-crime nation concerning crime within the *private sphere*, concerning *white-collar crime*, or in relation to what we could call *traffic violence*. Available research makes Japan's uniqueness dubious in those regards (Mieko, 1999, Kitamura *et al.*, 1999, Sugimoto, 1997). Consequently, I will disregard these types of crimes altogether. I will limit myself to 'traditional', predatory, public order crime. This means I will focus on illegal actions that directly and personally threaten people's property and/or physical security. In short, this is the crime people fear in their everyday life. It is the type of crime where the offender – either due to open aggression or as a result of an outsider status – is able to distance her/himself from an identifiable victim. It is crime committed by people who are loosely integrated into the established society, and who consequently have a conflictual relationship with society.[16] Like white-collar crime, this type of crime might also be described (as Durkheim did) as a strike against the well-defined states of the collective consciousness.

With these caveats, and concerning this type of crime, I support the conclusion that Japan has been a low-crime nation in the mentioned period. Each of the arguments presented in this chapter are not necessarily sufficient argumentation in itself. However, taken together it seems very unlikely that the unambiguous picture told by statistics, research, and popular literature should all lead us astray. Add to this a narrowing of our concept of crime to apply to predatory crimes, I think we should be on a fairly safe ground to start our research for explanations.

A final methodological challenge has to be addressed. Since I will focus on socio-cultural explanations of the unique Japanese crime rates, are there any alternative sets of explanations that first have to be checked? I will comment on two such alternatives: organized crime and circumstances related to economic variables.

Organized crime as a methodological challenge

As already mentioned, Japan has for many years had an extensive activity of organized crime (called the *yakuza*[17]). This is an activity which (like the mafia most other places) is strongly embedded in the society.[18] In a strange way the yakuza has a double and seemingly contradictory role in the Japanese society: it is responsible for serious crimes (20 per cent of all murders in 1975, according to Parker, 1978), while at the same time it is an integral part of the 'formal' social control which is given protection by the police (Kühne, 1994). Kaplan and Dubro (1986) are very explicit on this when they argue that the yakuza operates as an alternative police force in Japan. According to a book published by the US Federal Research Division (1994) 'the yakuza often receives protection from high-ranking officials in exchange for their assistance in keeping the crime rate low by discouraging criminals operating individually or in small groups' (Chapter 8). Henshall (1999) argues in the same way that in the past the police showed considerable tolerance towards the yakuza. As an illustration of the control function filled by the yakuza, Kaplan and Dubro (1986) mention that when President Eisenhower visited Japan he was protected by some 28,000 yakuza members. Von Hurst asserts that

> it is unorganised crime that really terrifies Japanese police, and it is the threat from such groups that can explain why there's so little street crime in Japan. Gangsters control the turf, and they are the ones that provide the security. 'If some odds come around the neighbour-hood and start making trouble, chances are the yakuza will reach them first. Japanese police prefer the existence of organized crime to its absence' (referred in *op. cit.*, p. 163).

Van Wolferen (1989) supports this perspective by arguing that 'the gangsters, who exert control over themselves within crime syndicates, help the police keep non-syndicate crime under control' (p. 101). It is well known that people running companies and restaurants in the big cities have to pay 'protection money' to the yakuza in return for safety guarantees. In this way organized crime takes direct responsibility for crime-preventing activities. Crimes committed within the control sphere of the yakuza will be addressed by this organization rather than by the police, which means that this organization takes care of police functions. Of course, this has consequences for the crime statistics.

What is the relevance of these remarks for the question of interpreting crime rates in Japan? I see four points: 1) When I subsequently analyse crime in Japan, I will do so with reference to strong *informal* social control. I will argue that group pressure and shame culture contribute strongly to the Japanese uniqueness in this regard. However, we also have to keep in mind that the existence of an 'auxiliary' police force (i.e., the yakuza) may be part of our explanation; an explanation that is less about a socially integrated society and more about a *forced* integration. In other words, little crime might as much be a signal of something bad as of something good in this society. 2) One should be aware that the borderline between suicide and murder is sometimes opaque. Kaplan and Dubro (1986) argue that the yakuza is responsible for 11 per cent of all suicides in Japan. People who are in debt to the yakuza are forced to seek this solution to their problems. One might define these suicides as a 'functional equivalent' to murder. What appears in the statistical data as suicide should obviously rather be registered as homicide. 3) With the yakuza so strongly embedded in Japanese society, there is reason to believe that people in authoritative positions will cover up a lot of its criminal actions, at least those with no obvious victims. 4) The yakuza functions in many ways as a kind of safety net for delinquent youth. Young people who otherwise would end up as lonely dropouts from society are absorbed by the yakuza and channelled into organized and 'controlled' (and rarely registered) forms of criminal activity. According to Dubro and Kaplan (1986) 'most new recruits are poorly educated, nineteen to twenty years of age, and are living alone when they join, according to data from Tokyo's National Police Science Research Institute. A surprising number come from broken homes: 43 percent have lost one or both parents' (p. 144).

All of this means that the existence of organized crime in Japan has a substantial yet uncertain intricate impact on crime in Japan. Probably, most of this impact points in the direction of under-communicating the crime problem in Japan. The yakuza represents a considerable deterring effect on potential criminal activity, and it also contributes to the 'evaporation' of a lot of criminal actions that otherwise would end up in the public statistics. When turning to our sociological interpretation of social integration and its effect on the crime pattern in Japan we also have to keep in mind the less flattering answer: social coercion.

Economic equality and low unemployment rates – alternative explanations to little crime?

Like quite a few other criminologists I argue that the unique Japanese crime rates should primarily be linked to explanations that can be traced back to the socio-cultural system. It is *sociological* dimensions, such as being a group society, and *cultural* dimensions, such as being a Confucian, other-directed society, that best explain the Japanese uniqueness. However, perhaps there is a simpler explanation that should be addressed, namely the way Japanese people are taken care of economically. As indicated in Chapter 1, criminologists have often focused on characteristics of the economic system when explaining crime. Unemployment/marginalization and economic inequality/ poverty have been two such dimensions that have been analysed. Perhaps the difference between Japan and the West is to be found in economic/material conditions? Perhaps the Japanese economy produces less marginalization than Western economies? The following questions have to be answered:

Do high unemployment rates and/or a high degree of economic inequality/ poverty have a crime-triggering effect? Are there any significant differences between Japan and the West concerning these questions? Has Japan during the relevant period had less unemployment and/or more economic equality than the West?

The link between crime and unemployment/economic marginalization can be put in this way: crime (for profit) can be regarded as an entrepreneurial action, that is, crime as a 'last resort' for survival (cf. the German writer Bertol Brecht: 'Erst das essen, dann die Moral!'). In such a case crime is an expression of absolute deprivation. Eventually, crime can be regarded in the perspective of relative deprivation, namely, crime as an action 'to keep up with the Jones'. Could differences in these regards explain little crime in Japan? Let me first give a general comment on the relevance of this way of explaining crime.

Balvig and Kyvsgaard (1986) underline the survival aspect of crime concerning earlier times. They show the close relationship that existed between crimes for profit and economic conjunctures. This type of crime increased (in Denmark) when prices on rye were high. A report from 1822 shows that two thirds of all thefts at that time were thefts of clothes, firewood, or what we could in short call bare necessities. Today this is the case in only one out of seven cases (in Denmark at least).[19] No doubt, during history many have survived by crime (Braithwaite (1993) and, in consequence, the criminal justice system has been an instrument of class control.

Hagan (1994) gives us a vivid picture of the relevance of this type of entrepreneurial crime for distressed communities and families even in modern society. In his article 'Crime, Inequality and Efficiency' he argues (with reference to the US) that crime can be understood as 'cultural adaptations to restricted opportunities for the redistribution of wealth' (p. 88). The youth invest their endeavour where it gives the best return, and that will often be within the criminal subculture.[20] In what he calls 'the new ethnographies of poverty' one can register how crime in poverty areas has become a short-term adaptive form of recapitalization for youth. Consequently, one can regard deviant formations as adaptive efforts to survive for individuals and their local communities. In the US, at least, it seems obvious that a significant part of the crime might be traced back to simple lessons from 'economic man': crime is the most rational choice in distressed and poor urban neighbourhoods. Fagan and Freeman (1999) present the same perspective, arguing that crime rates and expected legal wages are inversely related. According to recent ethnographic research, involvement in illegal work is often motivated by low wages and harsh conditions in legal work.[21]

This perspective of crime as an entrepreneurial action is not very different from Merton's (1968) theory on *Social Structure and Anomie*. In this classical work Merton argues that, 'some social structures *exert a definite pressure* upon certain persons in the society to engage in non-conformist rather than conformist conduct' (p. 672). He argues that deviant behaviour results from a disjunction between culturally defined goals to which most members of society aspire, and institutionalized norms (meaning acceptable means for achieving the goals). People who lack the necessary legitimate means to reach internalized cultural goals will turn to illegitimate means, for example crime. For Merton (or, in general, what we call 'opportunity theory'), *relative* deprivation becomes a causal factor that triggers crime in much the same way as absolute deprivation does. This brings us to the question of what kind of relationship exists between crime and economic inequality. Can high crime rates be linked to differences in economic and material wealth?

This question has been discussed by a number of authors. To drop straight to the conclusion I agree with those (see Chiricos, 1987, Watts, 1996b, Braithwaite, 1991, Skolnick, 1995, Taylor, 1998) who warn against simple answers on this topic. Even though Hagan (1996) maintains that research on crime focuses more and more attention on the criminal costs of social inequality, and even though Braithwaite (1989, p. 48) states that being at the bottom of the class structure (being unemployed or poor) increases rates of offending, it is difficult to bring forth empirical 'proofs' that unequivocally show poverty, unemployment or big economic inequalities to be directly causally related to crime. Of course, it is possible to make broad generalizations at an aggregate level that will show co-variation, for example between unemployment or poverty and crime.[22] But as Fukuyama (2000) argues, 'although there is plenty of evidence of a broad correlation between income inequality and crime, this hardly constitutes a plausible explanation for rapidly rising crime rates in the West' (p. 67). He argues that there was no depression in the period from the 1960s to the 1990s when crime increased rapidly, and that the great American postwar crime wave began in a period of full employment and general prosperity.[23] He also rejects the 'crime-income inequality' thesis by reminding one of increasing crime in other Western developed countries that have remained more egalitarian than the US.

This way of arguing is very much like Sutherland's when he tries to falsify the poverty-argument as causing crime. Those who are better off commit extensive crime. Consequently it is of little relevance to focus on unemployment and poverty as a main causal factor in crime – so the argument goes. This seems to me to be an unacceptable and oversimplified way of arguing. Nobody has declared that there is a simple univariate dependency between living conditions and crime. It is common knowledge that countries with a high degree of poverty are not necessarily identical to high crime societies, and in much the same way the opposite is also true. If crime analysis is reduced to simple univariate dependencies you can 'prove' almost anything.[24] According to Watts (1996b) 'close examination of the research done into the unemployment–crime link, and the second line of defence invoking the underclass argument and the political/policy advocacy use made of that scholarship, reveals that any simple links between unemployment rates and crime rates cannot be established' (p. 5). But this is not the same as saying that such links do not exist, which seems to be a fair interpretation of what Fukuyama (2000) thinks. Personally, I would – like Braithwaite (1989), Taylor (1990), Christie (1999), and Currie (1989) – argue that how you are economically situated is of huge importance as concerns the development of crime. Instead of relying on 'impossible' empirical evidence in this connection, we have to rely on more heuristic ways of reasoning, for example like Lea (2002):

the issues of crime control and the resolution of conflicts and harm cannot be separated from the achievement of the conditions necessary for effective dispute resolution. This means, it cannot be said often enough, substantive social equality. Under such conditions, other forms of power and conflicts such as gender and ethnic conflict will not simply evaporate but can be more effectively tackled (p. 190).

From such a point of departure my argument will start with two premises I put forward in Chapter 3: 1. It is a basic need for people to *belong* to a social network; and 2. It is a basic need for people to have a *predictability* and autonomous *control* (social and economic) of their everyday life. Of course, a developed welfare state will give people outside the labour market a certain predictability – as long as the benefits are above a minimum level and are reasonably safe in the long run. But an anonymous welfare disbursement does little to secure a feeling of belonging in the community. I therefore agree with Skolnick (1995) that

> although the causal relationship between crime and employment is complex, it cannot be dismissed. It is not only that people who have reasonably well-paying jobs are less likely to commit crimes than those who do not. It is rather that work is a fundamental aspect of social control. Work disciplines one's daily rounds. Work brings responsibility. Work supports the family life and moral values that conservatives complain we have lost (p. 2).

Consequently, unemployment is a risk factor for crime.

From this, the importance of employment will follow as a logical consequence of our sociological prerequisites concerning belonging and predictability/control. If we approach this with a kind of actor's (i.e. the unemployed) point of view, it seems fair to argue that 'people who cannot see the opportunity to work in either the present or the future, have little incentive to abide by the rules of a society which has rejected them' (Alder, quoted in Watts, 1996b, p. 4). Researchers who have tried to describe the everyday life of unemployed people give a fairly unison version of the problems they experience, namely loss of belonging and loss of control.

Braithwaite (1991) also uses a heuristic approach when he argues that inequality is relevant to the explanation of crime committed by poor people (as well as among the rich ones). He even extends the meaning of inequality to include inequality based on class, race and gender.

Braithwaite explicitly links his perspective to the tradition called 'opportunity theory'. In essence, his argument goes like this: even in modern society crime is motivated (at least in part) by *needs*. A society with inequality of wealth and power will be structurally humiliating and this will undermine respect for the dominion of others. Consequently, basic needs among the less well off will for some be satisfied by illegal means. At the other end of the scale of wealth, rich people will be tempted to commit crimes, not for use (as among the poor), but for exchange. Braithwaite argues that 'inequality causes crime by: (i) decreasing the goods available for *use* by the poor to satisfy needs; and (ii) increasing the goods available to rich people (and organizations) who have needs satisfied, but whose accumulation of goods for *exchange* constitute criminal opportunities to indulge greed' (p. 42).

This perspective is not only a simple argument of crime as a more or less mechanical and instrumental reaction to unsatisfied biological needs. It is a perspective including important psycho-social needs like self-respect and dignity. That is why he develops his thoughts under the headline *The social structure of humiliation*. In this regard he supports Katz's analysis, which makes it possible to include not only crime for profit, but also crime of violence in the theory. According to this perspective rage both recalls and transforms the experience of humiliation. It is an experience of a sense of righteousness that becomes the stepping stone from humiliation to rage.

Triandis (1994), using a socio-psychological perspective, reaches much the same conclusion as Braithwaite and Katz. His basic premise for individual well-being is the feeling of control with one's own situation. Without such a control, man will act irrationally. In societies with great inequality, people at the bottom level will experience frustration exactly because they are unable to control their everyday life. Accordingly, the greater the inequality of opportunity the greater the probability that some will act in aggression.

The 'frustration argument' is broadly accepted also in the literature on *rioting* among working-class youth and ghetto dwellers. Analyses of protests and confrontations in the US (the Kerner Report) and Great Britain (The Scarman Report) tell the same story. If you organize societies in ways where significant number of (especially young) citizens are excluded from the labour market, there should be no surprise if a gradual feeling of uselessness and despair finally turns into destructive rioting. Skolnick (1995, referring to the Kerner Report) reports that the typical riot participant in the US is between 15 and 24 years of age, and – in the Afro-American community – this age group experienced extraordinarily high unemployment rates (some 50 per cent). Skolnick then goes on to ask if it is merely a coincidence that this high-unemployment age group is responsible for a disproportionately high crime rate. His answer is negative.

Finally, at the *political/ideological* level the connection between inequalities and social disintegration has for long been recognized, not only within a leftist/social democratic tradition, but also within the social liberal tradition. The development of the modern Western welfare state, be it in the social democratic, the conservative, or the liberal model (see Esping-Andersen, 1990, Titmuss, 1974) can in many ways be interpreted as recognition of this knowledge. Bismarck initiated the German welfare reforms in the end of the nineteenth century not primarily as a means to relieve poverty, but as a means to avoid a threatening social disintegration with an accompanying political destabilisation. Today, after a long period where the authoritative economic philosophy has argued that an efficient economy demands increasing inequalities, one can register the same political worry within the EU. With 52 million people within the Union living below the poverty line, the threat this represents to the general order has been put on the agenda. In the report *European Social Policy: A Way Forward for the Union* (1994, referred to in Levitas, 1996, p. 8) it is announced that, 'the marginalisation of major social groups is a challenge to the social cohesion of the Union'. In another report (*Growth, Competitiveness, Employment*) the EU acknowledges that the market 'tends to underestimate what is at stake in the long run' (*op. cit.* p.10), and that the speed of changes affects different social categories unequally. As for Bismarck, it is not only pure humanitarian arguments that stimulate interventive action since social division has its obvious economic cost. As I will show in Chapter 3, these perspectives are closer to a communitarian than a liberalistic way of thinking.

The solutions proposed in the EU report to problems of exclusion are what the report calls 'collective solidarity mechanisms'. In practical politics this boils down to a programme to have people employed. The common sense philosophy behind this strategy is the simple fact that it is essentially more difficult to control people who are expelled from the ordinary labour market than those who are not. Within the EU there is obviously an increasing recognition that marginalization threatens social cohesion and makes crime a more probable outcome.[25]

I find it important to underline that a lack of unambiguous empirical 'proofs' to indicate a causal link between crime and unemployment/economic inequality does not falsify that such links nevertheless might exist. It is one thing to say that there is no mechanical relationship between full employment and little crime. It is another thing to deny that increasing unemployment or huge economic inequality does not increase the chances of increasing crime. In this paragraph I have tried to show that a kind of 'opportunity' and 'frustration' theory, linked with our general sociological perspectives on belonging and predictability/ control, makes it very reasonable to argue that it is important to consider different aspects of the economy to understand the crime level in a society.[26] In addition, we should not under-communicate that comprehensive reviews of aggregate research evidence have concluded that 'it is appropriate to argue that evidence favors the existence of a positive, frequently significant U–C [unemployment–crime] relationship' (Chiricos, 1987, p. 203).

So to my second question: has Japan during the relevant period had less unemployment and/or more economic equality than has been usual in most of the Western countries? Concerning unemployment the answer to that question is 'yes' if we talk about the period 1970–85. While the oil crisis from the early 1970s triggered an essential rise in unemployment in the West, Japan continued to sustain stable unemployment rates at about 2–3 per cent. It was only from 1995 that unemployment exceeded 3 per cent, and very slowly increased to 5 per cent in 2001. However, from 1945 until the early 1970s one cannot document any dramatic differences between most Western countries and Japan regarding unemployment. In this period crime was on the increase in the West while decreasing in Japan. This means that differences regarding the situation in the labour market hardly can explain the Japanese uniqueness up till the early 1970s. However, we cannot exclude that differences in unemployment (i.e. *not* socio-cultural variables) between Western countries and Japan have a role to play in explaining different crime patterns in this period.

What about economic inequality? Could little crime in Japan mirror an economic egalitarian society? In this regard it is obviously hopeless to operate with Western countries in toto. As we know, the US has essentially bigger economic differences between top and bottom than the Scandinavian societies. But what if we compare Japan to those Scandinavian countries? As I shall comment in Chapter 4, Japan is usually described as an egalitarian society. To the extent that we can rely on income statistics the gap between the highest and the lowest income groups has until fairly recently been among the smallest in the world. Clifford (1976) observes that 'poverty and underprivilege feature as prominently in the backgrounds of criminals and offenders generally who are brought before the courts in Japan as they do in other countries' (p. 78). However, he adds that there are few signs of class enmity or of the tendency to relate law-breaking to economics, social, or political protest. Nevertheless, there is no reason to regard Japan as more egalitarian than the Scandinavian countries and *these were countries with increasing crime* since the middle of the 1960s. As we shall see, complete income security for each citizen in the Scandinavian countries is probably essentially greater than in Japan because of a far better developed welfare state system.

So where does this take us? My summary of this discussion is as follows:

Crime is probably positively correlated with unemployment and economic inequality.

Low unemployment is *not* a guarantee for little crime.

The *extraordinary* low crime rates in Japan 1945–85 cannot be explained with reference to more favourable unemployment or (in)equality figures than in the West. However, rapidly increasing crime rates in the West since the early 1970s should to some extent be linked to changes in the labour market.

From this overview the hypothesis that little crime in Japan is due to socio-cultural variables has not been falsified even though we have to keep in mind differences concerning the unemployment situation since the 1970s in the two cultures.

The next step is to look into the sociological treasury to a) find appropriate tools for understanding crime in a sociological context, and b) identify relevant analytical dimensions for the discussion of Japanese society (Chapter 4). My intention is to give a general sociological background for understanding what kind of processes it is that might trigger crime.

3

Why Has Modernization in the West Been Synonymous with Increased Crime? Is Rapid Social Change Synonymous with Loss of Moral Sentiments and Loss of Community?

Let me repeat my main perspectives from Chapter 1. Different types of social problems (in casu: crime) have been regarded as a (more or less) necessary concomitant with modernization. Structural changes in society have challenged basic premises for social integration. Developments within the economic system have triggered technological, organizational and social changes, which run counter to fundamental prerequisites for the socio-cultural system. The basic values underpinning the economic system can – as an ideal type – be described as incompatible with the values underpinning the socio-cultural system. From a sociological point of view one can argue that a more or less one-dimensional fulfilment of calls for efficiency, competition and rapid change (generated in the economic system) will generate social changes with which a certain percentage of the population will have problems coping. They will become outsiders, and outsiders will be hard to control. The dreary story of crime preventing policies in the Western world can be regarded as the final proof of the truth of this perspective. No matter what interventionist measures governments have undertaken, and no matter how much money they have spent to prevent crime, the result has been deplorable.[1] Social turbulence means social up-rooting, and this again means a loss of belonging that (as a tendency) will trigger crime.[2]

This way of explaining social disintegration represents a 'positivistic' and deterministic position. The perspective is 'causal'. The final result ('The Great Disruption', to repeat Fukuyama's title) is caused by 'mechanical', 'universal', 'forces'. When crime seems to be the unavoidable consequence of modernization, this is an expression of such a nomotetic way of arguing. Sociology can tell us a lot about the general mechanisms and processes that are at work in this situation. The interesting question here is to what extent the link between modernization and social disinte-gration (crime) really does represent something like a nomotetic link. Is increasing anomie (lack of norms) really close to an unavoidable concomitant of rapid social change? Is moral collapse the only outcome in a market society based on merciless competition?

The case of Japan makes a more optimistic perspective possible. Social disintegration following rapid social change might be counteracted via a) strong normative regulation (which, as I will show later, could also be described as coercive or benevolent suppression), and/or via b) organizing principles that safeguard social integration. Be it religion, cultural values, morals, or the content of the socialisation process, it can be argued that disruptive forces can be kept in check via 'cultural bonding'. Such forces might also be counteracted if social life is organized in ways that take care of basic values such as belonging and predictability. While the positivistic perspective is causal and deterministic, the case of Japan invites a more volitional and libertarian perspective. The enigma of agency gives man a space for manoeuvring (McCann, 1998, p. 170). Individuals, and thereby cultures, will always have a 'freedom to choose' between different options.[3] From this point of view, the Marxian thesis that the 'superstructure' is nothing but a reflection of the 'base' has to be modified. The logic of capitalism and market ideology does not necessarily prescribe one and *only one* superstructure. As Berger (1987) has pointed out, Japan has demonstrated that 'individual autonomy is not an intrinsic quality of the economic culture of capitalism' (p. 170). In general, Confucian capitalistic countries in Asia fully illustrate this argument (at least until recently). Even if the economic system in two different societies is based on a capitalistic market principle, this leaves open a relatively wide space for distinctive development of culture. At least this seems to be so until recently, namely before the globalization process escalated.

To what extent the relative autonomy of the socio-cultural system should be defined only in terms of a 'cultural lag' (Ogburn, quoted in Smelser, 1967) or in terms of a real and persisting autonomy, is a ques-tion that has to be left aside in this connection. The interesting issue is the independent role of norms, values, moral, ideologies, social structures, etc. in a culture based on a market economy. Of course, such a discussion has to be more specific. Indisputably, *different* cultural value systems can go in tandem with the *same* economic system. However, it is another question to which extent cultures at a given time are 'free' to choose their future paths concerning normative structure. To put it another way, to argue that the case of Japan confirms the thesis of 'cultural autonomy', is something other than arguing that cultures can 'learn' and freely adopt whatever normative patterns they might decide upon. I will return to this discussion.

Obviously, Japanese culture triggers the in-deterministic idea that the basic value foundation of the socio-cultural system may have a determining influence on the value foundation of the economic system (cf. Fig. 1.1). Is it possible that values such as collectivism (vs individualism), altruism (vs egosim), time (vs efficiency), stability (vs change), social obligation (vs individual maximization), predictability (vs unpredictability), and security (vs insecurity), can 'defeat' their counterparts? Is it possible that an 'old fashioned' and (many would say) idealistic idea about 'morals' can counteract strong disruptional forces (turbulence, uprooting, alienation) at work in the economic system? Is it possible that 'traditional' social structures (like primary groups) might be carried on to modernized and urbanized societies?

To answer these types of questions we first have to address two specific topics:

1) *Since crime has been defined as a more or less unavoidable concomitant of modernization and urbanization, what, in more detail, is the logic behind this argument? Since scholars seem to postulate some kind of causal relationship between those two phenomena, what is the substance of this argument?*[4]

2) *Since the case of Japan seems to falsify the nomothetic character of modernization and crime, and since 'culture' (normative and social structures) seems to be the focal dimension, what has social science to say about the role of culture to explain social action? What is the status of morality as a strong and (more or less) independent preventive force in the literature of social science? Is the talk about values, norms and morality only phrases from a popular debate based on common sense prejudices, or does it have any 'scientific' relevance?*

Of course, those two topics are closely linked together. Social structures represent the 'underlay' for moral and cultural development.[5] Nevertheless, it is important to operate with an analytical distinction between those two perspectives since one of my main questions is the relative autonomy and the independent effect of culture in relation to economic/technological and social changes. So let's start with the discussion of crime as the dependent variable in, or crime as the 'unavoidable' consequence of, the modernization process.

Social disruption as the consequence of structural changes

I mentioned in Chapter 1 that social impacts of modernization are ambiguous. As Hirschmann (1986, cf. Giddens, 1990, Bauman, 2000a) points out in his essay 'Rival Views of Market Society', two schools contest the proper way of describing the fruits of capitalism. According to the 'Doux-Commerce' thesis capitalism would, via trade and industry, gradually have a civilizing effect on society. Commerce is regarded as a moralizing agent in that it brings about social harmony and civilized behaviour among people. The market expansion is supposed to restrain otherwise unregulated actions and, at the same time, restrain excessive and coincidental political forms of power.[6]

The 'Self-Destruction' thesis represents a contradictory perspective. From Marx to the Frankfurt School, from Toennies and Durkheim to the Communitarian School (Etzioni, Fukuyama), this perspective focuses on what Marx called the 'barbarian' aspects of capitalism. To understand why the turbulent market society triggers crime (as well as a lot of other social problems) we have to turn to this tradition. My intention here is to summarize briefly the logic behind what has been called the '*sociology of worry*' or the tradition of '*progress- and cultural-pessimism*' (Rasmussen, 1996). Even though most of the authors included in this tradition expressed some ambivalence to modernity, my mission in the present analysis is to purify the perspectives that focus on the eroding forces at work as market society develops. Or to put it in the words of Polanyi: 'The conflict between the market and the elementary requirements of an organized social life provided the century with its dynamics and produced the typical strain and stresses which ultimately destroyed that society' (quoted from Olofsson, 1999, p. 41). A schematic presentation is given in Figure 3.1.

One does not need to be a Marxist to identify the 'engine' behind the modernization process as being the economic system (Fig. 3.1, box 1), and by that meaning the capitalist market system. If we use the idea of a free market with open competition as an ideal type, it is fair to say that the market competition will *automatically* generate technological change. Each participator in the market system (on the production side) has to 'compete or die'. To survive in the competition one *has to* invest the surplus in new and more advanced technology. The alternative is to be eradicated.

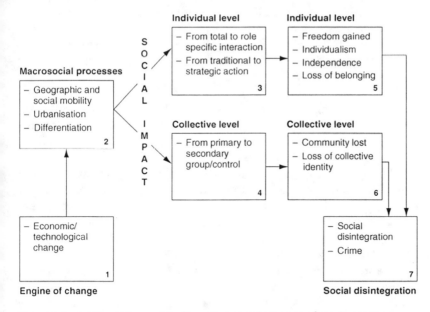

Figure 3.1 A schematic model of negative social impacts of modernization

New technology does not only mean changes in the *physical* means of production. It initiates huge spatial and social changes as well (box 2). As the criminologist Christie (1975) points out, a 'society of wheelbarrows' will create vastly different social structures than a 'society of trucks'. According to Christie, there is no doubt that these two societies will have very different levels and patterns of crime. Not only is the high tech society a more closed or expert society, but (as Illich, 1973, shows) this society will also kill alternative cultures of tools. The expelling process has started.

Classical sociology from Toennies, Weber, Durkheim and Simmel, to Parsons, Lockwood and Habermas has typically described the modernization process by the analytical categories *differentiation* and *rationalization*. Polanyi (in Olofsson, 1999) uses the concept 'disembedding' for describing this differentiation process. In traditional society (i.e. pre-industrial and pre-capitalist society) economic aspects were embedded into the general social web. During the period of industrialization and within the frame of a liberal market system society was split into different spheres (in what he called a 'disembedding process'). The consequence was a gradual de-coupling of the economy from its links to other subsystems. As the civilizing process went on, different spheres of society became more and more specialized and 'closed' to each other. Politics, economics, religion, etc. turned into more or less autonomous spheres, a development that many would read as a prerequisite for creating a liberal democracy (counteracting a centralized state power).

However, this process of differentiation and rationalization could be described as ambiguous in its consequences. While creating a fertile soil for both economic growth and an open and liberal democracy, it created an unwanted turbulence in the socio-cultural system. When the general concept of differentiation is specified to increased division of work, and social and geographic mobility (cf. urbanization), one can easily see that the differentiation process might create both *uncertainty/unpredictability* and a *loss of belonging/loosening of social bonds.*[7] According to Weber (1964) social action is directed to other people's way of behaving and, consequently, we have to presuppose that these actions are to a certain extent predictable. Cultures heavily based on customs, habits, consistent and universally accepted norms, laws, etc. will have good conditions for predictability. Situations of turbulence and rapid social change will easily undermine this cultural network. Furthermore, the importance of belonging is closely linked to social control/social bonding. According to the criminological tradition from Durkheim to Hirschi deviance will increase in societies where the ties to the conventional order of closely-linked primary groups are loosened/broken. When this process of specialization and differentiation not only flourishes in the economic system but gradually also takes place within the socio-cultural system, the feeling of uncertainty and loss of belonging will increase. Life in this modern world will represent a new challenge for each individual, especially related to what Weber called 'Sinnverlust' or a loss of meaning. When increasing differentiation goes in tandem with increasing rationalization,[8] the existential unity of life is split, and this will challenge the earlier experience of the life world as integrated and meaningful. In this modern world the individual has become more (socially) vulnerable than before.

Analytically speaking we can differentiate social consequences at two levels (Fig. 3.1, boxes 3 and 4): the *individual* and the *collective/communal* level.[9] Let me start with the last one.

A more mobile and turbulent society means that the so-called *secondary groups* (i.e. groups of shorter durability, and with a more limited and specialized aim) increase in importance, while *primary groups* ('the nursery of human nature' as Cooley, 1964, called them), like the family, become less important. This change in the group affiliation of the individual will affect the way people exert informal social control on each other. The *primary control* exerted through close ties with 'significant others' will more and more be replaced by the *secondary control* exerted by formalised agents (like the police). The traditional viewpoint among sociologists and criminologists is that the effect of the primary control exercised by the primary group is far better and more far-reaching than the secondary control.[10] Accordingly, so the argument goes, crime and deviance will hamper life in the modern urban setting.

If the important change at the collective level is the transformation from primary groups exercising primary control to secondary groups exercising (a weaker) secondary control, how is this change experienced at the individual level? Two types of answer can be given – one related to a perspective from 'role sociology', another related to 'action theory'.

Let's return to our concept of primary control and ask why primary control is more effective than secondary control? A simple answer given from the perspective of *role sociology* would be 'because people will control each other as total persons'. What does this mean?

One implication of the differentiation process will be an ever-increasing specialization of roles. Specialized functions means specialized roles. People who know each other as total or whole persons will exercise a stronger control of each other than those interacting only along role-specialized dimensions. 'The more I know about you, and the more you know about me, the more we will control each other' – this is the essence of the argument.[11] Role specific interaction, where the persons involved disclose only parts of themselves, will be less controlling than interaction among total persons.

The relevance of this perspective to understand crime in Japan will soon become very obvious. Japan is first of all a 'group society'. Every citizen is linked to structures of primary relations that very likely will have a crime preventive function. Or to express it another way: if the Japanese group structure does not have such an effect, then the sociology of deviance should be fundamentally revised.

Another perspective regarding consequences of social change at the individual level follows if we use a perspective from *action theory*. Differentiation and rationalization are accompanied by an increasing *secularization*. In the pre-modern world the human being would find meaning in a metaphysical worldview. Imaginations of 'heaven and hell' gave some kind of meaning to life. Religion was one way of coping with different kinds of existential problems.

However, according to Weber, the process of modernization is at the same time a process of rationalization, and this increasing rationalization of the life world undermines the ability of the individual to experience her/his life as meaningful. The rationalized life leads to a change in pre-conditions for the reproduction of our basic life motivation. In other words, the paradoxical situation Weber describes is how man's searching for logic and explanation undermines the basic meaning of existence. Man gets captured in a cold 'iron cage'.

In modern society an increasingly instrumental type of rationality takes control. This means that people will increasingly follow a strategic, calculative way of behaving which in turn, may create a distance between people. This aspect of modern life has been described as a typical trait among urban dwellers (Park, 1952, Wirth, 1938, Saunders, 1981).

What is the relevance of these perspectives to my analysis of crime in Japan? Japan can in some respects be described as a 'value rational' society (as opposed to an 'instrumental rational' society) in spite of being highly modernized and urbanized. The omnipresence of a unique combination of Confucianism, Buddhism, and Shintoism, makes Japan in many ways a more value-oriented society than Western societies (Chapter 4). This, of course, has effect on basic attitudes and ways of addressing other people. I will return to the criminological implications of this later on.

Let me next (Fig. 3.1, box 5) continue to specify (as 'ideal types') some *negative social impacts* of modernity, and now move from the individual to the collective level again.

To simplify the story, much of the sociological worry about modernity can – at the community level – be described as different series of 'loss of....' – statements. A résumé of the relevant literature has given me the following list of typical characteristics used by these 'worried sociologists':

A loss of community
A loss of collective identity
A loss of social context
A loss of transcendental moral and religious order
A loss of communal solidarity
A loss of emotional communities
A loss of density of acquaintanceship
A loss of collective memory
A loss of a common symbolic universe
A loss of trust
A loss of relatedness
A loss of meaning

Part of the communitarian movement (see the second part of this chapter) expresses many of these 'demonic' characterizations of life in modern society. Even though it is wrong to argue that classical sociology (in toto) can be described as a one-sided representative of the self-destruction thesis, there are many examples of a pessimistic attitude towards modernity within sociology.

Toennies is a central character in this tradition. Traditional society, presented by Toennies with the concept of *gemeinschaft*, is characterized by close and intimate bonds between people. Toennies describes tribe-like situations where people are linked together by a common language, common culture and a common belief. The concord among people is based on consensus and a feeling of solidarity. All these characteristics are fundamental for social integration into society. As we shall see, many authors use exactly the same concepts to describe Japanese society today.

Toennies does not romanticize traditional society, but he is obviously very worried about how the modern 'gesellschaft' society destroys fundamental aspects of the social web.[12] Toennies is definitely (like Cooley) a 'conservative' sociologist.

Even though Durkheim expressed ambivalent perspectives about the qualities of modern society, and even though he was more preoccupied with safeguarding individual rights than many people used to think, he should also be regarded as a 'conservative' sociologist. Nygaard (1995) gives us this evaluation in support of such a conclusion:

> Durkheim is most of all occupied by, and worried about, the social conditions of his own times. In his different analyses he continually points to the inhuman sides of modern society, and he puts forward traditional social structures and values as positive alternatives. For Durkheim, the cultural rationalisation and the accompanying secularisation and differentiation represented an evil. It meant dissolution of the inner relationship between the actor and the actor's social surroundings; in modern society the social structures have an alienating effect as for the actor's self-reflection and opportunities for action. However, at the same time, he meant that one could not stop the human development and return to traditional society (p. 32).

One main argument supporting the description of Durkheim as a conservative sociologist is his *focus on the collectivity* (like conservatism in general). In many ways I think Durkheim would have fancied the Japanese society in this regard. This is the quintessence of Durkheim's writing in support of such a conclusion:

Durkheim is certainly a central author when the topic is preconditions for social order. He refutes the liberalistic idea that order and harmony are natural consequences of modern utilitaristic and individual action. The individual freedom that might be gained through a more efficient, rationalistic and calculating way of acting will easily be perverted into the dreadful opposite unless society itself manages to ensure a collective identity that can express the moral of solidarity and concord. The integrated society is, for Durkheim, a society where the totality is present in the conscience of each single person. From this perspective modernity represented a possible threat to society in so far as it meant a strengthening of the individual conscience at the cost of the collective conscience (in contrast to Rousseau who was worried about the threat modernity represented to the *self*). But it is important to stress that Durkheim, like Rousseau, was not an anti-modernist. Alienated individuals *might* be the result of rapid social change, but this was definitely not a *necessary* concomitant of modernity.

Durkheim, stressing the importance of a *collective identity*, and a *collective conscience* to secure social integration in society, is very relevant to our understanding of Japan. It has been argued that every Japanese citizen in her/his everyday life behaves as if Japan is an integral part of her/him. Such behaviour is a precise illustration of a very strong collective mentality. When Durkheim writes (theoretically) about how a collective conscience contributes to link the individual actors together, this could very well have been an empirical description of Japanese society.

Another aspect of Durkheim's sociology that is relevant to Japan is his discussion on *moral tightness*. This concept covers social situations where the individual has moral conceptions not only in relation to her/his own primary group, but also to members of a broader social system.

In a society with a collective conscience one will find that people will experience symbolic bonds between each other in ways that are obligatory. Sennett (1998) comments on this in his book *The Corrosion of Character*:

A place becomes a community when people use the pronoun 'we'. To speak in this way requires a particular though not a local attachment; a nation can constitute a community when in it people translate shared beliefs and values into concrete, daily practices. Rousseau was the first modern writer to understand how deeply the workings of politics are founded on these rituals of everyday life, how much politics depends on the communal 'we'. One of the unintended consequences of modern capitalism is that it has strengthened the value of place, aroused a longing for community (pp. 137–8)

The opposite situation is a society where people first of all talk about 'I', 'my point of view', or 'I would like' rather than 'we'. According to Durkheim, the process of modernization will easily weaken the collective conscience and strengthen the individual conscience. As a tendency this will contribute to loosening of bonds between members of society and, in extreme cases, create anomic social circumstances.

These theoretical observations are definitely relevant to the case of Japan. Japan is usually described as a homogeneous and uniform society. The so-called 'nihonjinron'-debate (about being Japanese) shows that there is a strong tendency – not the least among Japanese scholars – to talk about the uniqueness of the Japanese. This implies an assertion about a common culture and moral foundation which, in consequence, suggests a specific 'moral tightness' in this society. I shall return to this and an opposing viewpoint.

Finally, an author who represents a very explicit negative view regarding social impacts of modernity is Polanyi. However, in contrast to Toennies and Durkheim, and though he has been accused of romanticizing pre-market societies (see Olofsson, 1999, p. 38), he represents a 'radical' critique of the market mentality.

In Chapter 1 I presented my main research question in the following way: does Japan represent a case where the economic system does not dominate the socio-cultural system altogether? Polanyi argues that findings of historical and anthropological research show that economic affairs as a rule have been submerged in social relationships. However, with the development of the capitalistic market system the influence goes in the opposite direction. 'Instead of economy being embedded in social relations, social relations are embedded in the economic system' (quoted from Olofsson, 1999, p. 44). To Polanyi, this turns the market economy into a dominating and even imperative force. 'For once the economic system is organized in separate institutions, based on specific motives and conferring a special status, society must be shaped in such a manner as to allow that system to function according to its own laws' (*op. cit.*, p. 45). Expressions like these sound like a mechanical materialistic perspective. When social scientists talk about 'laws', this echoes a determinative Marxian perspective.

For Polanyi it is a primary concern to make the social impacts of this autonomous economic system explicit. He regards them as 'catastrophic'. For many people, it is not just the modern factory that becomes a 'satanic mill', but the whole of society! 'According to Polanyi, the serious and harmful transformation brought about by market society was not the economic standards of living (focused by the historians' "standard of living debate"), but the *loss of the social context*' (Olofsson, 1999, p. 42).[13]

However, with the development of the Western welfare state, a 're-embedding process' starts (or a 'de-commodification process' to use Esping-Andersen's (1990) concept). This has contributed to counteract some of the stresses on the socio-cultural system.

The interesting question is whether Japan, as a capitalistic market society, but without many of the Western welfare arrangements, has managed to avoid social disintegration and, if so, how has this eventuality been achieved?

If we search for a kind of common denominator of negative social impacts on the collective level, this would be the term '*a loss of community*'. Sociology tells us that the Thatcher slogan 'there is no such thing as society', is absolutely incorrect. Societies (or, better, 'communities') do exist, not only as given realities, but also as social and mental constructions (cf. Cohen, 1989, and Hunter, 1974, writing about symbolic communities). Gold (1985) points out the important difference between a town and a settlement, a distinction that reminds us that collectivities are something more than just individual aggregates. When Dahrendorf (1985) talks about the 'weakening of ligatures' (p. 25),[14] when Durkheim talks about 'anomie',[15] when Fukuyama (1995) talks about 'loss of trust' in society, when Freudenburg (1986) talks about changes in 'the density of acquaintanceship', when both Burke, Durkheim and the communitarians talk about the weakening of 'emotional communities' (see Guneriussen, 1999), when Polanyi talks about the 'loss of social context', when Kawai (1998) talks about 'loss of relatedness', and when Lockwood (1999) talks about the 'loss of communal solidarity', these are all expressions that confirm Durkheim. Society is something 'sui generis'. As a soccer team consisting of eleven individual players is something more and something different from the aggregate of the eleven players, a society is something more and something different from the sum of citizens. The very moment a society turns into nothing more than a settlement, we are back to a Hobbesian situation. Translated to our present discussion this means that situations approaching something like a 'loss of community' will certainly also mean a high level of crime.

Let me next (Fig. 3.1, box 6) try to identify what these processes might *mean* at the individual level. Watts (1996) has demonstrated that the preoccupation among the founding fathers of sociology is with the problem of social order in changing societies and that this has 'resulted in a privileging of the public and the structural over the private and the motivational' (p. 128). Such a statement could easily invite a discussion on the never-ending topic between micro- and macro-perspectives in sociology. I will not enter this controversy (for a good summary, see Mouzelis, 1995). But I do support the Weberian thesis that sociology should search for explanations that are both 'Sinn-Adequate' and 'Kausal-Adequate' (i.e. explaining social phenomena both as result of individual meaningful actions, and as the result of 'autonomously', 'externally', and 'mechanically' operating forces). When the focus is on understanding 'Japanese uniqueness', it will be obvious how important it is to analyse both the structural and cultural (meaning aggregate) level, *and* the individual and micro level (especially the socialization process).

Berger (1987) sums up the impacts of the modernization process on the individual level with these words:

> There is strong evidence that all over the world, at least in nonsocialist societies, modernisation has an individuating effect – not, to be sure, in the fullfledged Western or American sense of 'individualism' but in the sense of freeing the individual from the constraints of traditional groupings, such as those of kinship, village, caste, or ethnicity. Put simply, modernisation, at least under conditions of capitalism, increases individual autonomy (p. 176).

As supporting evidence for this thesis, Berger refers to Toennies (gemeinschaft/gesellschaft) and Durkheim (organic/mechanic solidarity). However, from this general statement Berger goes on to make an important (and for our analysis interesting) reservation by saying that the interesting question is whether East Asia offers another exception in this area: 'Has the cultural substance of Western modernity "infected" East Asia along with its external forms? To what extent has East Asia succeeded in modernising itself under capitalist conditions without the process of becoming more "individualistic"?' (p. 167).

Let me concentrate here on the last question concerning the assertion of *increasing individualism*.

The 'community lost' effect at the collective level is corresponded by a 'freedom gained' effect at the individual level.[16] Especially related to analysis of the modern urban life style one will find arguments supporting this viewpoint. Those scholars focusing on the positive aspects of modern individualism stress how the urban personality is characterized by openness, self-confidence, tolerance and an unprejudiced way of handling people.

On the other hand, representatives of the 'Chicago school' (Park, 1952, Wirth, 1938) stress the more negative story concerning the individual level. The urban personality is described as superfluous, unconcerned, reserved, cold and blasé.[17] Modern life is characterised by turbulence, many and continually changing impressions, and short-term relationships, which in turn will lead to a non-involving way of behaving. The 'front stage' becomes the most important arena for judging people, and this stimulates a performative, status-seeking,[18] and unauthentic behaviour. As a consequence, people will to a decreasing degree behave in a caretaking and bothering way.

The concept of *independence* is that which best describes the lifeworld of modern, urbanized man. Focus on individuality, on individual freedom, on individual rights in a culture of social and geographical mobility will (as a tendency) contribute to loosen the reciprocal dependency between people. Modern Japan deviates quite a bit from this description. While a basic aim in socializing children in the West is to create independence, the situation is the opposite in Japan. Here, dependency between people represents a positive value, which, consequently, is stressed in the socialising process. According to Sennett (1999) dependency has more and more come to have a negative meaning in the West:

> The social bond arises most elementally from a sense of mutual dependence. All the shibboleths of the new order treat dependence as a shameful condition: the attack on rigid bureaucratic hierarchy is meant to free people structurally from dependence; risk-taking is meant to stimulate self-assertion rather than submission to what is given. Within modern corporations, there is no honorable place for service – the very word conjures up the last refuge of the time-server. John Kotter's celebration of consulting as the acme of flexible business behavior supposes that the consultant is beholden to no one. None of these repudiations of dependence as shameful, however, promotes strong bonds of sharing (p. 139).

Since this perspective is central in contrasting the West and Japan, let me refer to another paragraph from Sennett:

> Similarly, in many societies there has been little or no shame attached to more public experiences of dependence, where the weak are in need of the strong. The ancient Roman client asked his patron for favors or help as a matter of course, and the patron lost face if he could not take care of those who looked to him. Louis Dumont and Takeo Doi

have documented how in Indian and Japanese societies dependence has similarly carried no hint of self-abasement. In early capitalism, as Albert Hirschmann has shown, trust in business relations arose through open acknowledgement of mutual dependence – which is not quite the same as an honorable relation between strong and weak, but still a recognition that alone one is insufficient to support oneself. Jacques Savary, the seventeenth-century author of *Le parfait négotiant*, declared that divine providence wills 'that men would trade together and so that the mutual need which they have to help one another would establish ties of friendship among them.' And when traders admit to mutual need, Montesquieu observed a century later, 'commerce ... polishes and softens barbarian ways' (p. 140).

From this quote we can see that Sennett agrees with Berger (1987) that the 'freedom gained' effect of modernity has the price of increased root-lessness. His perspective has strong links both to a Marxian *alienation* perspective and to a Durkheimian perspective on *anomie* (even though Durkheim's term applies to *social*, not to individual circumstances).[19]

Weber, focusing 'Sinn Adequate' explanations, asks how the individual will experience huge structural changes in her everyday life. Modern life is for Weber synonymous with a more or less rationalized life. Increasing rationality, however, does not deliver what it seems to promise, namely precise answers to man's many basic questions about life. As secularization increases modern man is more and more bereaved of the old 'meaning-creating' institution of religion. This, for Weber, is conducive to creating a *problem of meaning* at the individual level, which will make life more troublesome. When Weber talks about an increasing 'Sinnverlust', he talks about changes in the individual lifeworld where the different spheres of life are no longer linked together in a meaningful whole.

This aspect of modernity is also of relevance in our discussion of Japan. Do 'beliefs' like Shintoism, Buddhism and Confucianism in Japan operate as 'functional equivalents' to traditional Western religion, and do these value systems represent an active force in everyday life in modern Japan?

Another example of a 'loss of' – feeling at the individual level can be found in Durkheim's writing on *limited and satiable needs versus unlimited and insatiable needs.*

According to Durkheim, man is different from animals in one important way: without externally imposed restrictions, human needs have no limits. When they have finished eating, animals retire and rest. This is different for man. We continue our search for satisfaction of new needs in an endless process – unless someone imposes a normative restriction upon us. Our ability to reach need satisfaction is consequently dependent on a kind of regulation of these needs. This regulation should (for Durkheim) be made by 'society'. Durkheim also underlines that our ability to define the limits of our needs is dependent on our ability to acknowledge our place in society. As we shall see, a central hallmark of Japanese culture is, precisely, to take one's proper station.

The *anomic* society is a society with lasting and considerable differences between aspirations and real possibilities for realizing these aspirations. Societies undergoing a boom (eventually a bust) are thus vulnerable to anomic processes. Expectations of personal spin-offs can easily exceed what can be realized in real life. In such a case, different types of 'a-social' reactions might be the result. In Japan it is not personal but group spin-offs that matter the most.

One important aspect of this phenomenon is the problem of *relative deprivation*. What classical theorists remind us is that people might be very frustrated even though a growth process is Pareto-optimal (i.e. somebody improves their situation while nobody becomes worse off). People's feelings of social and material well-being is not so much a question of absolute as of relative standards. It is your own position *in relation* to important reference groups that matters the most if you want to understand people's subjective experience of satisfaction. In other words, if people *expect* some kind of profit and they do not get it, it is of little comfort to remind them that this is a status quo situation. And this is especially so if a colleague or a neighbour succeeds in what you missed out on. Both your own expectations as well as your lifeworld's ability to cope with a new challenge will determine your own degree of satisfaction.

Theories of relative deprivation have been central to criminology for a long time. Best known is perhaps Merton's perspective (elaborating Durkheim). In the American society everybody will internalize the aim of material wealth and success. But everybody will not have an equal chance of reaching this aim. In the run for success some people start lagging behind. But these people nevertheless have the same wish for goal-attainment. If they can't manage this by way of legal measures, they will use illegal strategies. In short, crime becomes an opportunity for reaching material wealth. According to this theory, societies with a low degree of economic inequality will have less crime than those at the opposite end of the scale (cf. Chapter 2).

Not only relative deprivation, but (of course) also absolute deprivation might trigger crime. As Hagan (1994) shows, crime can be regarded as 'cultural adaptations to restricted opportunities for the redistribution of wealth' (p. 88).

Let me end this discussion by turning to the perspective of social psychology. Are there any general lessons to be learned from this discipline concerning the individual level? Man has few instincts and is consequently in need of a high degree of institutionalization (Berger and Luckmann, 1966, Wrong, 1994[20]). Man is an 'ordering creature'. Our only way to create predictability is through institutionalization. Institutionalization also helps us avoid uncertainty.

In *The psychology of control*, Langer (referred to in Triandis, 1994) shows how man has a basic need for control in his everyday life. Hagan (1994) shows in a similar way that people living in slum areas use crime as a way of getting control of their everyday life. Braithwaite (1991, referring to Clark) stresses the same point as for the function of crime in olden-days Australia. According to Triandis (1995), cultures that do not have collective networks as a kind of buffer, will experience more stress than cultures that have such networks.

Japan has certainly a higher degree of predictability than Western countries, both if we refer to the family sphere and if we refer to the employment sphere. According to Komiya (1999) 'the Japanese can almost anticipate their position 20 or 30 years hence. This high predictability narrows the gap between aspirations and expectations as the source of strain. This strain was thought to drive people to commit crime according to Merton's "strain theory"' (p. 385).

To sum up our discussion of social impacts on the individual level, a strong tradition in social science underlines the importance of collective framing of individual life conditions. The existence of a social community is a prerequisite for becoming a socialized person, and it is a prerequisite for reaching a shared understanding of the world. The ability to 'take the role of the other' (Mead, 1934) assumes a reciprocity of perspectives where 'society' represents a given framework. Society comes first, then comes the individual (Bruun and Christie, 1985). Being a human being will always imply living with a tension between individual freedom/autonomy and dependency/sociability.

Let me finally pull together some of the threads from this section. Life in modern society is definitely characterized by a 'freedom gained' effect compared to life in traditional society. The consequences of this increased freedom are ambiguous. While the liberals argue along an optimistic logic (a belief in rationality and in progress and modernization, a more open society), others (be it conservatives, communitarians or quite a few social scientists) will argue that what the liberals designate 'liberation' for some others will mean 'dissolution'. Guneriussen (1999) supports the aim of freedom and autonomy, but points out that, at the same time, it is difficult to find in this philosophy a clear picture of the content of 'the good (social) life'. We should also add, like Magnussen (1983, p. 8), that the value pluralism we find in modern society is something that the strong-minded among us enjoy, while others will pay a price for this pluralism.

So, if we limit ourselves to focus only the possible negative aspects of modernity we can argue in this way:

A loss of meaning and a loss of unity of existence can accompany increasing rationalization and secularization. This development is not compensated with other meaning-carrying institutions – at least in the West. For the individual, this can be experienced as a threatening development. Our question is whether this description of modernity fits less well in modern Japan, due to its 'religious substitutes' or what sociologists call 'functional equivalents'.

Not only loss of meaning, but also a loss of belonging might be an aspect of how the individual experiences modernity. This is linked to the description we gave of 'independence' as a cherished value in the West. Increasing independence from significant others can definitely be described as a freedom gained, but it is at the same time a freedom from both important social and emotive support, and from important social control. The situation is very different in Japan, where an understanding of 'the anatomy of dependence' (Doi, 1976) is basic to an understanding of its culture.

Modernity invites situations where people are stimulated to behave like 'kids in a candy store' (Leonardsen, 1996). In a society of unbridled individual consumerism people are seduced into thinking that each individual, more or less by herself, should try to get hold of everything the commercials say one needs. Life turns (as Durkheim describes it) into a 'strained life string' with a lot of stress. Japan will not be very different from Western societies in this drive for affluence and success. But again; in Japan it is more the success of the group than that of the individual that counts. That may make a difference.

From what we know about human reactions to rapid social change, we can say that unpredictability and uncertainty have a negative impact on most people. As we shall see later, it *may* be that an average Japanese citizen, in spite of a modest welfare state, has a higher degree of predictability and certainty than most people in Western societies.

Where does this take us? From a sociological point of view modern society implies a structural change with potentially disintegrative effects.

It can obviously be argued that what Fukuyama (2000) describes as 'the fall of social order' is closely linked to massive turbulence in the wake of modernity.[21] However, in very guarded terms I have also suggested that Japanese society might seem to have succeeded in 'separating' structural economic changes on one side from social/cultural changes on the other side. Even though modernization along some dimensions seems to develop in a predictive way, in total, this process should not be described in deterministic terms. The case of Japan – at least until the early 1990s – might suggest that the socio-cultural system has a relative autonomy to which the West has paid too little attention. If modernity represents a threat to stable primary group relations, to feelings of belonging, etc., then there still seem to be ways to safeguard basic social values, at least if these values are operationalized as 'crime'.

In this section I have analytically focused on *structural* aspects of the modernization process (even though I have also indicated more substantial aspects). I have been mainly interested in 'social forms' rather than 'cultural content'. Of course, these dimensions are closely linked together, but again, not in a deterministic way. Structural forms constitute an important framework for cultural transmission, but this framework far from determines the content of this transmission. In the preceding discussion I have presented a very general perspective on possibly negative aspects in the wake of the modernization process. Implicit in this presentation is the assumption that these negative aspects also will have a crime-triggering effect. In a few subheadings I have linked my presentation to Japanese society and culture and (so far) only hinted that the unique Japanese crime patterns *might* have a connection to unique Japanese social structures.

On the other hand (or perhaps in addition), one could also argue that *cultural content* (values, morals), rather than social structures, is the important independent variable to explain social integration in Japanese society. At least at an analytical level one can make a distinction between these two dimensions. This is the question I will follow in the next section: what role do values and morals play in explaining individual behaviour in social science?

Social disruption as the consequence of cultural and moral decay

As Parsons (1951) points out, values held in common constitute the primary reference point for the analysis of a social system. Nevertheless, perspectives inviting 'morals' as a relevant dimension to understanding social action have easily been accused of carrying an idealistic bias and, consequently, have had a secondary status in sociology.[22] Value-based explanations easily turn out to be tautological (actions are explained by referring to values, and values are explained by referring to actions, cf. Østerberg, 1988). Nevertheless, we would jump to conclusions if we – *at the collective level* – rejected the relevance of cultural values as an important aspect of cross-cultural differences in social patterns (for example like crime).

Consequently, let me (still at the general, theoretical level) give a short presentation of the role of value- and moral-based explanations in social science. Starting with the founding father of liberalism and ending with today's communitarian movement my intention is to show that the moral dimension both has had, and still has, weight within the social sciences.

Adam Smith is often regarded as a typical representative of the period of Enlightenment. In his famous book *On the Wealth of Nations* from 1776 he presented the basic principles of liberalistic thinking. In popular presentations of this (and corresponding texts) man is reduced to an economic animal, tracing restricted, but rationally calculated, economic goals, applying cost–benefit analysis in his/her decisions and priorities, pursuing egoistic rather than altruistic goals and, in consequence, lacking a broader culturally based and value oriented reference for decisions and actions. In a state of the pure cultivation of this perspective the common good is best attained if each individual pursues her/his own interest. The assumption is that the good or moral society will appear as the aggregate effect of individually-based benefit calculations. What is good for the individual is good for society.

Even if this version of classical liberalism is very common in present day discussions in political economy, it is a very incomplete and unfair presentation of Smith's economic philosophy. Smith was not only an excellent economist, but also a prominent philosopher. He was definitely not a dogmatic and single-minded advocate of the ego-interest as the only motivating factor behind human actions. On the contrary, he stated very clearly that

> how selfish soever man may be supposed, there are evidently some principles in his nature, which interests him in the fortune of others, and renders their happiness necessary to him, though he derives nothing from it except the pleasure of seeing it. Of this kind is pity

or compassion, the emotion we feel for the misery of others...
(Smith, 1976, p. 9).

Seventeen years before Smith published his fundamental thoughts
about economic liberalism he published *The Theory of Moral Sentiments*
(1759) in which he left no doubt about how dependent the free market
society was on other values than the egoistic self-interest. In this work
he showed that the competition in the market is constructive only
because people are already linked together at a deeper emotional level.
An open competition in the market, where there is a war of all against
all, and the operating rule is the survival of the fittest, will be very
damaging to the social web of society unless there exist strong moral
sentiments among people.[23] According to Smith it is the built-in restraints
derived from morals, religion, custom and education that prevent
undue harm to the community from egoistic market transactions.

The importance of a world of morality, religion, other-directedness,
trust, etc. was obviously a stronger ingredient in the liberalistic era than
we tend to think today. Guneriussen (1999) shows that it was not only
a short-sighted rationalism that characterized the eighteenth century.
Sentiments and passion, moral philosophy and social analysis were part
of the Enlightenment tradition, and the most fundamental source for
social solidarity was thought to be the ability to feel sympathy.

The awareness that the capitalistic market system very much needs
strong counter-balancing forces based on a social, cultural and moral
foundation, received new attention towards the end of the twentieth
century.[24] Hirsch's influential book *Social limits to growth* (1976) is of
central interest in this connection. Hirsch (and later on Hobsbawm[25])
talks about the *moral legacy* that capitalism has inherited from pro-
ceeding eras (for example the feudal order).[26] However, this legacy is
depleted by the market system itself. The *moral foundation* that is a
prerequisite for the well-functioning of this system is eroded via the
market competition:

> The social morality that has served as an under-structure for economic
> individualism has been a legacy of the precapitalist and preindustrial
> past. This legacy has diminished with time and with the corrosive
> contact of the active capitalist values – and more generally with the
> greater autonomy and greater mobility of industrial society. The system
> has thereby lost outside support that was previously taken for granted
> by the individual. As individual behaviour has been increasingly
> directed to individual advantage, habits and instincts based on

communal attitudes and objectives have lost out. The weakening of traditional social values has made predominantly capitalist economies more difficult to manage, that is, to guide by state intervention (Hirsch, 1976, pp. 117–18).

From this passage we can deduce that Hirsch ascribes to 'traditional social values' a relatively strong autonomous status. For a very long time these values have counteracted the corrosive influences of an 'a-moral' market system. Paradoxically tradition has represented a strongly-needed civilizing force that has saved us from the barbarities of an unregulated capitalism.

Since my main topic in this book is Japan, and how moral duties might affect the social integration in society, it is interesting to notice that Hirsch makes exactly this point. In the introduction I talked about the value-conflict between 'basic needs' in the economic and the socio-cultural systems – a conflict Hirsch expresses as a conflict between individual maximization of consumption and the stress on duty and social obligation.

The important dilemma in this connection is not only the 'damage' which a free market economy inflicts on the socio-cultural system, but also the challenge this represents on the economic system itself. Without due attention paid to morality and sociality the market system will dig its own grave:

> The problem here is that the pursuit of private and essentially individual economic goals by enterprises, consumers and workers in their market choices – the distinctive capitalist values that give the system its drive – must be girded at key points by strict morality which the system erodes rather than sustains (Hirsch, 1976, p. 117).

Thus, Hirsch focuses on *morality* as an autonomous force that must be nurtured to avoid a one-dimensional society. At the political/economic level the social democratic movement has tried to construct the basic prerequisites for such a moral society by introducing Keynesian economics as an attempt to 'save capitalism from the stupidity of its managers' (*op. cit.*, p. 123.)

However, while Keynes wanted to save the capitalistic market economy through macro-economic interventions at the state level, Hirsch seems to be more focused on the *general value content* in society. Even though he does not elaborate his point, he is clear that only a decent internalized value system can be the solution:

Generally, restraints on individual behaviour imposed in the collective interest can be enforced most effectively when the sense of obligation is internalised. These restraints grow more necessary as communities become physically larger and socially more transient (p. 139). Without this internalisation, and with reduced 'neighbourly policing', collective interests will be neglected (p. 140).

As for the content of the internalized value system, Hirsch argues that truth, trust, restraint and obligation are the social virtues that have to play a central role to counteract the destabilizing forces of a contractual economy. At this point Hirsch joins the sociological tradition and underlines the functional aspects of religion, which Comte and Durkheim have elaborated.

A point to which I will return is that this moral foundation of society will be important if we want to understand the main differences between Japan and (many of) the Western countries. And to bring my topic on crime into focus, let me add: if crime can be defined as an action against the collective society, the question is what kind of moral climate will make people restrain from individual advantage, and 'join in a cooperative effort, to obey the spirit as well as the letter of the law'? (Hirsch, *op. cit.*, p. 143.)

Hirsch turns a central perspective in liberalism upside down. Adam Smith (and later on Friedrich von Hayek, 1944, and Milton Friedmann, 1980) argued that the common good would best be achieved if everybody followed her/his own private interests. For Hirsch it is more sensible to reverse the line of argumentation:

> Rather than pursuit of self-interest contributing to the social good, pursuit of the social good contributes to the satisfaction of self-interest. The problem is that the latter pursuit needs to be deliberately organised under existing standards and instincts of personal behaviour. So the invisible hand is presently unavailable where it is newly needed (p. 177).[27]

Hirsch echoes Adam Smith when he extends the perspective on necessary preconditions for the functioning of the free market society. The decentralized and self-interested market mechanism can only function when it operates in tandem with some moral and social principles. This means that if we want a solidaristic, low-crime society, we have to speak out on behalf of the socio-cultural system and its basic needs to function well. The question is, what are these 'needs' or preconditions? This question will follow us all through this book, but at this point, let me indicate this answer:

The capitalist market system must be carefully protected against itself if it is to survive. While Keynes wanted to protect market capitalism by way of economic and political macro interventions, Hirsch is more focused on the inoculation of the citizens by internalizing a moral philosophy based on obligation, restraint, truth and trust. As we shall see, these are values that are not alien to classical sociology, to Japanese culture, *or* to the *communitaristic* movement of today.

In recent years communitarianism has had a strong revival in the Western world, and it is especially interesting to notice the strong support of these collectively based values in the number one country of individual freedom, the US. What is the message presented by this movement? There are at least four types of communitarianism (Hughes, 1996). For my discussion, it is sufficient to simplify to a few general headlines.

The general starting point for the communitarians is the opinion that Western societies are characterized by an increasing social disintegration.[28] Their critical arguments towards modern Western societies can be expressed in the following way:

Too many rights	— Too little responsibility/moral obligation[29]
Too much individualism	— Too little communitarianism
Too much inner-directedness	— Too little other-directedness
Too much attention to interest groups	— Too little attention to consensus-making
Too much state	— Too little civil society
Too much market	— Too little volunteering
Too much 'me'	— Too little 'we'

Even though the communitarianism of Etzioni is a mixture of both the political left and right,[30] it is essentially a very *moralistic* movement. In *The Spirit of Community* Etzioni's (1994) introductory chapter is about 'A New Moral', and the title of Part I is 'Shoring up Morality'. Since Etzioni's description of Western societies represents a clear contrast to the traditional picture of Japan (as a very orderly society), I would like to quote the following passage from his book:

We require a general shoring up of our moral foundations. Since the early sixties, many of our moral traditions, social values, and institutions have been challenged, often for valid reasons. The end result is that we live in a state of increasing moral confusion and social anarchy. Once we were quite clear about what young couples were supposed to do – and refrain from doing – even if many of them did not fully live up to these expectations. The trouble now is not that the traditional family was undermined; it did deserve a critical going-over. The trouble is that no new concept of the family – of responsibility – has emerged to replace the traditional form (p. 12).

According to Etzioni we live at present time in a vacuum. Many of the traditional values and institutions have been destroyed, but little has been done for reconstruction. This will take time, and in the meantime we are finding ourselves in a floating and confusing situation.

But as for the remedies, Etzioni's communitarianistic project leans strongly towards an idealistic and voluntaristic approach. It is very much about shoring up the social foundations of morality 'so that communities can again raise their moral voices, families can educate their youngsters, and schools can graduate individuals who will become upstanding members of their communities' (p. 14).

The strong focus on morality and the need for reconstructing the family[31] and civil society as the normative centre in society is also to be found in Lasch (1979) and Fukuyama (1995, 2000). According to Fukuyama it is today almost universally accepted that civil society is a precondition for a healthy economy:

'Civil society' – a complex welter of intermediate institutions, including businesses, voluntary associations, educational institutions, clubs, unions, media, charities, and churches – builds, in turn, on the family, the primary instrument by which people are socialised into their culture and given the skills that allow them to live in broader society and through which the values and knowledge of that society is transmitted across the generations.

A strong and stable family structure and durable social institutions cannot be legislated into existence the way a government can create a central bank or an army. A thriving civil society depends on a people's habits, customs, and ethics – attributes that can be shaped only indirectly through conscious political action and must otherwise be nourished through an increased awareness and respect for culture (p. 6).

Fukuyama is critical in his analysis of the market economy, and though he proclaims that neoclassical economy is 'eighty percent right'[32] (wherever he gets that figure from), he strongly warns against a tendency 'to regard economy as a fact of life with its own laws, separate from the rest of society' (p. 6).

Different critics of the capitalistic market system use different terms to headline their analyses. For Fukuyama the main cement in society is 'trust'. He argues that it is a general lesson that a nation's ability to compete, and thus survive economically, is conditioned on the level and radius of trust[33] inherent in the society. At the other extreme, the social disintegration that (for example) the US has experienced the last decades is for Fukuyama a natural consequence of the decline of trust and sociability, or in short, a decline of basic cultural values that safeguards the social web of society.

What we can read from the above presentation is that 'the relevance of the moral dimension seems quite evident', to quote Etzioni (1991, p. 376). As I have indicated, such an assertion is obviously controversial within the social sciences, and a lot more could be elaborated at this point. However, for my case study of Japan, it is sufficient to point out that 'culture', 'morals' or 'values' are all concepts that for a long time have been regarded as important dimensions of social disintegration. In my opinion, this has special bearing on Japan. The cultural 'superstructure' of Japanese society is essentially different from Western countries. The collectivistic values in the Confucian and Buddhistic tradition give a qualitatively different guidance for action from the individualistic Christian culture. We have to be open for the independent significance of this reality for understanding differences between East and West.

In addition to this value-founded perspective, we must also bear in mind the *structural* perspective presented above. The development from a gemeinschaft and primary group based society to a secondary and gesellschaft based society will easily challenge two basic 'prerequisites' in the socio-cultural system: *predictability and group belongingness*. Rapidly changing societies that leave their citizens with a loss of control of their everyday lives (and consequently little predictability), and (eventually) without basic membership in some kind of a permanent collective, will sacrifice social order. Increasing crime rates will be but one expression of such a development.

In this regard we have to remember the fact that it is *young* people who primarily commit crime. The most obvious reason for this is – in accordance with my argument above – that this group is in a *transitory* stage. Those who get involved in crime in more than an accidental way and on more than a short term basis, seem to be victimized in both regards mentioned above: they have become 'outsiders' (cf. belongingness), and they have little control of their everyday life (cf. predictability). They are (as an ideal type) outside their (consanguine) family, they have not established their own family, they are school dropouts, and they are without a foothold in the labour market. Consequently, they are also without much control of their everyday life situation. Not disregarding the complex interaction between cause and effect in these processes (do you become a criminal because you have no family involvement, or do you have no family involvement because you are a criminal?), I will argue from a sociological point of view that belongingness and predictability are the two main prerequisites for social adaptability.

It can be argued that the transition from childhood to adulthood has become more complicated since the 1970s, both in the West and in the East. The social construction in modern society of an interim period, called 'youth', is an expression of this fact: Where youth in the early 1960s, being tired of school, could leave school and enter directly into the adult world of fairly safe employment and steady salaries, this is no longer the situation. In addition, cultural changes have brought other challenges as well. Today, young people are 'culturally set free' (Ziehe and Stubenrauch, 1983) and they have to choose their style of life within a market of plural choices. For those with the worst odds to succeed in this struggle, options have become fewer and uncertainty has increased.

The interesting challenge from here is to analyse to what extent Japan is characterised by social structures and cultural values that, with reference to the present chapter, clearly indicate that it is a more socially integrative society than the average Western society. Let's now turn to the presentation of the Japanese society to find an answer to this question.

Part II
Japan as a Low-Crime Nation

4
A Cultural, Sociological and Criminological Description of Japanese Society

Introduction

In this chapter I will present a broad cultural and sociological presentation of Japan. Understanding crime is about understanding basic questions concerning cultural values and social structures. My main interest is to find out in which way modern Japan diverges from Western countries struggling with social disintegration. Is Japan differently 'constituted' (culturally and sociologically) from most Western countries? This will be further probed with a more criminological related discussion. Sociology (in general) and criminology (in particular) have for a long time suffered from a 'level problem'; conclusions have too easily been drawn from a general sociological perspective to individual actions like crime. However, one cannot simply make deductions from a dimension like 'employment situation' or 'moral sentiments' to individual actions, whatever they might be. Poverty is certainly a relevant topic when discussing crime, but most poor people are not criminals. Moral values are likewise important to understand crime patterns, but religiosity has definitely both induced as well as hindered crime through history. After all, crime consists of *actions* committed by *individuals*. By saying this I want to stress the importance of making sociological perspectives criminologically relevant and to identify macro processes at the micro level. My intention in this chapter is to establish such a link.

Not least in the literature discussing crime in Japan will one find that individual actions are explained with reference to broad and vague categories like 'economy', 'homogeneity', or even 'Asian values'. There often seems to be a kind of 'missing link' in the deductions that are made. My hope is to be a bit more specific about the processes leading or not leading to crime. A first task is to go into the cultural foundation of Japanese society.

On the definition of culture

Fenwick (1985) has given us this evaluation of the relation between culture and crime in Japan: 'Cultural traditions/values may be the pivotal element in understanding Japan's astonishing post War record of crime control'. What kind of cultural traditions/values are we talking about here?

Of course, general announcements like the one above very easily become tautological. If 'culture' includes both subjective (norms, values, etc.) and objective (structures, tools, etc.) aspects (see Triandis, 1994, p. 2), then Fenwick *has to* be right. If culture, as an illustration, is defined with Herskovits as 'the human-made part of the environment' (see *op. cit.*, p. 16), then we have not increased our understanding much by using the label of culture. Of course crime is (has to be!) linked to something 'human-made' (all laws are human-made).

What I myself mean here by culture is rather something in the direction of 'manifest or latent normative premises for action'. On some occasions people act 'deliberately'; they reflect consciously about what to do and not to do. But most of the time our actions are carried out more or less mechanically (cf. Berger and Luckmann, 1966). In both cases our actions are meaningfully situated within a cultural setting that is more or less a given fact and something that we (more or less) take for granted. Or to quote Ito (1998), 'cultural patterns are deeply embedded in their taken-for-granted realities' (p. 621). Even though we should not regard people as 'cultural dopes' (Garfinkel, 1967); even though people can display a lot of creativity in their daily lives; and even though cultures change as a result of deliberate individual and collective actions, people do perform their roles within given 'manuscripts'. This way of delimiting the concept of culture comes close to Hofstede and Bond (1988) when they say that culture is 'the collective programming of the mind that distinguishes the members of one category of people from those of another' (p. 6). If the human being is the computer, then culture is the computer program that controls behaviour, or 'the software of the mind' as Hofstede calls it (see Triandis, *op. cit.*, p. 6).

However, the distinction between 'computer' and 'computer program' above is incomplete for my own analysis since it is missing a *structural* perspective. In my concept of Japanese culture I will also include structural or organizational principles. How a society is organized, especially what kind of group structures you will find in this society (i.e. no matter how people are 'programmed'), is essential for the final 'output' of actions. Consequently, when I use the concept of culture I will include both values (the programming of the mind) and structural arrangements surrounding the individual.

Also, I would like to add that culture is a concept that applies to an *aggregate* level. One cannot make unreserved inferences from cultural aspects to individual behaviour. I will come back to the point that Japan (like other countries) is not a monolithic collectivity without regional and individual varieties (see Miyanaga, 1991, Sugimoto, 1996, Sano, 1995). However, my presentation of Japan has to be regarded as a Weberian 'ideal type' and, as such, I find it meaningful to describe Japanese culture as essentially different from a Western culture, a viewpoint I share with a lot of scholars (Nakane, 1970, Smith, 1983, Triandis, 1994, Westermann and Burfeind, 1991, Numata, 1999), and which Hofstede and Bond (1988) have documented empirically.

If a cultural perspective is relevant to explain low and high crime societies (i.e. at an aggregate level), then we are saying that some cultural patterns will induce crime more easily than others. If this is so, what kind of cultural patterns are we talking about?

As explained in Chapter 1 I have – until recently – found little confidence in explanations of crime that take 'values' or 'mentality' as the starting point. In my point of view, these norm-based approaches have mixed the dependent and the independent variable. I have been more comfortable with a perspective that regards people's way of acting as (more or less) a mirror of basic social structures than the other way around. Or to express this differently: I have supported a Marxian rather than a Hegelian way of understanding human action.

The Japanese experience has made me change, or at least revise, my opinion. I really think that 'Asian values' are basically different from Western values, and I think that these differences are important for the way people behave in these cultures.[1] Also, I do think that those values have an autonomous status in Japanese society that makes the dependency relation between the socio-cultural and the economic system different in Japan from that in the West. To support this assertion I think Hsu (1975) has presented the most convincing documentation, concluding that, 'I am of the opinion that all these developments, and especially Japan's rapid industrialisation, are built on Japan's traditional social structure, not the Western pattern of human relationships' (p. 150, cf. pp. 223–4). By supporting this position I know I invite an old debate on 'the myth of Japanese uniqueness' (to use the title of Dale's 1986 book) or the so-called *nihonjinron* discussion (theories about the Japanese).

I will comment on this later, but let me very shortly add that to me there is a huge difference between saying that Japanese culture is significantly different from Western culture and arguing that Japanese culture in a positive meaning is unique in the world. I will definitely not argue along such lines. But I find it important both to study what Japanese values are all about, and to find out how these values are 'implemented' into society. That's what this chapter is about.

Japan: a country that needs 'thick description'

If Wrong's (1961) expression of 'the over-socialised conception of man' ever had relevance, it would have to be in Japan. Singer (1973) has given a precise description of the space for individual action in Japan in the following statement:

> it is one of the most characteristic traits of Japanese life that it has reduced the realm of genius to a bare minimum, with rigour unknown in any other great civilization (p. 94). (...) The ultimate purpose of this system of ritual-like customs seems to be the transformation of everyday life into a quiet stream, reflecting a state of mind that is close to unconsciousness (p. 66, cf. much the same description in McVeigh, 1997).

The vast amount of tourist books about 'The inscrutable Japanese' (Hiroshi, 1997) or 'Culture shock – Japan' (Shelley, 1993), giving advice concerning ways to behave and not behave, is a pregnant expression of Japan as a 'jungle of norms'. Japan would have been an eldorado for Goffmann (1958) and his disciples within symbolic interactionism, and it would have given new substance to Riesman's (1961) categories on tradition-, inner- and other-directedness. It is difficult to imagine a modern society that has spun to the same extent a web of norms, traditions, rituals, expectations, obligations, etiquette, etc. around the individual. It is difficult to imagine a modern society that has managed in the same degree to stick to traditional codes in spite of social revolutions, wars, urbanizing and modernizing processes.

This means that it is not easy to find analytical dimensions that give justice to the cultural complexity that Japan reveals. Geertz's call for 'thick descriptions' is relevant to Japan. Above all, Japan should be characterized by one word: *ambiguity*.[2] (cf. Henshall, 1999, Levine, 1985, Benedict, 1967). For my own analysis, I have found it useful to describe Japanese culture along five analytical dimensions (which are *not* mutually exclusive). I would like to stress that the basic cultural values that underlie these five dimensions go very far back in time (I am talking about more than 2,500 years). The religious and moral ethics that constitute the web of Japanese society are primarily based on Shintoism, Buddhism, and Confucianism. Instead of giving a separate presentation of these 'isms', I will comment on each of them under each of my five dimensions. My analytical dimensions are all chosen from the criteria of being criminologically relevant.

Japan is a society with a high degree of value continuity (over time), value consistency (across society), and unity concerning main aims[3]

A. General description

The heading of this section contains three assertions, each with a potential criminological relevance: a low-crime society is dependent on a) a certain historical stability concerning its value foundation, b) a common core of mutual compatible values transmitted throughout society, and c) a certain unanimity concerning the main aims. Let's look a bit closer at each of these propositions and, next, evaluate their relevance for crime.

Re. value continuity over time   Social integration is – at the individual level – very much about belonging. Belonging is about being deeply rooted, both in time and space. We have seen that Western sociologists regard social change as 'a full package'; economic and technological changes generate social and cultural changes, and this will generate tensions. In the words of Ogburn 'changes in material culture proceed at a faster rate than changes in adaptive culture – customs, beliefs, philosophies, laws, and governments – and the result is continuous social maladjustment between the two types of culture' (quoted from Smelser, 1967, p.703). It has almost become a truism that you can not have one (economic change) without the other (cultural change). In this perspective modernization applies as much to mores and values as it applies to technology and material growth. To use an analogy, the essence of this argument is that when the physical structure of a road changes from a cart track to a motorway, and when the medium of transportation changes in a corresponding way, then the navigating principles will change as well.

From this argument it follows that social change will invite some form of uncertainty and unpredictability, at least for those who passively adapt rather than actively take the initiative.[4] The stock of 'tacit knowledge' in such societies is shrinking, and this may challenge the feeling of mastering one's situation. In an (idealized) stable society the situation is rather different. As Schutz and Luckmann (1974, p. 7) put it '[S]o long as the structure of the world can be taken to be constant, as long as my previous experience is valid, my ability to operate upon the world in this and that manner remains in principle preserved'. Triandis (1994) applies the same type of logic to 'tight' societies: 'One of the major advantages of tightness is that people know what they are supposed to do and how they are supposed to behave in every important situation' (p. 164). However, in the modernized, unstable and loose society (ideal type!) the 'previous experience' of the individual is rapidly deflated. Old knowledge, and knowledge possessed by old people, is no longer valid. For young people this means that traditional values like 'respect for the elders', 'filial piety', or even 'respect for authority' will devalue. If culturally-based values can be regarded as an important prerequisite for our 'ability to operate upon the world', then rapidly changing societies inhibit cultural transmission. It would appear that in important ways Japan is not a rapidly changing society.

The gist of my argument regarding value continuity over time is that, since 1945, Japan has gone through the same economic, technological and demographic changes as the West. However, this has affected the 'equilibrium' of the socio-cultural system to a far lesser degree than in Western nations. Put simply, Japan has industrialized and modernized itself, but without having become westernized. To a surprisingly large extent traditional society lingers on in a nation that is at the very forefront of technological modernity.[5] Let me support this assertion (concerning Japan) by giving a few illustrations.

In the book *Iemoto: the heart of Japan* Hsu (1975) argues that the 'iemoto' is the most important and characteristic form of secondary groupings in Japan. When Hsu uses the expression 'the heart of Japan' it is due to both the prevalence of this type of group ('the iemoto characteristics are to be found in all aspects of Japanese society, in religion, in business, in schools and universities, in workshops and offices' (p. 69)), but also (and most important to my argument) because it tells us something about how the Japanese relate to each other. The iemoto is based on a vertical principle called 'kin-tract'. It consists of a master and his/her disciples. This relation is fixed and unalterable, it is hierarchical, people participate voluntarily and they follow a common code of behaviour, they have a common ideology and common objectives. In other words, this type of secondary group, to which every Japanese person belongs, in a manner of speaking, is based on a very *traditional* foundation of values. Becker (1988) gives us a very good illustration of how this functions, writing about different forms of arts iemoto. Japanese society has never allowed adults to return to college after periods of employment or marriage. Consequently, it has become very popular for different groups of individuals to attend groups where they can be taught flower-arranging, tea ceremony, planting and brush-writing, self-defence and flute-playing, judo, calligraphy, painting, archery, horsemanship, singing, cloth-designing, miniature gardening, cooking, the art of manners, incense burning, dancing, drama, etc. In these groups one not only learns 'techniques' related to each subject, but also discipline and morality. Becker concludes that 'upright character and selfless moral action are seen as indispensable prerequisites for mastery of any of these arts. In an era dominated by concerns for efficiency and economy, those arts emphasize timeless discipline and values more important than money' (p. 429).

From this perspective Japanese people have confronted modern times with a weaponry consisting of group structures based on the traditional values of obedience, discipline, adaptation, loyalty, and filial piety. At the same time, they are structurally linked together in a system of dependency and reciprocal obligations. This means that the Schutz/Luckmann statement above is highly apropos in Japan: previous experiences really are valued in this country. The iemoto structure, with its master–disciple principle, has 'facilitated the growth and maintenance of the industrial system with an ease unmatched by Western societies. The transition from traditional Japan to modern Japan did not involve fundamental social changes, requiring great psychocultural reorientation on the part of a majority of the people' (p. xi)[6] (Hsu, 1975).

Westermann and Burfeind (1991) also provide historical explanations in explaining how Japanese society has confronted modernity. In their book *Crime and justice in two cultures – Japan and the United States* they argue that Japan has absorbed most aspects of modernity but, at the same time, has clung to values that have developed over nearly two thousand years of history. Japanese people are very conscious of their history and they celebrate history through both drama and rituals. Referring to Hall and Beardsley, Westermann and Burfeind argue that the Japanese are 'intensely proud of a distinctive cultural heritage that has become a living tradition' (p. 8). The basic ingredients of this cultural heritage are Shintoism, Buddhism, and Confucianism, with Confucianism having an especially strong influence even today. Westermann and Burfeind put it this way:

Confucianism – with its emphasis on tradition and loyalty to that tradition, its acceptance of hierarchy and position, and its teaching that morality is to be found in the fulfilling of the duties and obliga-tions of status – has profoundly affected Japanese values. The Japanese sense of belonging, which gives identity to the person, certainly develops out of the ideas of corporate responsibility found in Con-fucian ideology. The Confucian desire for peace and order has also strongly influenced the Japanese concept of wa, or harmony. These ideas have remained very much a part of the secular religion of modern Japanese culture (p. 17).

At this point I would like to focus especially on one 'ingredient' of the Japanese cultural heritage, namely the dominating value of *harmony*.[7] My assertion is that *wa* (or harmony) is perhaps *the* pivotal concept in Japanese culture. From this Confucian core value we can deduce many virtues that characterize Japanese society (like consensus orientation, other-directedness, belly-communication, etc.), and these virtues will again have important implications for crime and crime policy (not being obtrusive, avoiding conflicts or confrontations, etc.).

The value of harmony has a long history in Japan. As long ago as 604 AD we find this principle expressed in the Constitution of Prince Shotoku:

Harmony is to be valued and an avoidance of wanton opposition is to be honoured. All men are influenced by partisanship, but there are few who are intelligent...Let us cease from wrath and refrain from angry looks. For all men have hearts, and each heart has its own leanings. Their right is our wrong, and our right is their wrong...How can anyone lay down a rule to distinguish right from wrong? So...let us follow the multitude and act like them (quoted from Becker, 1986, p. 79).

This quotation is of course very interesting in itself. However, at this point I want to stress the argument relating to value continuity over time: *in Japanese society of today this article is still seriously studied by schoolchildren*! Indeed, it is not only studied, but very carefully and thoroughly *practised* as well. Of course, in all nations you will find that students have to learn about their own history and culture. You will probably also find that this culture is 'activated' and 'propagated' in contemporary life. But on few occasions will you find a living cultural history as in Japan. Confucian values permeate the everyday life of Japanese citizens to an extent that can only be described as unique – at least compared to the Western societies. Consequently, it is not an exaggeration to assert that no matter the amount of economic and technological changes during hundreds of years in Japan, the cultural 'superstructure' seems to remain intact, both as an ideology, but also as an everyday reality.

Value continuity can also be found in relation to another cultural heritage: the striving for *perfection*. Rooted in native myth, in Confucianism, and even in Buddhism, is the idea that human beings have nothing more than this life and this world (Smith, 1983). It is not in a life to come, but in the very world one lives in that important goals can be attained. Like a corollary to the liberal ideology ('if every citizen maximise his own profit, then society in general will profit as well') the logic goes like this: if each individual follows the rationality of perfection, then the society as a whole will become perfect. This constant search for perfection is one of the more characteristic features of Japanese society today – but the principle has a history of hundreds of years.[8]

Ruth Benedict (1967), in her much celebrated and discussed book *The sword and the chrysanthemum*, has titled one of her chapters 'Debtor to the ages and the world'. Her message is that Westerners pay very little attention to the world and what it has given them. They owe nothing to anybody, and they have no sense of indebtedness to the past. In contrast, 'righteousness in Japan depends upon recognition of one's place in the great network of mutual indebtedness that embraces both one's forebears and one's contemporaries' (p. 68). Even though Japan used to be described as a non-religious society, they nevertheless stay in close contact with their forebears, especially their parents. Each individual has received an 'on' (obligation) from one's parents. This 'on' makes up the basis of the filial piety that permeates Japanese society, and gives parents what Benedict calls a 'strategic position of authority' over their children. All through life the individual will be aware of the debt one carries in relation to parents and even grandparents. 'In this world the living bear the heavy burden of an unrepayable debt to the collectivity of the ancestors who gave them life, and each must strive to contribute what he or she can to the patrimony of those who will come after' (Smith, 1983, p. 124, cf. Doi, 1976, p. 62). Much the same perspective is presented by the psychiatric/anthropologist de Vos, who argues that the Japanese are possessed by a feeling of guilt in relation to their parents. It is this feeling that directs and guides much of the individual actions, according to de Vos. Again, the desirability of this kind of dependency relation to history stands discussion, where, for instance, living with a permanent pressure of always trying to be better than one's parents will create both stress and in-authenticity. In terms of sociological *functions* the continuous presence of the values and the principles of one's forebears links each individual at a minimum to a more consistent and broader value foundation than would otherwise have been the case. If loss of collective memory, common symbolic universe, transcendental moral and religious order, and relatedness represent a challenge to modern man, then Japanese people confront modernity with a sense of belonging that is very different from Western man. This sense of belongingness is to a large extent based on deep-seated historical values, especially influenced by Confucian ethics.

Consequently, the illustrations of historical presence in Japanese society are ubiquitous. The omnipresence of *historically-oriented rituals* is perhaps the most pregnant expression. Both in collective ceremonies and in everyday language and customs you will find old-time codes kept alive within the most modernized settings. According to Hsu (1975) 'the Japanese in all walks and stations of life, far more than their Chinese counterparts, have always adhered stringently to rituals and ceremonial details handed down from the past' (p. 108). Any observer of Japanese society will register how much they love festivals, and there is hardly a time of the year – or a place in the country – without their own festival, a *matsuri*. Those festivals are a pretext for having fun, and many of them have been arranged every year for many centuries. As remarked in Chapter 3, sociologists often describe modern Western societies with the term 'community lost' (Leonardsen, 1996, 1998). The individual is socialized in ways that confirm her status qua individual, but the collectivity (the family, the local community, the neighbourhood, etc.) has few opportunities to have its identity, qua collective unit, confirmed. In addition, the individual is given few opportunities to have *her* identity as a part of a community, confirmed. Japanese culture is very much founded on collective identity confirmations. Rituals and ceremonial functions are mainly based on very old cultural traditions with roots in Shintoism, Buddhism, and Confucianism. According to De Mente (1992) Japanese society has 'hundreds of festivals and ceremonial functions that are so much part of the life of every Japanese' (pp. 22–3). Miyoshi (referred to in Smith, 1983, p. 37) argues that rituals and ceremonies express the most essential values of Japanese culture, and this contributes to a framework of unity in society. The Shinto culture especially represents a rich heritage for collective celebrations.

We should note that ceremonial functions very much include the younger generation. Both children's festivals and maturity rituals are celebrated all over the country. The most famous of these is the *shichigo-san* ('7–5–3 festival'). On this red-letter day girls (aged 7), boys (aged 5) and girls and boys aged 3 will wear their finest costumes, they will be taken to a Shinto shrine, and here they will express their gratitude for having reached their respective age and ask for blessing for the future. Every 5th May all boys participate in 'The Boys' Festival' which is heavily permeated with symbols from Japanese past. The girls will celebrate their own 'Dolls Festival' on 3rd March. On this occasion tradition is also very important, with dolls representing the Court of the Emperor ('Japan', 1985). There is little doubt that the ubiquitous presence of ritual celebrations gives the individual Japanese a feeling of historical and collective belonging that is uncommon in the West.

Japan has in many contexts been defined as a 'wrapping culture', that is, a culture where forms and face are more important than content. (Hendry, 1993, Ben-Ari *et al.*, 1990). One very important aspect of this 'wrapped-ness' is the historical wrapping of this nation. If it is true as Bell argues (see Guneriussen, 1999, p. 258), that we should talk not only about communities of place and psychological communities, but also of communities of memory, then Japan must be a typical illustration of this.[9] Of course, all nations will have their own collective memory; that's what makes them a culture. Our thoughts and moral ideas will always rest on past times. However, the argument I put forward here is that this is much more of a living reality in Japan than in the West.

Let me very briefly add that so far I have commented neither on the *content* of the Japanese cultural legacy, nor on the way this legacy has been *used* by the governing elites through history (see Dale, 1986, Henshall, 1999, Hidaka, 1980, McGormack, 1996, Takahashi, 1991, Smith, 1983, Sugimoto, 1997). It is no secret that functionalistic and pragmatic attitudes have been basic guidelines determining public policy in Japan. It is no secret that Buddhist and Confucian values have been implemented with an obvious intent to reach political aims. How ideas and values contributed to harmony and equilibrium in the Japanese society has been more important than an evaluation of what ideals these values represented.[10] However, an elaboration of this type of critical remarks will have to wait.

Re. value consistency and predictability across society　In Chapter 3 it was noted that one aspect of 'the sociology of worry' was that the emphasis on diversity and individual choice in (post)modern society represents a special challenge to the younger generation. Freedom to choose within a pluralistic culture represents a cherished value in modern society. But this freedom is (historically) something fairly new. Up until the early 1960s Western countries could be described as relatively monistic or as having a high degree of value unity. Mass media in the form of national broadcasting conveyed a relatively unified and consistent message to every citizen and there was little diversity between broadcasters. They transmitted very much the same ideological and moral message. In addition to media and popular culture, carriers of cultural values including parents, schools, the workplace and the broad network of voluntary organizations all conveyed similar idols and ideals. At the same time, the universe of choices for each individual was essentially more diminished. Employment options were also much more predictable than they are in (post)modern society. The life career was limited but predictable.

Ziehe and Stubenrauch (1986) have coined the concept 'cultural free setting' to describe the situation of youth (in the West!). The term is very telling. To be 'set free' implies (looking backwards) emancipation from historical bonds, and (looking forwards) that one is 'free' to choose among different cultural packages. In an historically new way modern man is free to design her/his own life. Life has become a project. This is exactly what Western culture has been striving to achieve, but it is not without consequences. Without a basic and unified 'rationality' (i.e. common values and norms) each individual has to trust her/his own judgements and choices, and this implies risks and uncertainty. Accordingly, predictability decreases,[11] people constantly question the established beliefs and certainties, while at the same time they become more self-reflexive. Without an embedded biography and life trajectory with which to meet a plurality of values and beliefs, many will experience a loss of ontological security (Giddens, 1991).

Bruun and Christie (1985), writing about drug problems (and obviously inspired by Ziehe and Stubenrauch), give this critical assessment of the socializing process in modern, Western societies: 'We do not know if our time in total is more conflictual and more difficult than earlier. However, we do argue that today is a time that offers extraordinary difficulties concerning how to find out *who you are*.... Emancipated from cultural heritage and a lot of material tasks youth is left with the task to find out who they really are – or are in danger of becoming' (p. 37). What these authors focus on is that differentiated modernity with its unlimited opportunities and choices has a price. For a majority (cf. the term 2/3–1/3-society) the new challenges represent – yes exactly – an interesting *challenge*. But for a (in this context an unspecified) minority it will represent trouble. As a psychiatrist might express it, '[t]he value pluralism, the possibilities to choose, and the diversity we experience today, and which the best equipped among us can enjoy and appreciate the freedom of, others will have to pay a certain price for. It is difficult to grow up with too many offers as for values and lifestyle' (Magnussen, 1983). This viewpoint is echoed by another Norwegian psychiatrist who argues that, 'a challenge in our days is the experience of sufficient unity and connection. How can we convey an inner unity and connection?' (Skaarderud, 1998, p. 24).

Following my definition of crime earlier, our question is not why so many apparently manage to cope with this situation but why there are still many who seem to fall outside and commit deviant actions? One way of answering this question is to look at the degree of consistency of norms in 'tight societies'. Even though such a wide concept will hide important nuances, I support Triandis (1994) when he concludes that the tight society is less ridden with crime. One important characteristic Triandis emphasizes in this connection is consistency of norms: 'Tight cultures have clear norms that are reliably imposed' (while 'loose' cultures have unclear norms) (p. 160). Etzioni (1993) supports such a perspective and links his arguments explicitly to crime when saying that 'it is not enough for families to be strong, or schools to be fine educational institutions, and so on. To minimize crime all of these elements must reinforce one another' (p. 190). How does all this link to Japan?

Both at the institutional and at the cultural level Japan is a very uniform society. According to Nakane (1970, p. 14) Japan developed a system of institutional homogeneity as early as the Tokugawa period (1603–1868), and this system is still powerful. The values propagated from different Japanese institutions also share a high degree of unity. For hundreds of years the central government has had strong control over the ideological 'superstructure'. Consequently, centralised cultural hegemony has filtered down to the smallest cell of the community. The result has been that the family, the school, neighbourhood organizations, voluntary organizations, and companies – in short all types of primary and secondary groups – have been conveying much the same ideological and value-based message.[12]

I am well aware of the danger of conveying a picture of Japanese society as 'a Teutonic singularity' (see Dale, 1986, p. 214) with little or no diversity in ethnicity, class, gender, regionalism, etc. As Dale stresses, there has for a long time been a dominant ideological hegemony in Japan where cultural nationalism concerned with the ostensible Japanese uniqueness has been dominant. I would also like to emphasize the signs of a new pluralism appearing in Japan today (see Miyanaga, 1991, Sugimoto, 1997), which warns against simplified, ideologically infected, and sweeping generalizations. Nevertheless, with our focus on the years up to the 1990s, and with a clear demarcation against the *nihonjinron* protagonists, I support this description given by Vogel (1979):

> Japan has become a homogeneous country not only because of the new national media like radio and television but also because there is a common core of culture transmitted to virtually the entire population. The Japanese encourage diversity in culture, art, cuisine, and style of life, but it is to be in addition to a very substantial common core. This core reduces the danger that cleavages will disrupt the social fabric and increases the chance that the populace will work together against crime and disorder and pull together when the national interest requires it (p. 180).

As long as by 'homogeneous society' we include only those cultural aspects that Vogel mentions here, I accept the label of Japan as a homogeneous society. The educational system especially represents a fundamental force in moulding Japanese citizens into one standardized mass of people, each being a carrier of the same 'mentality'. Ben-Ari (1997) documents how pre-schools all over Japan are characterized by a far-reaching uniformity and standardization. In their daily routines, in their behaviour management and in their educational goals, one will find a significant homogeneity among pre-schools.[13] This pattern continues in the primary and secondary education system. Via textbook censorship, curriculum guidelines and conformist patterns of socialization the central government has created a uniformity and regimentation that trickles into every little cell in the Japanese school system. Japanese school children spend very long hours in educational institutions, and while there they are exposed to very much the same regimentation and the same influence (Sugimoto, 1997).

Sociology tells us that shared sets of values, shared understandings, and shared commitments to rules of conduct are basic for creating social order (Wrong, 1994). Values held in common constitute perhaps the primary reference point for the analysis of a social system, and value consistency is important to create an integrated society. Westermann and Burfeind (1991) confirm the criminological relevance of this perspective for Japan when they argue that, 'because there is a single moral tradition, internalized in the home and reinforced by the educational system, the Japanese appear to be people with strong self-control' (p. 41). From this perspective we can conclude that Japanese society possesses one important prerequisite for social order.

Re. unity concerning main aims in which everybody can participate   A common sense experience tells us that a group working together with a common aim, supported by all the members, will satisfy one important prerequisite for being an integrated 'society'. The best example to illustrate this argument can be found in sports. Soccer teams are primarily organized to fulfil the aim of winning their matches. Every player is important to reach this aim, and everybody is heading in the same direction. They identify with the aim of winning each match, and they are proud of giving their individual commitment to the collective best. Players who pursue their own egoistic aims are not welcomed since they contribute to conflict rather than unity. Such players will easily end up sitting ringside; they will become 'outsiders'.

This logic can be applied to society in general (Leonardsen, 1996). Societies with some main unifying aims with which most people can identify, and which can include most groups, will – *ceteris paribus* – have a solid foundation for being socially integrated. One important 'latent function' of the Second World War was to unite each country, first to beat back the enemy, and, next, to rebuild all that was destroyed during the war. There is a strong case for arguing that the years of reconstruction were years of unity as regards overarching aims in most countries.[14]

What is specific to Japan is that those years of unity concerning common aims continued for a much longer time, and were more consistently proclaimed than in the West. As McCormack (1996) shows in *The emptiness of Japanese affluence*, postwar Japan replaced war with the three 'C's: construction, consumption and control. According to McCormack 'in no country is social life so structured around the imperatives of economic life, or are people subjected to more pressure to consume' (p. 289). The military defeat by the Allied countries was a terrible blow to a culture with so much pride invested in its national identity. If Japan lost the *military* war, it became more important to win the *economic* war against the US: '[s]hame over a self-perceived backwardness was a major spur for "catching up and overtaking" (*oitsuke, oikose!*) the West which formed the external model for modernisation' (Dale, 1986, p. 176). The corporate warrior replaced the military warrior. Consequently, right up to the burst of the bubble economy and the Kobe earthquake in the early 1990s the Japanese nation was in an incredible way united in the task of catching up with the West. Triplets like washer, vacuum cleaner and refrigerator (1954), car, cooler (air conditioner) and colour TV (1966), and career, class and clever (1996), have all been ingredients in an ideology aiming at turning Japan into an economic superpower (see Field, 1996, p. xvi).

Consequently, there are few other nations that can boast the same duration of unity and commitment among citizens to a one-dimensional aim which, for Japan, was the post-Second World War period run on material goods. This commitment can be expressed in figures. Referring to the statistics from the Japanese Labour Ministry, Shelley (1997) reports that in 1986 only 28 per cent of Japanese workers enjoyed a five-day working week. Seventy-eight per cent had a two-day weekend at least once a month. Firms in Japan do not report all overtime hours, and they rarely pay for them (a practice called 'service overtime work'). Total working hours per annum is much higher in Japan than in most Western countries (Sugimoto, 1997, p. 93). Reading these figures we must remember that workers in addition have commuting times that usually range from 60 to 90 minutes one way (Takahashi, 1991, p. 2). On average, Japanese workers take only half of their paid annual vacation – a vacation that usually is not longer than 15–20 days, and employees normally use part of their annual paid recreation leave as sick leave (Sugimoto, 1997, p. 93). The most dreadful expression of this complete commitment to the company (called 'marugakae', meaning completely enveloped) is that every year more than 30,000 white-collar workers are killed in the workplace due to the amount of work they are expected to do (Takahashi, 1991, p. 2).

The only way to attain such blind discipline is by way of strong personal allegiance and obedience coupled with intense group pressure. To break out of this 'marugakae' would mean to leave the rest of your colleagues with extra work, which would be impossible in a strong collective culture. However, in the analytical perspective I convey in this section, my argument is that the striving for material affluence happened in a less atomistic setting than in the West. While modernization in the West meant a differentiation process where the *individual* conscience was strengthened, this did not happen in Japan. On the contrary, it was the *collective* conscience (Westermann and Burfeind, 1991 speak of a 'national conscience' (p. 89)) that was nurtured, and the basic aims and values were regarded as obligatory to all citizens. 'If you produce, you may presume upon your superior's indulgence!' as Dale (1986, p. 148) formulates it. The specific group mentality in Japanese society was the ideological soil that made this collective effort possible and that made people submit so uncritically to this 'economism'. Education, discipline and altruistic behaviour became the efficient tools to be invested in this new economic war.

The Japanese are dedicated not only with regard to economic functions. In their spare time you will find them busy in group-organized activities.

Komiya (1999) refers directly to this phenomenon as part of his explanation of the low crime rates in Japan: 'it may be worth mentioning, in passing, that the Japanese are often too busy with group activities to find time to commit crime or even think about it' (p. 385). Though I would not exaggerate the autonomous strength of this argument, the way the Japanese live as part of a well-orchestrated, overarching organized plan is criminologically telling. Let's look a bit closer at this.

B. Discussion

I will address two main topics for discussion. 1) I argue that Japan is a society characterized by value continuity (over time), value consistency (across society), and unity concerning main aims. This invites a short discussion on the asserted *homogeneity* of Japanese society. 2) Is a homogeneous culture automatically a low-crime society? Among criminologists studying Japan there seems to be an overwhelmingly tendency to argue both that Japan really *is* a homogeneous society, and also to infer (more or less without further argumentation) that homogeneity is an important prerequisite for social integration and consequently low crime.

For many decades Japan has been described, both by natives and by foreigners, as a unique culture encompassing every citizen. With regard to history, language, ethnicity and belief systems it has been stressed that Japanese people are extremely homogeneous.[15] For the last 20 years this perspective has invited critical voices, saying that too much attention has been paid to the asserted exotic otherness of the Japanese (Henshall, 1999, Sugimoto, 1994, Dale, 1986, Miyanaga, 1991, Stevens, 1997, Singer, 1989). These authors have all emphasized Japan's internal variation, its social stratification, its diversity, its subcultures, and so on. They have also argued that much of this talk about Japanese homogeneity and uniqueness is political propaganda distributed with obvious political aims.

In many ways I regard this discussion as rather futile. With no agreed yardstick for what is meant by 'homogeneous culture' or 'unique culture' both sides will be right in their assertions. I have no trouble accepting Japan as a class society, a strongly gendered society, a society with regional diversities, a society with considerable generational variations. I also agree with Dale's (1986) emphasis on the myth of Japanese uniqueness. However, this does not overturn the view that value consistency in time and space and a high degree of unity concerning main aims also characterize Japanese society. Compared to most Western countries it is possible to describe Japan in toto as a culture characterized by uniformity. If by homogeneous society we mean a society with a high degree of unity of values (in time and space), and a broad commitment by most citizens to some main aims, then Japan deserves the homogeneity label.

The next question is trickier. Is there any link between cultural uniformity and crime?

Concerning the relevance of *value continuity over time*, I argued in Chapter 2 that crime could be regarded as an expression of exclusion; of having an outsider status in society. I will definitely not argue that being outside a 'community of memory' is a crime-triggering factor in itself. In that case immigrants would all be criminals. But one *can* argue that historicity is one aspect of a 'tight society', in this connection meaning a society with clear norms. Even though Japanese society is strongly influenced by Western principles, especially regarding criminal law and justice, a strong core of Confucian and Buddhist philosophy has dominated during the last four centuries (Takahashi, 1991, Sano, 1995). As we have seen, these norms stress the importance of filial piety. The importance of 'family honour' and the fear of disgracing one's family will probably function to deter crime. The case of Japanese immigrants to the United States and the Hawaiian Islands in the early 1900s might illustrate this argument. Crime among descendants from these immigrants is virtually unknown even today. In-depth interviews with a representative sample of these off-spring show that the 'historical connection' was a recurring explanation. 'Pride in Japanese ancestry', 'to avoid bringing shame on the family and to the family name', 'hopes and expectations of our parents', and 'respect for the elders'; these were the typical answers to the question why Japanese Americans rarely if ever violated the law. One of the respondents refers directly to the importance of obligations to the forebears. 'Our parents taught us to be considerate of others, respectful to our elders and older people. Constantly we heard the terms duty (*giri*), obligation (*on*), and shame (*haji*)' (Westermann and Burfeind, 1991, p. 23).

At least within a conservative/Durkheimian logic it can be argued that this historical tradition represents a 'glue' in the Japanese society that is of criminological relevance. The social Darwinist William Graham Sumner (Wrong, 1994, p. 30) echoes this perspective when describing how societies control the individual. To Sumner it was the habits and customs of 'Folkways' (the name of his 1906 book) that functioned as the guiding principles for succeeding generations. One aspect of the 'community lost' debate is about loss of the time-dimension in modern life. Clarity of norms is a function of time. No doubt, this time dimension, or historical belonging, is much more present in Japan today than in most Western countries. The omnipresence of different rituals in Japan contributes to a strong confirmation of this historical belonging. When van Wolferen (1989) writes about rituals in his comprehensive book on *The enigma of Japanese power* it is under the heading 'Order through ritual'. According to van Wolferen, conflicts in Japan are not solved via substantive discussion and appeal to reason, but through rituals.

As for the criminological relevance of *value consistency in space* I will argue in this way: When Durkheim developed his theory on anomie, he started by stressing the importance of *normative restrictions on human beings*.[16] Like Rousseau, he noted that our degree of satisfaction was less dependent on the amount of goods we possess than on the level of our aspirations. Our ability to reach a satisfaction of needs is consequently dependent on a kind of regulation of our needs. This regulation should be made by 'society'. Durkheim underlined that our ability to define the limits of our needs is dependent on our ability to acknowledge our place in society. However, if society does not regulate our needs, and if different socializing agents do not give us consistent and 'realistic' aspirations as to what is possible to reach, then the individual will experience a kind of infinity urge. Even if institutions like the family or the school try to implant one set of values (for example related to discipline, altruism, and modesty), other institutions, like media or advertising might boost conflicting values (like hedonism, egoism, and impudence). In principle, everything is attainable! Boomtown communities give us good illustrations of the confusion that might be created on such occasions, here expressed by the Director of a psychiatric clinic in one such boomtown: 'And then there were all these new kids coming in, who were doing a lot of other things, other kinds of drugs and so on, and it was like being in a candy store. They didn't know which way to turn. . . . That seems to be one of the stresses – it's easier to have a well-defined situation than one where there's a lot of blending' (quoted from Freudenburg, 1986, p. 46). Modern Western societies do not represent a 'well-defined situation' for the young generation. On the contrary, they are characterized by a wide variety of offers and possibilities. Up until fairly recently, the situation in Japan has been quite the opposite of this, with well-defined and predictable tracks of life for most people.

To state this very explicitly, the general sociological perspective tells us that *anomie* (normative disintegration) develops when older norms lose clarity and bonding power. Increasing division of labour will, as a tendency, have a centrifugal social effect, while a *common* system of norms counteracts this and has a centripetal social effect. When traditional norms are not enforced in a consistent and vigorous way, and when competing norms are given broader attention, the net result is (to quote Westermann and Burfeind, 1991) 'a sort of moral laissez-faire – social control is greatly diminished and crime and delinquency flourish' (p. 26). A situation of diversity and lack of strong moral tradition or consensus will, according to those authors, lead to uncertainty and confusion (cf. Adam Smith's concept of 'moral sentiments', Hirsch's focus on 'moral legacy', and the communitarians interest in 'shared moral values'). This conclusion is deduced from a general theoretical perspective that 'social disorganisation and anomie theories of social control suggest that when there is a lack of strong consensus about values and norms, traditional rules no longer apply, and the amount of 'deviance' is likely to increase' (*op. cit.* p. 42). Research by Shaw and McKay supports this conclusion. In the first two decades of the twentieth century they studied the turbulent social changes in Chicago, and concluded that in the areas of low rates of delinquency there was more or less uniformity and consistency of conventional values. On the other hand, high crime areas were characterized by competing and conflicting moral values. Sellin also researched the effects of clashing norms in societies characterized by increased complexity and concluded:

> Culture conflicts are the natural outgrowth of processes of social differentiation, which produce an infinity of social groupings, each with its own definitions of life situations, its own interpretations of social relationships, its own ignorance or misunderstanding of the social values of other groups. The transformation of a culture from a homogenous and well-integrated type to a heterogeneous and disintegrated type is therefore accompanied by an increase of conflict situations (referred in Adler, 1983, p. 145).

If the above description is correct, then we are approaching an important juncture for understanding the extent of crime in Japan. Westermann and Burfeind (1991) have made this point about the importance of value consistency as a crime preventive dimension in Japan very explicit: 'Japanese commit less crime because there is essentially a single set of basic values that are shared among a tradition-oriented people' (p. 151). To this I think we should add a Braithwaite-inspired perspective about shame. His theory of reintegrative shaming is based on the assumption that there is a core consensus in society about basic values. The more diversity, the more pluralism, and the more inequality you have in a society, the more you will hamper those social control mechanisms that are based on shaming.[17]

Let me finally comment on the criminological meaning of *unity of main aims*. If we stick to the conception of crime as actions committed by outsiders, we have to link the question of unity of aims to the question of 'participation for all'. Conflicting aims in society stem from or coexist with: a) diversity and economic inequality, and b) subcultures. Diversified societies may, or may not, have conflicting aims. However, diversified societies that also have essential economic inequalities will rapidly develop subcultures with conflicting aims vis-à-vis the greater society. The problem of social exclusion during the last 20 years in the West gives us a good illustration of this (see Jordan, 1996). Unity of main aims is very difficult to attain in a society with essential economic inequalities and social dropouts. Crime – the way I have defined it – is primarily committed by people who have little to lose by deviance. These are the disadvantaged who have little chance to play a significant role in established society, who have failed in the educational system, in the family system, and in the labour market. By implication, these are the ones that can hardly identify with the main aims of society.

From this perspective, unity of main aims is unavoidably linked to the question of economic equality and participation for all. As we have seen, Japan (until 1990) has been a society with low unemployment and a 'reasonable' low level of inequality (and in this connection it is important to repeat that some 90 per cent of the Japanese define themselves as belonging to the middle class). As long as the Japanese government, both ideologically and economically, managed to integrate each citizen into a corporate army, where everybody could define themselves as soldiers in Japan Ltd, few would walk out of line.

It may be reasonable to conclude that crime is less of an option in a society that succeeds in instilling a collective direction where everybody can have a stake. In this regard unity of main aims is one dimension of Japan's crime story.

Japan is a social-conservative, group and shame based society

A. General description

Understanding the omnipresence of group structures in Japan is key to understanding the crime pattern in Japan. Chapter 3 presented a general sociological perspective on modernisation and dissolving processes. We found stable primary groups (friends and family) were significant for their role in giving the individual a feeling of belonging and collective identity. If this is a correct observation, then Japanese 'groupism' will go a long way to explain the low crime rates in this country.[18]

At the ideological level, Japanese society is based on a *collectivistic* philosophy. If we were to describe this culture in terms of Western traditions, we would have to start with classical social-conservatism: according to this ideology the individual is weak and irrational and will consequently have to be subjugated to authority. The individual belongs to different types of collectivities, and it is necessary to organize society along hierarchical principles. Values like stability, harmony, group-conscience, tradition, authority and allegiance are, according to conservatism, basic navigating principles for the individual. By implication, the problem of social order is a main preoccupation in this ideology.

Japanese society values order, and – like conservatism generally – it is run by a 'functionalistic group ideology':[19] it is the stable functioning of the nation, company, family, etc., which determines individual dispositions. In this culture of utility, what is important for the group is given priority, and individual wishes must be subjugated accordingly (cf. Ito (1998): 'Ones individual blossoms fully only when one is part of a family, a society, the natural world, and the universe' (p. 628)).[20] The concept of 'kaisha' is an expression of the community or group to which one belongs, and the group consciousness linked to this is (according to Nakane, 1970) all-important in one's life: 'The power and influence of the group not only affects and enters into the individual's actions; it alters even his ideas and way of thinking. Individual autonomy is minimized. When this happens, the point where group or public life ends and where private life begins no longer can be distinguished' (p. 10). Doi (1976) argues in a comparable way when he says that people in Japan so strongly fear being isolated from the group that they are willing to put up with anything to avoid such a situation (p. 138).

In providing the leading account of Japanese 'groupism', Hsu (1975) starts with the assumption that the nature of man's relationships with fellow men represents the key determinant of human behaviour.[21] However, it is not human relationships in general that are of primary interest to Hsu, but a network of those relationships of which the individual is a part, and which she/he defines as important.

Hsu's main concern is not with the traditional primary group called the family, but with the secondary groups occurring between this level and the tribal or national level. These secondary groups are called 'iemoto'.

As discussed in Chapter 3, modernity is characterized by a high degree of role differentiation. One important consequence of this differentiation process is (according to Hsu) that role has become separated from affect. As the worker has been removed from family labour, she/he has also lost the traditional bases for affective ties with her/his co-workers. And as the worker has been moved to the assembly line, she/he has in a comparable way lost the affective ties to her/his tools. This process is defined by Western social scientists as a universal and inevitable process. As modernization develops, human beings will gradually become more impersonal towards each other. However, this type of conclusion suffers from an ethnocentric bias. According to Hsu, the case of Japan directly contradicts this type of conclusion. Due to the all-encompassing existence of iemoto structures in Japanese society, this nation has embarked on modernity with a very different cultural legacy. The core structure of the iemoto is (as already mentioned) the master–disciple relationship marked by mutual dependency. This dependency is 'soft'. The relation between the master and the disciple is defined in sort of pseudo-kinship terms. 'From this point of view each iemoto is a giant kinship establishment, with the characteristic closeness and inclusiveness of interpersonal links, but without kinship limitations on its size' (p. 152). This means that whatever turbulent processes the individual experiences (cf. geographic and social mobility), on most occasions the individual will be linked to supportive and caring personal relations: 'the all-inclusive, interlinking mutual dependence among members of any two levels in a large hierarchical organization has the effect of extending the feeling of intimacy beyond those situated in the closest proximity' (p. 152).

The effect of this iemoto system is that Japan, all through an enormous modernisation process, has been embedded in cultural stays that have had a preserving and conservative function. Basic principles for human relations have been little affected by economic and technological changes. The way the individual Japanese feels about himself and about the world around him has changed far less than has been the case in the Western countries. Or to let Hsu conclude in his own words:

> The Japanese have reached modernisation and industrialisation via a very different psycho-social route than that found in the West. Japanese non-heirs were not, as were their Western counterparts, encouraged to seek, or bent on seeking, their own fame and fortune on their own terms. Their kinship system encouraged them to look for mutual dependence instead of independence. Therefore, instead of individualism and freedom, the Japanese proceeded from their iemoto system based on the kin-tract principle. They developed newer and larger groups with non-traditional objectives, without feeling a need for significant changes in their traditional pattern of human relationships (pp. 223–4).

Earlier in this section I supported the expression that Japan had modernized without being westernized. Hsu has explained to us exactly what this might mean. Contrary to both Marxian and cultural-lag theories, important aspects of the socio-cultural system seem to remain intact within the frames of a market economy. Durkheim may have approved of the way Japanese society has avoided the dangers of a social process leading from functional differentiation to increased individualization. In one way (but I say this with a reservation) one could argue that the moral tightness (which for Durkheim means the way members of a society are morally relevant to each other) has been taken care of within the structure of iemoto.[22]

The group ideology is in a very systematic way transmitted through the socialization process, and follows the individual throughout life. Starting in the family, continuing in the kindergarten and the school system, via the work place, the same message is confirmed: the group is everything, the individual is nothing. This perspective is 'double-edged'; it is not only a celebration of collectivity, but also a denial of the self. Singer (1973) underlines this, saying that

> in his everyday existence the Japanese acts, feels, thinks, decides, as if Japan would act through him; if asked to what extent his acts emanate from himself, and to what extent from his group, he would not only be unable to give a rational account but he would also be unwilling to admit the validity of the question. He stands to his group in a relation in which we imagine the life of a cell stands to the life of an organism; or, at the very least, it approximates to that relation in a degree observable on no other civilised nation. If the Japanese wants to sever these congenital bonds, there is no choice left for him but to destroy all ties of birth and allegiance, withdrawing not only from his group but also from the whole world of impermanence, entering the Buddhist path which promises to lead to the complete annihilation of 'this fleeting world' (p. 110)

This description is contradictory to basic assumptions in Western philosophy. Wrong (1994) points out that attachment and obligations to other people in our culture are often regarded as a burden, 'a painful constraint preventing them from pursuing desires and interests of their own' (p. 3). He adds that the conflict between the individual and the demands of society is 'a human universal'. This line of arguing is a Western way of constructing the world. It is not that the Japanese are born altruistic (and Westerners are born egoistic), but the obliteration of the self in Japanese culture makes the question of 'burden' and 'constraints' on the individual a much more complex topic than it might appear from a Western point of orientation.

The pathway into the group and the community in Japan is formed in subtle ways. Adults will rarely behave as visible and distinct centres of authority. The phenomenon is better captured by Rohlen's (1989) concept of 'the empty centre'. Necessary guidelines for the individual are put forward more as unexpressed expectations from the group than as manifest directions for action. Consequently, social order in Japan has opaque and floating power structures, vague ideological hegemonies, and an unproblematized culture of consensus and harmony. Singer (1973) argues that there is little 'you must not' in Japan. Adults will instead manoeuvre in ways to avoid coming in direct confrontation with children. The individual, by anticipating feeling the resentment or withdrawal of the group will rapidly adapt to the common rules and norms. It is as if a Rousseauian 'general will' (but in this connection at the micro level) exercises the necessary pressure on the individual. And it will not be felt as an improper invasion of individual freedom, since the group is regarded as the better manifestation of the individual.[23]

From what I have said so far, it appears that the individual is of little worth apart from the group. According to Schneider (1992) 'the individual achieves social status and respect only through the status of the group of which he is a member. The individual receives his identity, his self-awareness only through social bonds' (p. 313). From social psychology we know that even in individualistic Western cultures you will have to pay a high price for standing outside social networks. In the collectivistic and group-oriented Japanese culture this is much more so. In her book, *On the margins of Japanese society*, Stevens (1997) gives this strong support. She describes life for those (few, but increasing) who fall outside the culture of iemoto (unemployed, day labourers, ethnic minorities, travelling gamblers, the elderly, the disabled and social activists) as challenging the Japanese call for order and embeddedness. Although social marginality is defined in Japan as belonging to an ambiguous group, ambiguity is regarded as dangerous and undesirable since it challenges the social order. Somewhat ironically, 'marginal categories are created to label and control the disorder' (p. 16). It is probably somewhat worse to play the role of outsider in a collectivistic than in an individualistic culture.

As I have already noted, historical rituals permeate Japanese society. I have referred to these events to illustrate how traditional values are kept alive in present-day Japan. As might be understood, these historical rituals also play a significant role in confirming the collective identity among people. However, such processes are not only based on historical rituals and traditional values. Everyday Japanese society is pervaded by gatherings that continuously link the individual to a collective setting. According to Singer (1989) 'Japanese people wrap themselves in rituals' (p. 332), and if there is one characteristic that differentiates the Japanese from both Westerners as well as from other Asian people, it is in the extent of their ritualistic behaviour. Within kindergartens (Ben-Ari, 1997) and schools there are a lot of gatherings that will mark the start and the end of the day (different red-letter days, etc.). Within a general Confucian ideology the children are taught how individual self-sacrifice is necessary for group success. An extensive use of uniforms and common symbols help visualize the broader collectivity of which the individual is a part. All primary schools, middle schools and even high schools have their own school song which is sung at morning assemblies, sports events and ceremonial occasions, all with the intention of promoting psychological uniformity and cohesion among the pupils (Sugimoto, 1997, p. 123). Åm (1981), who undertook participant observation in a Japanese kindergarten, argues that all the collective markings that took place in her institution functioned as 'fittings'. While Åm has a rather positive evaluation of this 'collectivity drill' for pre-school education, Sugimoto (1997) seems more sceptical regarding its use at the next level. He describes the ideology in Japanese schools as a 'militaristic ethic for personality formation', a 'quasi-military age-based hierarchy', and a 'militaristic discipline in classroom' (pp. 122–3). An important aspect of the collective identity building is the use of school uniforms, and even in this regard a semi-military style is fairly common, at least among the boys. Arimoto (1995, p. 383) supports Sugimoto's description of the strict control in Japanese schools. From his point of view Japanese school children have to learn self-sacrifice, discipline and skill mastery.[24]

Moving from the educational system to the working life, much of the same pattern can be identified. The almost obligatory use of the black suit among the 'sarary men' (from English: salary) is comparable to the school uniforms the children use, and daily rituals are as common as in school. According to Hsu (1975) most Japanese corporations reinforce their employees' identification with the company through different types of ceremony. He gives an example from Matsushita Company, where workers and employees start each day's work by singing:

> For the building of a new Japan
> Let's put our strength and mind together,

Doing our best to promote production,
Sending our goods to the people of the world,
Endless and continuously,
Like water gushing from a fountain.
Grow, industry, grow, grow, grow!
Harmony and sincerity!
Matushita Electricity!' (Hsu, 1975, pp. 210–11).

Hsu adds that this type of song is in no way unique to this particular corporation.

The contrast to this celebration of the group spirit is the invisibility of ceremonies that support *individual* identity. Individual birthdays are given very little attention in Japan ('Japan', 1985, p. 134). For a long time the Japanese custom was to define a newborn child as one year old, and then two years old on the next New Year's Day. Consequently, all children born in the same year had their 'birthday' on the same day. Even if this custom has gradually changed, the collective festivals like the '7–5–3-festival', the 'Boys' Festival', or the 'Doll Festival' are regarded as much more important than individual birthdays.

The low priority given to individual values has an interesting semantic correspondence: the word 'I' (and also 'no') is rarely used (Shelley, 1997). The Japanese avoid using the subject form and will rather say 'we' where Western people would say 'I'. The concept of 'man' reflects this other-directed way of thinking. The parallel Japanese word is 'ningen', and the original meaning of this concept is 'between people' (Umehara, 1992, p. 11. See also Fenwick, 1985, Becker, 1988, Henshall, 1999). However, 'ningen' is originally a Confucian word, and it has to be understood in this context. The relationship between people within this ideology is not horizontal but *vertical*. As we have seen in the presentation of the iemoto-relationship, in this cultural context it is always a question of a master–disciple relationship, with devotion to your master as one important ingredient.

Creighton (1990) points out that the Japanese word for 'myself' (*jibun*) means 'my part', implying my part of some *larger whole*. She then goes on to quote Joji's characterization of the Japanese personality as a 'shell-less egg', indicating a personality with only a soft fluid outer membrane but no hard shell outside it (as in the West). 'Who is 'I' and who is 'you' is not defined absolutely, but is always being redefined according to the nature of 'I' and 'you' relations' (*op. cit.* p. 294). I will return later to the point that this also illustrates the strong contextual aspects of Japanese culture.

Another semantic illustration of the ignoring of the individual person can be found in the concept *kanjin* (meaning contextual person). In the West we are used to thinking of the individual as a separate unit with the point of reference located in itself. The Japanese describe this type of person with the term 'kojin' (meaning separate person), and it is definitely a negatively loaded word. 'Kojin' has connotations of social immaturity and self-centredness, while 'kanjin' expresses the Japanese ideal: the other-directed person (see Henshall, 1999, p. 148).

As we can see, the opposite to the cultivating of the group and the group identity is the wiping out of the individual self. Singer (1973) traces this tendency to obliterate the individual back to Buddhism:

> Buddhism has taught him, or has encouraged him in this tendency, to deny the very existence of an individual soul. To conceive of his own interior sphere of mind as an articulate, structured, self-creating mental fabric is an idea utterly alien to him. He does not feel an urge to make his ego a microcosmic image of the universe, to become god-like by shaping himself after a divine image. He does not wait for the decisive challenge that he must take up if his true self is to be realised. Life to him is not a substance which is to be given shape, form, order, but a force to be suffered patiently or to be received in one violent moment of fulfilment (pp. 50–1).

With so little space for individual identity, there is correspondingly much more space for group identity. As we have seen, this space is demarcated in many ways. From early childhood, in kindergartens, in schools, and in the company, Japanese culture will always give priority to collective values, to symbols and events that strengthen the group. Nothing starts until everybody who is supposed to participate has found his/her place. There are distinct ceremonial openings and closings of everyday activities (e.g. start/end of the day, a lesson, etc.), and these markings contribute towards including absolutely everybody in the appropriate group. In this way, people at the margins of their social context will be 'forced' into a structure that transcends their own self.[25]

B. Discussion

Dennis H. Wrong has nicely put the essential sociological lesson in this section:

> The power of the group over the individual, of the Many over the One, through the effective psychological medium of what Georg H. Mead

called the 'generalized other,' is usually more ubiquitous and more successful in inducing conformity than the efforts of particular persons to control the conduct of others. The rule of expectations in this broad sense is basic to the achievements of social order (Wrong, 1994, p. 44).

From what I have presented above, three points follow concerning groupism, collectivism and crime: One is that the rich culture of rituals and celebrations in Japan contributes to a consciousness of unity and solidarity of the group. The next is that the pervasiveness of groups in Japan creates a structure of social control which is deeply pervasive. The third is that the fear of conflict between group members structures action. My first point will focus on questions related to identity formation in an age of cultural disembedding; my second point will focus on the visibility aspect of primary social control; and my third point will focus on moral shame related to a group of significant others.

Re. celebrations and ceremonies   In sociology the social functions of religion have always been a central topic, and ritual ceremonies have been a critical concern. Durkheim stressed the importance of common symbols to the sustenance of group unity and group identity. To Durkheim, this was a prerequisite for social solidarity. Such symbols would create a consciousness about the importance of a common history, and establish a collective memory regarding important events in the history of the group. This contributes to the formation of a group identity. In his writings on the socialization process, Durkheim carried this perspective further. He argued that an essential part of the socialisation of the younger generations was to introduce them to the symbolic universe of the group. In a more mobile society the links between people might get looser, especially the links with the elderly, who he regarded as the most important 'carriers' of tradition and collective identity. Modernization meant to Durkheim increased individualization, which again meant a detachment from important social bonds. If people lost their common symbolic universe and their collective memory the result would be an increasing feeling of loneliness.

Collective celebrations and ceremonies make it possible to create and sustain a consciousness about the unity and solidarity of the group. Bruun and Christie (1985) have commented on the criminological importance of this. As a background for discussing drug cultures in the West, they research the negative effects of the loss of collective celebrations. The almost complete absence of collective rituals (in the West) undermines the chances for giving individuals the experience of collectiveness. 'We are content to take the absence of rituals as one of many expressions of a long developed individualism, or, rather, the absence of experienced collective orientations' (p. 35). While this development has offered increased freedom (since conventions and traditions have lost their significance for the individual), it has also left the individual more vulnerable in his/her own cultural choices. Consequently, the social web around the individual will be looser, and the barriers for crime will be fewer.

Komiya (1999) comments explicitly on the collectivistic ceremonial aspects of Japanese culture in his discussion of the low crime rates in Japan. The fact that the Japanese regularly and frequently engage in ritual group practices contributes to the assurance of group conformity. According to Komiya the vast amount of ceremonial settings lends the Japanese a strong awareness of how people should behave and this imposes a strong pressure to conform. Crime is a less probable alternative within structures of this type.

In a functionalistic perspective it can be argued that Japan, partly due to its celebration of collective events, has avoided some of the problems linked to a loss of collective identity, emotional community, common symbolic universe, and collective memory. The individual Japanese is less atomized and more socially embedded than the individual Westerner. In a Weberian perspective it can be argued in a comparable way that Japan has 'compensated' itself for modernity's loss of meaning ('Sinnverlust') with traditional and modern ceremonies. At a very general level this probably contributes towards making certain aspects of modern life less difficult. One can argue that the Japanese are moved by a kind of 'organic mentality' where – as Singer (1973) has argued – the individual stands to his group as a cell stands to the life of an organism. Sugimoto (1997) describes the implicit conformity pressure in the Japanese ceremonies as 'emotive moralizing'. The extensive use of collective singing, for example, will play an important role in generating group solidarity. No doubt, this could also be described in a somewhat less complimentary way.

Re. structural aspects of groupism: control and regimentation   If we move our perspective from a social conservative and functionalistic frame of reference to a critical social control perspective, we can find another type of answer to the Japanese crime paradox. In this perspective the answer is less related to a 'positive' perspective of belonging, and more related to a 'negative' perspective of total control and fear of reprisals.

According to Sugimoto (1997)

> Japanese society has various forms of regimentation that are designed to standardize the thought patterns and attitudes of the Japanese and make them toe the line in everyday life. While these pressures exist in any society, in Japan they constitute a general pattern which one might call friendly authoritarianism. It is authoritarian to the extent that it encourages each member of society to internalise and share the value system which regards control and regimentation as natural, and to accept the instructions and orders of people in superordinate positions without questioning (p. 245. Cf. comparable perspectives in Dale, 1986, and Komiya, 1999).

To attain this system of 'repressive tolerance' the system of small groups permeating all aspects of life is used as a basis for mutual surveillance and deterrence of deviance. Komiya (1999) maintains that instead of simplified propositions about 'homogeneous population' or 'strong group consciousness', it is the locality-based group formation that gives both security and repressive rules. Setting aside arguments in support of specific Japanese moral qualities, Komiya argues that everyday life in the inner circle (called the *uchi* world) is so entrenched with watching eyes that the individual soon internalizes this *external* control into a severe *self*-control. Clifford (1976) underlines the same perspective in a chapter entitled 'The Japanese self-image: The internal policeman'. This self-image is totally dependent on the opinion of the outside world, and 'cannot be overestimated in considerations of the control of behavior whether that behavior be individual, group, or national. The individual takes his point of reference from outside and is, therefore, pressured to conform' (p. 8). Hechter and Kanazawa (1993) support this point of view by stressing the wide variety of 'mechanisms of visibility' that keep people in the vice. Be it in schools, workplaces, neighbourhoods, or in the family, the individual will always be visible and consequently accountable for his/her behaviour. They argue that more important than Confucian values (values that are found in less orderly countries like South Korea and China) are the structural or institutional mechanisms that encompass the individual. Or in the words of van Wolferen (1989), this totalising control can be expressed as an 'inescapable embrace'. Van Wolferen calls Japanese police 'nurses of the people' and 'nagging and instructing nursemaids'.[26] He describes in detail how the average Japanese citizen is supervised at all times and in almost all places. Like Clifford, he argues (quoting Belsey) that Japan is a paradise for the police because 'Japanese society polices itself' (p. 187). More detail on the social control exercised in neighbourhoods and in schools will illustrate this point.

Neighbourhood control   Back in feudal days (twelfth to sixteenth centuries) neighbourhoods were organized into the so-called *gonin-kumi*. This was a group consisting of five families, hierarchically organized, with a leader who took responsibility for his whole group. The groups were designed to keep law and order among themselves and were held responsible for delivering up offenders. During the Tokugawa period (1603–1868) this system was made the most of to suppress potentially disruptive forces. Via a system of peer pressure and group accountability everybody had responsibility for what other group members did. People, who in earlier periods behaved in unexpected ways, risked severe punishment, even execution. Henshall (1999) maintains that the criteria for what would be defined 'not correct behaviour' were very obscure and, consequently, 'it is hard to imagine a more effective means of enforcing conformity and suppressing individualistic behaviour' (p. 151). Even though this system was formally abolished during the Meiji restoration (1868) this did not hinder the continuous functioning of this system up until modern times.

Today, Japanese neighbourhoods have both formal and informal institutions with a wide variety of functions, and the cultural heritage from earlier days is still very much alive ('neighborhood associations persist, and are pervasive' (Ashkenazi, 1991, p. 386)). Even though participation in the *chokai* (neighbourhood association) is formally voluntary, it seems that no household refuses to belong. In his in-depth study of a neighbourhood in Tokyo, Bestor (1989) lists the following functions as central to the *chokai*: fire and crime prevention, traffic safety, public health and sanitation, festivals and support for the local tutelary deity, activities for women and youth, expressions of condolence, and 'other issues that may become important' (p. 126). The *chokai* operates in close co-operation with the police (e.g. by distributing public service announcement notices on how to prevent crime), and it has a very effective system of communication with its members. But, more important than 'technically' prescribed functions, is the informal social control of this system. Residents are watching each other, they are watching the youngsters, and they admonish misbehaviour. Children who stay out late will be reported to their parents.[27] This means that the fairly newly invented Western system of parental night patrols is historically incorporated into the social web of Japanese society. Empirical research (in Hechter and Kananzawa, 1993, p. 475) indicates that Japanese society has a high level of neighbourhood intimacy. Comparing the US with Japan, Hechter and Kananzawa conclude that 'it seems that the level of neighborhood association and involvement is about twice as high in Japan as it is in the United States. More involved with their neighbors yet subject to their strict social control, the Japanese are under their neighbors' and friends' watchful eyes to an extent that is unimaginable in other countries' (p. 476). According to van Wolferen (1989, pp. 184–5) a number of embezzlement cases have been discovered due to tips from neighbours who noticed stolen goods being delivered to a home.

In addition to this formal and informal network of neighbourhood associations, there exists a network of voluntary associations with the single aim of preventing crime. The 'Crime Prevention Association' consists of ordinary citizens, and the main objective is to co-operate 'spiritually and practically with the various activities of the police' (Clifford, 1976, p. 101). These associations are organized into a national network ('The National Federation of the Crime Prevention Association', established in 1963) and by the end of the 1960s there were some 410,000 liaison units within this system. Like the neighbourhood associations, they carry out a variety of crime-preventive activities. Also, there exists a network called 'Vocational Unions for Crime Prevention', which consists of professional or business people most likely to be affected by crime (7,742 such vocational units in 1969).

Most scholars will describe the police–citizen relationships as consensual and reciprocal. To a certain, descriptive, extent I will subscribe to such a conclusion. There is little doubt that the civil and voluntary participation in the whole chain of the criminal justice system is extensive and apparently consensual. However, I must warn against superficial conclusions at this point. It is not easy to determine the real meaning of a concept like 'consensus' in this connection. Japanese police operate within a cultural and institutional framework characterized by hierarchy, respect for authority and a continuous stress on the ideal of harmony. Traditionally, Japanese law has been an instrument of constraint used by the authorities to control its citizens. Consequently, one might as well argue that, 'the public is not undivided in its admiration of policemen. To some extent they are still feared' (van Wolferen, p. 185). Komiya (1999) supports this evaluation by saying that 'the Japanese have an antipathy to law and do not take law seriously' (p. 372). In Japanese culture one makes a clear distinction between people who belong to the inner circle (called *uchi*) and those who belong to the outer circle (called *soto*). In relation to people not belonging to one's *uchi* Japanese behaviour can be repudiating and even hostile. From this perspective it would be misleading to present police–citizen relationships as harmonious. As both Benedict (1967) and Levine (1985) argue, Japanese culture – or Asian culture in general – should first and foremost be characterised by the word *ambiguity*. As discussed in Chapter 2 the 'reality' is a social construction, and what you see is dependent on where you stand. In a perspective defined as a 'functionalistic and harmonic' one might describe police–citizen relationships as almost symbiotic. However, wearing more critical or conflict-oriented glasses it is easier to discover forced and suppressive structures in this relationship.

School control   The focus on visibility and direct control that is found in the neighbourhood system can be seen within the schools as well. Even though the postwar education system in Japan is formally based on an American model, the way the school day is organized is very different. The main difference relates to the topic of control.

In many ways Japanese society can be described as an integrated society. However, a glance into the Japanese school system indicates that this is very much a *forced* integration. Rohlen (referred in Hechter and Kanazawa, 1993, p. 469) compares the schools with egg cartons. Even high school students have their clearly designated compartment for the whole day, and the location of any student at any time of day can easily be determined. Students will often wear uniforms, unique school insignia, and nametags can even be applied. The students have no free periods and they do not participate in any form of individual tasks. This means that teacher supervision is very tight. Teachers planning school trips will pay a lot of attention to the overarching aim of keeping control. The structural control of the students is accompanied by a complimentary ideological control: Japanese schools are permeated by slogans, goal for the day, or aim for this month, and normally have a very moralistic nature. 'Let us not run in the corridors', 'Let us try to answer the teacher clearly', and 'Let us keep our school toilets clean', are typical requests (see Sugimoto, 1997, p. 124). The teachers will administer a lot of exercises designed to keep the pupils in line and, in addition, they will exert their control via special pupils in charge of school discipline.

Henshall (1999) provides further examples of the surveillance of Japanese schoolchildren:

> They are subject to numerous rules and regulations often of a very pedantic nature, almost 'army-style' in that they sometimes seems to

be just rules for the sake of rules. For example, there are regular inspections, at junior high school level in particular, to ensure that hair is of an appropriate length and style, that trousers are properly creased, and that skirts are of the right length and with the right number of pleats. Some schools even have a set procedures for asking questions, with arms having to be raised to a set angle in a set direction, and set phraseology used (p. 114).[28]

In addition to strictly monitoring the everyday life of the children, a really effective strategy to make the children conform is the use of so-called 'lifestyle committees', made up of students themselves. Members of these committees are responsible for quite extensive surveillance functions in relation to their own peers, reporting to the teacher if any irregularities are detected. Even though peer group control is not unique to Japanese society, control systems are extraordinarily developed both in substance and extension. Singer (1973) supports such a conclusion:

> it is a peculiar trait of the Japanese way of upbringing that with them discipline and constraint, at least during their decisive stages, are imposed less from outside, by men of greater age and terrifying authority, than by members of the same group. In a Middle School, and still more in a higher School, it is the pupils of the same form who tighten the network of 'ought' and 'ought not', according to their sentiment, belief, or waywardness (p. 34).

There is no doubt that all this regimentation in schools and kindergartens is exercised with the deliberate aim of ensuring control. From the 1970s schools increased teacher control of pupils, which reflected the political unrest in the 1960s and increasing school violence: 'To suppress potential deviance from school norms, school administrators and teachers tried to tighten their grip on students by shaping their outward behavioural patterns into a uniform code' (*op. cit.*, p. 125). Even though this process was met with protests and demonstrations, there is no doubt that demands for rigidity, stringency and regimentation got the upper hand in this conflict.

In short, scarcity of individual/private *space* (but also scarcity of *time*) has turned life in Japanese schools into a kind of quasi-military pattern (cf. class room leader shouting 'stand up', 'bow', and 'sit down' at the beginning of a session). A combination of structural, symbolic and ideological measures is used to see that everything runs smoothly. While school children all over the world are controlled in a variety of ways,

Japan has developed systems of control that leaves extraordinarily little space for 'voluntary' commitment and 'self-generated' adaptation. However, increasing problems related to bullying in school indicate that not everything is under control.

The general picture of Japanese schools as a kind of 'total institution' continues from primary to secondary level of the education system. In a study on juvenile delinquency, Foljanty-Jost and Metzler (2003) comment on the omnipresent control in Japanese junior high schools. They report that students are kept so busy that there are almost no chances for 'slipping away' into undesired activities. Under the headline 'structural control' they remark that 'social interaction and behavior is clearly defined by school regulations, teacher guidance materials, and rules self-imposed by the students' (p. 40). Furthermore, there is a 'general control' in these schools that permeates every aspect of the students' everyday life. Social behaviour that does not fit in with a very pro-social pattern is automatically defined as delinquency. Finally, by means of a 'specific control' every form of delinquent behaviour (e.g. forbidden red ribbons or shoelaces) is swooped down on. These authors conclude that the focus on delinquency is so intense that it functions, not as a self-fulfilling prophecy, but as a self-preventing, prophecy.[29]

I have limited myself to mentioning neighbourhood and school control as illustrations of what we might call the 'visibility aspect' of crime control in Japan. The same principles will also be in operation in other arenas, like the workplace, company housing residencies, and the family. There is little doubt that life in Japanese society is based on principles of dependence and visibility that should be described as quite unique. So what is the criminological relevance of these structural aspects of Japanese groupism?

There is broad agreement among criminologists that informal social control is the basic prerequisite for effective crime prevention (cf. for example Braithwaite (1989): 'It would seem that sanctions imposed by relatives, friends or a personally relevant collectivity have more effect on criminal behavior than sanctions imposed by a remote legal authority', p. 69). The two most important aspects of such informal control are *visibility* and personal *dependency* (Christie, 1975). While the most fundamental mechanisms of social control are to be found in the normal processes of interaction, the increasing differentiation and size of institutions we live within has made it more complicated to see each other. The conditions for delivering wrinkles or praise (as Christie expresses it) have declined at the same speed as invisibility has increased. In consequence, the informal social control is weaker in modern societies than in traditional ones. In Christie's vocabulary, societies with both a high degree of visibility and a high degree of reciprocal dependency are *tight societies*. These are societies where the primary control will have good preconditions to function. Without commenting on the mechanisms for attaining the high visibility in Japan, there is little doubt that informal control via high visibility is much higher in Japan than in the West. It seems that Japanese authorities have a 'cultural history' for using mechanisms of tight visual control to supervise its citizens, and it is hardly a coincidence that responsibility for maintaining street lights on dark back paths and alleys is defined as the *chokai's* major current contribution to crime prevention (Bestor, 1989, p. 128). In Hechter and Kanazawa's (1993) analysis of *Group solidarity in Japan* the visibility argument is their main proposition: 'We argue that the relatively high visibility of the Japanese fosters normative compliance' (p. 468). Rather than saying that a shared heritage of Confucian values is the primary explanation of little crime in Japan, they focus on a more 'cynical' perspective: Since both South Korea and China have much of the same cultural foundation as Japan, there seems to be more power to a belief that maintains 'various institutional arrangements that foster dependence and visibility in its constituent groups' (p. 486). Furthermore, Westermann and Burfeind (1991) emphasise in their analysis of low crime rates in Japan that individuals live under the constant scrutiny of the groups to which they belong.

Re. shame as a crime preventive factor   One popular explanation of little crime in Japan has been the so-called 'shaming theories'. According to these theories 'crime is best controlled when members of the community are the primary controllers through active participation in shaming offenders' (Braithwaite, 1989, p. 8). Although in this perspective factors that may *prevent* crime are examined, little is said about crime *triggering* factors. In his much-debated book *Crime, shame and reintegration* Braithwaite uses Japan as a case to illustrate the effectiveness of shaming. Although this is not the place to debate Braithwaite's contribution, I will shortly argue that without linking the question of individual shaming to a wider historical and cultural perspective, we run the risk of limiting ourselves to a classical social-conservative and functional-istic analysis. From my point of view, Braithwaite is right in focusing on 'shaming' as an explanation of low crime rates in Japan. However, without commenting on topics like power, hierarchy, gender, or suppression, he might easily be accused of conveying 'ideologies of harmony'.

If we were to arrange Japanese values in a hierarchical system, we would definitely have to put *harmony* (or *wa*) as the main, overarching value. Singer (1973, p. 62) calls it 'the law of harmonious flow', and argues that this principle has acquired the force of a 'biological instinct' in the life of everyday Japan. Shelley (1993, p. 142) defines harmony as 'the cardinal value of interpersonal Japanese interrelationships'.[30] As already mentioned, this Confucian value has for many centuries been effectively exploited by power elites to control the people.[31] To serve this aim of control, authorities used the strategy of 'enrolling' the whole population into self-surveillance groups. These groups were organized on a hierarchical principle, with one leader (or rather master) responsible for the whole group. At the same time, each member of the group would in any setting represent the group of which (s)he was a member. This has important consequences from a criminological perspective. Japan has, right up to modern times, been a 'representing society'. No matter in which arena the individual plays her/his role, she/he will always represent a group of other individuals. As already mentioned, the individual person is at best of secondary importance. What matters the most is not the rights and the justice of the individual, but the smooth running of the community. As long as I know that my own actions will have consequences for other people to whom I am closely linked, I have to strive for spotless behaviour. This is especially so if I know that my whole group might be regarded as responsible for my misconduct. The principle of collective responsibility was implemented by the Tokugawa shogunate to suppress all kinds of opposition. Henshall (1999) describes this system in the following way:

> This included peer pressure in the form of group accountability. If one member of a group stepped out of line (moreover a tightly pre-scribed line), the whole group risked severe punishment. It is easier to control groups than individuals, especially if they are very conformist groups that regulate themselves in fear of dire consequences if they fail to do so (Henshall, 1999, p. 151).

The same principle is practised within Japanese schools today. A class is divided into *han* groups (a working group of five to eight children) that carry out both social and academic activities. All the members of such a group are responsible – *as a group* – for accomplishing their goals (for example cleaning the school. Benjamin, 1997). Sugimoto (1997) describes the neighbourhood system of control that I referred to above as a 'quasi-espionage organization', where families were required to watch each other and report any signs of deviant activities. But even today the principle of group accountability is practised in Japanese society. Sugimoto reports:

> When one or a few members of a unit indulge in culpable behavior, all members bear the blame collectively. When one pupil plays a mischievous trick or disobeys the rules, teachers sometimes punish the entire class by making all pupils stay late, organizing a soul-searching session, or, as in one controversial case, ordering all boys in the class to cut their hair short. If a member of a promising high-school baseball team engages in delinquent behavior, the principle of shared responsibility can force the entire team to withdraw from a national tournament. The whole group assumes collective responsibility (*rentai sekinin*) for the wrongdoings of each member (p. 247).

The principle of collective responsibility is applied even within today's criminal justice system:

> Much can be expected of the threat that the suspect's family will become involved. In a fair number of recorded instances, relatively simple-minded suspects were told that their father and mother would also be arrested if they did not confess... A vague belief in collective guilt survives from centuries of military government, so that even today the family of a criminal suspect may be ostracised by the community (van Wolferen, 1989, p. 189).

The degree to which this extended responsibility is still alive in Japanese society is illustrated by the following case (reported in *Japan Times*, 16 November 2000). For some weeks Japanese newspapers launched hard attacks on a well known actress, because her 20-year-old son was arrested for drug use. Since this was not the first time her son had been in trouble with the law, she was given the 'Bad Mother of the Month Award'. This woman won this dishonourable award because she was defined as being negligent, self-centred, prioritizing her role as actress more than as mother (to a 20-year-old son). Her worst sin was to state in a TV interview that she had told her son that once he became an adult he had to be responsible for his own actions. According to the *Japan Times* the press made mincemeat of such statements. It noted: 'Parents are always seen as being responsible for their children's actions, no matter how old the children are, they also have a claim on their children's accomplishments, no matter how little involvement they have in those accomplishments'.

Obviously, the individual in Japan finds her(him)self in a web of constraints that gives very little freedom. If we apply a Western standard, there are very few opportunities for self-expression in Japan. The group has full control. Once the individual self is extinguished, and once the dependence of the group is established, it follows that each individual will fear doing something that may harm the group. Since the collective identity is more important than the individual identity, it follows that a wrongdoer will hurt her/his collective identity more than her/his individual identity. In such a society the social implications of shame and apology will be essential. Schneider (1992) reports:

> The stigmatization of a family causes problems in the search for partners for the children. Family members have difficulties finding employment. The mass media increase the pressure of conformity by publishing the names of adult offenders. Being a member of a respectable enterprise has a criminality-preventing effect insofar as a loss of job must be expected if an employee is convicted of a crime (p. 314).

As long as harmonious relationships are directing Japanese morality, the individual will have to avoid actions that will bring shame not only to the individual, but to the group. He/she will also have to avoid actions that lead to humiliating processes of apology and redemption. As Creighton (1990) argues, the connection between shame and belongingness is so strong in Japan that shame may be invoked even if the individual acts independently of the group. 'Shame is a more effective sanction in a society where rejection or ostracism from the group generates a greater anxiety than the fear of punishment' (p. 295). As long as – metaphorically speaking – morals are incarnated as the 'Group' (cf. the Constitution from 604 A.D.: 'Let us follow the multitude and act like them'), the individual will be effectively tethered in a web of obligations.

From the above I have to add that shame in Japanese culture should rather be regarded as an 'effect' than as a 'cause': From a *culture* cultivating harmony, and a *structure* utilizing the group as a means to attain this value, it follows – almost as a necessary implication – that shame will play a pivotal role in structuring options of action. In this regard 'shame' is not an isolated mechanism that can be implemented around the world independent of a broader cultural and structural network. Shame is effectual only in communities where people are already integrated. (For a further critical discussion of 'limits to shame', see Massaro, 1997.)

The Japanese 'groupism' creates a network for the individual with an obvious criminological relevance. The omnipresence of groupism creates a tight society that functions preventively regarding crime (cf. Triandis, 1994). If we – in line with Guneriussen (1999) – differentiate between three types of group fellowship – a community of place, a community of memory and psychological communities – then we can safely argue that Japanese society at least has realised the two last forms. And that should definitely be of criminological interest.

Japan is an other-directed, relational and contextual society

A. General description

The stress on harmony in the group leads naturally to an ideology where personal relations and etiquette are important ingredients.

> The Japanese believe that an intimate knowledge about personal relations (*ningen kankei*) is of superior importance. This belief is derived from the notion that society consists of interactions and interdependency of its members. In Buddhism (in a text called Garland sutra) no human being has its own innate 'self-nature'. Rather, the individual self is constituted through an infinite number of relations with other people, and it is these relationships that define each being (Kawai, 1998, p. 14).

Consequently, the Japanese value group affinity and group identity. They only trust those with tangible and close personal relations. Group affinity or identity can develop only through sharing actual everyday life experiences with others (Mori, 1994, p. 98). Less favourably, people who do not stick to the Japanese code concerning correct behaviour will end up in embarrassing situations.[32] That is why we find an extreme alertness among Japanese people with regard to how they influence one another's behaviour.[33] Van Wolferen (1989, p. 333) uses strong imagery, maintaining that the Japanese adhere to an etiquette like that of an old-fashioned royal court.

The strong focus on social relations in Japanese culture has been documented in different empirical research (referred to in Triandis, 1995, pp. 69–70). Lebra reports an interesting difference between the answers she received from interviews with Japanese and American women. While American women told her a lot about themselves, but very little about their relationships with others, it was the opposite with Japanese women. Lebra learned a lot about Japanese women's relations to the outside world, but almost nothing about themselves. The same pattern can be found in 'independence tests'. American men and women regard themselves as much more independent than Japanese men and women. For a Japanese person the main ideal is to have a large number of successful relationships with others, while the American ideal is to reach great accomplishments. The other side of this coin is the fear of being in conflict with other people. This can be seen in a lot of situations, including the classical Japanese reluctance to make decisions without extensive consultations (Goldman, 1994). Radford *et al.* (see Triandis, 1995) reported that Japanese subjects have less confidence when making decisions than Australians. They reported complacency, avoidance, and hyper-vigilance more frequently than the Australians in relation to decision-making, and also more stress when they had to make decisions without consultation. It seems quite obvious that all these illustrations express the overarching importance in Japanese culture of harmony in all type of relations.[34]

It is a common experience that Japanese people continually have their radar turned on. This high degree of other-directedness is deeply buried in religious and cultural traditions. This is implanted from early childhood in the concept of *amae*. *Amae* denotes the primary dependency that is said to exist between all people. In his much debated book *The Anatomy of Dependency*, Doi (1976) argues that *amae* must be our starting point if we want to understand not only the psyche of each individual, but the whole social structure in Japan.

The verb *amaeru* can be translated as a wish to 'be an object of love from others', 'a wish to be allowed to behave like a spoiled child', and 'to pretend being a baby' (Kalland, 1986, p. 67). According to Doi this is a primary human need which Western cultures have neglected. While Westerners will stress independence and self-confidence in the child, the opposite is emphasized in Japan. The child will be taught that the 'outside world' is full of dangers, and that the mother is the only protection against these threats. To indulge in the family (the mother!), to trust in the protection from the group, will be the only way to survive. 'To play on amae and the need for care and love, the Japanese mother will develop an aversion in the child as for taking decisions alone, and a fear of being isolated from family and friends' (Åm, 1981, p. 103). Usually, Japanese mothers will try to make their children behave appropriately not by rebuking, but by a kind of withdrawal of love (or what Creighton, 1990, calls 'maternal ostracism' (p. 298)), and through ridicule. To Westerners the use of ostracism against the children may seem cruel: children being locked out of the house may be left screaming for their mothers for a long time. But since the mother on such occasions has defined the child as 'non-existent' she will argue that she is not really locking anyone out (*op. cit*, p. 299). The principle of locking children out of the community with significant others is also applied in Japanese kindergartens (Åm, 1981). A person who experiences ostracism from his family has in reality lost her/his identity (Kalland, 1986, p. 74). Anyone who cannot find her/his place in the group is a *hikokumin*, or non-citizen.[35]

Benedict (1967) also comments on the great importance of finding acceptance. She portrays a world that from a Western point of view seems almost terrifying:

> Gradually, after they are six or seven, responsibility for circumspection and 'knowing shame' is put upon them and upheld by the most drastic of sanctions; that their own family will turn against them if they default. The pressure is not that of a Preussian discipline, but it is inescapable. In their early privileged period the ground has been prepared for this development both by the persistent inescapable training in nursery habits and posture, and by the parent's teasing which threatens the child to accept great restraints upon himself when he is told that 'the world' will laugh at him and reject him. He clamps down upon the impulses he expressed so freely in earlier life, not because they are evil but because they are now inappropriate (p. 201).

Research carried out by Caudill and Weinstein (referred to in Kalland, 1986, p. 64) discloses that the process of interpreting the kind of behaviour that is expected starts early in a child's life. Already at the age of three to four months infants in Japan and America have incorporated different and culturally appropriate forms of behaviour and these forms seem to be consistent with later social expectations. The authors continue: 'In Japan, the infant is seen as a separate biological organism who from the beginning, in order to develop, needs to be drawn in to increasingly interdependent relations with others. In America, the infant is seen more as a dependent biological organism who, in order to develop, needs to be made increasingly independent of others' (*op. cit.*, p. 64). According to developmental psychology, shame develops in the pre-oedipal or bonding stage, which is exactly the phase that is mostly emphasized in Japan. In the US more emphasis is on the separation stage, and this is the phase at which guilt develops.[36]

One important implication of Japanese child-rearing is that it gives rise (much more than in the West) to the implantation of shame. As long as it is a kind of social evaluation rather than an internalized, self-contained ethical code that matters the most, the children will always direct their behaviour according to what is 'appropriate' in the given situation.

It is quite common to hear Japanese mothers remark 'I am happy' when the children behave well, and by saying 'I am sad' when they don't. On most occasions the feedback to the children's behaviour will be relatively non-verbal, using a very discreet signal system to communicate their message. In this way 'the Japanese thus learn to pay attention to how others feel and to change their behaviour so that others will feel good. Thus, the Japanese learn as much when an important other person gets rewarded as when they themselves get rewarded' (Triandis, 1994, p. 35). Even if such a description may seem valid for a lot of other countries in the world, Japanese child-rearing is clearly different from what will be found in Western countries (Zoellner, 1992, Kalland, 1986, Henshall, 1999, Singer, 1973). In spite of an almost total emotional involvement from the mother, it has been pointed out that, in reality, the child is implanted with a basic absence of confidence during the first years of living (Dale, 1986).

At this point it is important to add that in return for conformity to the group the individual can expect loyal and omnipresent support. Even if Japan can be described as a disciplined nation with people behaving in a strictly conformist manner, we must also remind ourselves of values like tolerance and understanding. As Clifford (1976) argues

> the need to relate behavior to the group pressures is balanced to some extent by the individual's confidence that, in return for his loyalty and conformity, he can expect to be 'looked after'. He belongs to his group and conforms to its expectations because at the same time it provides him with security and an understanding of his basic needs (p. 16).

This means that the individual can count on both support and tolerance whenever that should be needed. It is well known that superiors in Japan have to meet the needs of their inferiors to an extraordinary extent (from a Western point of view). A loyal employee can expect that his boss will take an active part in his life, by inviting him (and here it is correct to say him) for drinks, acting as a marriage broker, and taking responsibility for errors committed by the rank and file.[37] People who get drunk and run into trouble when out drinking with friends will rarely end up in a police station. Loyal group members will always be taken care of by those nearby. This intra-group tolerance is learned at an early stage. As already mentioned, naughty children are indulged far more than in the West.

The stress on the *amae* relation is consequently an important brick in building Japanese culture. You will not be long in the company of Japanese citizens before experiencing the fruit of this upbringing: their tendency to apologize. So omnipresent is this apologetic culture that van Wolferen (1989, p. 188) argues they sometimes give the impression of thinking that their mere presence is a nuisance to others. According to Doi (1976) this is because 'they fear that unless they apologize the other man will think them impolite with the result that they may lose his good will' (p. 31). To lose the good will of the other is in an *amae* perspective very threatening. Since it is the relation to other people that is important for the individual, anything that may weaken this relation will be fatal. Wagatsuma and Rosett (referred to in Haley, 1998) add to this description that, for the Japanese 'the external act of apology becomes significant as an act of self-denigration and submission'. Through this act the Japanese can show her/his 'commitment to a positively harmonious relationship in the future in which the mutual obligations of the social hierarchy will be observed' (p. 850). By apologizing one will also express accountability and a willingness to put matters right. As we have seen, the custom of apologising is still an integral part of the criminal justice system. An offender is expected to express total contrition for what infringement has been committed. For even minor offences the perpetrator will have to sign a letter of apology. Although this practice is not an integral part of the formal statutory system, it is held on to because 'the offenders need to cleanse their spirits completely to conform to social norms in the future' (Sugimoto, 1997, p. 253).

Amae relations will create both a type of dependency and a socializing discipline that in turn create a foundation for the Japanese group mentality. At the same time values like empathy, sensitivity and self-synchronizing are encouraged (Dale, 1986, p. 110). The 'ideological' basis for this sensitive culture can be traced back to four basic concepts in Confucianism (see Goldman, 1994): *Jen, shu, i* and *li*.

Jen,[38] or humanism, means the duty of each individual to aspire to cautiousness, warmth, and attention while communicating with others. Self-interest and self-attention are foreign words, while the focus is on empathy and the search for other people's feelings and viewpoints. The implication of this is that non-verbal communication is valued, something that presupposes the abilities to observe and listen. It will also mean a demand that each individual exerts a high degree of self-control (Nosco, 1998, p. 2).

Shu can be translated as reciprocity. Confucius is said to have expressed that 'there has never been a case where a man who did not understand reciprocity was able to communicate to others whatever treasures he might have had stored in himself' (McNaughton, referred to in Goldman, 1994, p. 32). *Shu* is often mentioned in connection with the concept *heragei*, which means something like 'belly communication', but which even the Japanese themselves have difficulties in explaining. It has a strong affinity to the concept *enryo*, which is defined as 'polite hesitation', 'restraint' or 'holding back'; a key concept in interaction in Japan (Stevens, 1997, p. 19, Doi, 1976, p. 38). It is important to be very attentive towards other people, and always seek harmony. This means that a Japanese will always try to avoid open conflicts, avoid losing face and, of course, never hurt anyone.[39] These cultural characteristics are mirrored in the often-noted fact that Japanese people avoid taking a case to the court. As a consequence, Japan has essentially fewer lawyers than Western countries.

A further consequence of this attentiveness is an extreme awareness of nuances in body language and the paralinguistic language. This means that *shu* is closely linked to *jen*. According to Triandis (1994) it is a typical characteristic of collectivist cultures that more attention is paid to context (emotional expressions, touching, distance between bodies, body orientation, level of voice, eye contact) when they communicate than do people from more individualistic cultures. This, of course, is linked to the importance of keeping relationships with in-group members at their best. The important thing is to interpret the whole setting, where the spoken word is only one minor aspect of the total communication.

I denotes a principle of seeking the best for the group, not the individual. Be it the family, the company, the local community or the nation, it is always the best for the group that matters. In a Mertonian perspective this means that even though the Japanese might seem to have a lot in common with Western people concerning a success culture, success in Japan is not linked to individual endeavours but to the collectivity. Alternatively, if one single person is given some kind of honour, this will not necessarily devolve on the right person, but the one with a senior position or highest status.

Li applies to how the three above-mentioned principles are to be put into operation. Japan is a culture with an extremely fine-meshed culture of norms, where rules for conduct cannot be learned except via a bodily socialization. The practical rules for interaction between people is expressed in *li*; the outer manifestation of '*jen*', '*shu*' and '*i*'.

Another important aspect of the Japanese other-directedness is their basic view of the human being. Cross-cultural studies have found significant differences in the way people interpret other's actions. Individualistic cultures will often have a tendency to make *dispositional* judgements about people, while collectivist cultures will make more *contextual* judgements (Triandis, 1994, p. 96). This means that people in the Western cultures will base their interpretation of actions on *finalistic* or motivational models, while people in Asian cultures will stick to more causal and contextual models. It is very important to notice this difference because it has deep implications for the way we interpret social patterns that at face value might appear strange to us. As Clifford (1976) underlines, 'it is difficult then to seek understanding by simply applying Western standards of rationality to the Japanese phenomena. They have to be perceived on their own terms, and apparent opposites or contradictions (to the Western mind) have a place within a more integrated whole than we can conceive' (p. 34).

While in the West one can talk about the 'character' of an individual, and by that mean consistent, lasting and relatively situationally independent characteristics, the Japanese think in more contextual and relational categories. This is linked to the basic meaning of reciprocal obligations that permeates the whole society. Two central concepts in this connection are *on* and *giri*. It is difficult to give an exact translation of these concepts, but if we simplify, this is about the diversity of obligations a human being can have towards her/his fellow man. In this connection we do not only talk about negative burdens like social debt, but also positive virtues like friendliness, love and loyalty. *On* refers to indebtedness for a favour given, and it is a debt that has to be repaid. *Giri* 'refers to the obligation to act according to the dictates of society in relation to other persons' (*Keys to the Japanese Heart and Soul*, 1996, p.87). According to Benedict (1967) there exists a fine-meshed network of duties (to your family, to non-related people, to one's name, etc.) that traps the individual totally in obligations. As an illustration, let us return to the debt of gratitude that each individual has in relation to his/her parents. The sacrifice that parents have shown children will, even after the death of those parents, follow the children like 'a constant shadow' (Benedict, 1967, p. 81). This way of thinking will permeate all types of important relations for the individual, be it towards the Emperor, a neighbour or a work colleague. In this way the Japanese citizen is involved in a multitude of dependency relations which will subsequently create insoluble dilemmas. Is the obligation in relation to the spouse or to the job most important? Should one give priority to one's own children or to those of one's colleagues? No matter what choice is made, the individual will end up in situations where loyalty and obligations will have to be broken. In this situation, the Japanese contextualism is helpful. Instead of looking at the individual in isolation and with specific characters ('good' or 'bad'), the Japanese will rather describe each other in relation to what Benedict calls different 'circles':

> They see the 'whole duty of man' as if it were parcelled out into separate provinces on a map. In their phrase, one's life consists of 'the circle of chu' and 'the circle of ko' and 'the circle of giri' and 'the circle of jin' and 'the circle of human feelings' and many more. Each circle has its special detailed code and a man judges his fellows, not by ascribing to them integrated personalities, but by saying of them that 'they do not know 'ko' or 'they do not know giri'. Instead of accusing a man of being unjust, as an American would, they specify the circle of behaviour he has not lived up to. Instead of accusing a man of being selfish or unkind, the Japanese specify the particular province within which he violated the code. They do not invoke a categorical *imperative or a* golden rule. Approved behaviour is relative to the circle within which it appears (p. 137). (*Chu* is loyalty to the Emperor, *ko* is deference to your ancestors.)

For a stranger it is difficult to imagine the extent and the meaning of all these types of dependency relations. However, it seems obvious that Japanese culture has a very tight, invisible social web that links the citizens together in a unique – some will say frightening – way (see Triandis, 1994). To an extent that we are not familiar with in the West, everyone (so to speak) in Japanese society is interrelated to other people, and the rightness of their actions is dependent on the context within which it appears.[40]

This strong relatedness is also mirrored in the language. The Japanese have many expressions for saying 'thank you', which expresses the difficulties with receiving things. *Arigato* (thank you) means 'oh this difficult thing'. In modern business life people used to say *sumimasen* (thank you), which in reality means 'Oh this will never end', i.e. 'this is something I cannot possibly repay'. *Katajikenai* is another word for thank you that directly translated means 'I am insulted' and 'I am grateful'. This will express a feeling of shame and insult because the recipient is not worthy of receiving such a present. I will comment further on politeness in Japanese language in the next section.

According to Triandis (1995) 'collectivists shift their behaviour depending on context more than do individualists. This is seen clearly when we study social behavior toward ingroup and outgroup members' (p. 74). Contextualism may be further appreciated by way of three Japanese conceptual dyads. Though Western societies are familiar with the distinction between a back stage and a front stage (cf. Goffmann, 1958), the importance of these concepts in Japanese everyday life is much more fundamental. In Japan, the concepts of *tatemae/honne, omote/ura*, and *soto/uchi*, give us a better understanding of the extension of and limits to Japanese contextualism. These conceptual dyads are related to the importance of making a distinction between front and back stage, appearance and reality, domestic and foreign policy.

I mentioned in an earlier section that Westerners regard Japanese culture as very ambiguous. Some people visiting the country describe the Japanese as the friendliest people in the world, while others reach quite opposite conclusions. 'Foreigners who are not aware of these variables – and even some who are – can end up dismissing the Japanese as erratic and inconsistent, or even duplicitous and "two-faced"'(Henshall, 1999, p. 163). Benedict (1967) gives a very vivid description of how confusing Japanese behaviour may appear:

> The Japanese are, to the highest degree, both aggressive and unaggres-
> sive, both militaristic and aesthetic, both insolent and polite, rigid
> and adaptable, submissive and resentful of being pushed around,
> loyal and treacherous, brave and timid, conservative and hospitable
> to new ways. They are terribly concerned about what other people
> think of their behavior, and they are also overcome by guilt when
> other people know nothing of their misstep. Their soldiers are disci-
> plined to the hilt but are also insubordinate (p. 2).

Sugimoto (1997, p. 26) supports this description by saying that double codes are often legitimized in Japanese society. This creates a world behind the surface, a world that may be not only different from, but even contradictory to the experienced world. Again, this seeming duplicity is appreciated by way of conceptual pairs.

Tatemae and *honne* refer to performative versus honest aspects of an action. *Honne* refers to our true feelings while *tatemae* is about strategic correctness. *Omote* designates what is permissible and correct, while *ura* has connotations in direction of something hidden, wrong or unaccept-able. Finally, *soto* is used to describe the sphere outside one's primary belonging. *Uchi*, on the other hand, refers to the 'inside', to the back stage where people can be open and honest in relation to people being a member of the same in-group. In the *soto* sphere we say 'them', but in the *uchi* sphere one should rather say 'we'.

In sum, Japanese 'morality' first and foremost may be described in 'group functionalist' terms. What contributes to the harmony of the group is the guiding determinant for individual behaviour. Justice for the individual person is not necessarily the best remedy to safeguard this value. Individual rights may need to be subsumed under the collective good. If society is like an organism, then it is a holistic and utilitarian approach that should guide individual actions. In Japan 'holism' stems from primary group(s). It is what the *ura* world defines as important that guides the actions of each individual. But since group harmony is the leading principle Japanese have a 'flexible' attitude towards truth (*honne*). To a Japanese it is regarded a greater sin to hurt anybody than to tell the truth, in much the same way as it is regarded a worse sin to hurt anybody's soul than to hurt her/his body. Finally, transparent and forthright interaction between people might both hurt and be dysfunctional. On some occasions one will have to arrange things in the *ura* sphere to avoid unwanted consequences (for example pay *ura* fees to pay your children's way into important schools through the *ura gate* (back door), see Sugimoto, 1997, p. 26).

In contrast to Western justice, in which formal, abstract law is the decision-making template, in Japan the concrete particularity and 'situational ethics' of group expectations is key. Japanese are embedded in the vertical relations of different *iemotos* where everybody has to find her/his place and the individual will always be bonded to others via different types of obligations. This system of tightly interlocked parts of Japanese culture, Creighton (1990) argues, is based on 'situational ethics': 'Japanese morality tends to judge the value of an act in a situational context based on its impact on significant relationships' (p. 297). The *giri* is an integral part of this system because it comprises a code of behaviour that guides the individual towards other-directedness and, at the same time, defines proper behaviour relative to each circumstance.[41] As a consequence, actions will then be regarded as good or bad depending on the situation. Creighton (*op. cit.*) concludes that it is impossible to define negative behavior except in an extremely abstract sense; 'bad is bad when bad is bad' (p. 297). While Western tradition is concerned with inherent and abstract evil and puts an emphasis on guilt sanctions, the Japanese don't talk about 'sin'. When they have done something regarded as 'wrong', they will apologise by saying *machigai*. The direct translation of this concept is very telling: It means 'misplacement in context'. The guiding principle for superior behaviour is to become a master of life, and this is synonymous with being a person who never makes mistakes judging the correct combination of context and action. A 'situational ethic' has obvious implications for deviant behaviour. As long as the individual has found her/his place in one or many *iemotos*, the individual is both emotionally and materially dependent on this group, and the group in return operates with a collective responsibility for its individual members, the social web is fairly closely knit around each person.

B. *Discussion*

A main perspective in my presentation of 'the sociology of worry' was that an increasing differentiation and specialization will weaken primary control mechanisms. An urbanized life style will generate a more role specific way of interacting between people, and this will loosen the social embeddedness of the individual. In the language of Christie (1975), modern people meet each other like 'ships in the night'; we can only observe the lantern of the other ship, which, translated into sociology, means that we have a society with a far-reaching role specific communication. First of all, this is a society that makes it more difficult to identify ourselves with others. 'The other' is a stranger and, consequently, is of limited interest to us. It is at the same time a person that has little control over me. Modern society is a society with low visibility and low dependency. Modern society is a society where the individual is independent of other people and where each person acts on behalf of her/himself. Modern society is a society with weakened social bonding and consequently with weakened social control.

Hirschi (1969) has developed this Durkheimian perspective further in his social control theory.[42] His main argument is that unless human beings are socially bonded in an adequate way they will engage in deviant actions. To Durkheim social bonding was primarily about the internalization of common norms in society: 'We are moral beings to the extent that we are social beings' (i.e. have internalized social norms, Durkheim, here referred from Hirschi, 1969, p. 18). Hirschi has tried to specify the concept of bonding a bit further, differentiating between *attachment*, *commitment*, *belief*, and *involvement*. For my present analysis it is the two first concepts that are of primary interest.

By *attachment* Hirschi thinks of to what extent an individual feels morally linked to his fellow men. An attached individual is an individual who is well aware of, and strongly sensitive to the needs and wishes of other people (cf. what I earlier said about people being 'morally relevant' to each others). Hirschi regards crime as an act contrary to the wishes and expectations of other people: 'If a person does not care about the wishes and expectations of other people – that is, if he is insensitive to the opinion of others – then he is to that extent not bound by the norms. He is free to deviate' (Hirschi, 1969, p. 18). In short, this perspective is very much about *sensitivity* in relation to people around us.

Commitment refers to an individual's rational self-interest to engage in conventional activity. This self-interest can be positively or negatively motivated and, for Hirschi, fear of losing respect and recognition from others will be a crime-preventive mechanism.

In Japanese society it is very important not to lose face, and in this connection we are also talking about a 'group face'. In this culture one has traditionally attached overwhelming importance to one's name, 'even to the point where it regulated one's actions' (*Keys to the Japanese Heart and Soul*, 1996, p. 61). The value of one's name occupies a central place in the psychological makeup of the Japanese, and it embraces both the family and ancestors. 'Shame' is not only shame in relation to one's own person but even more so in relation to ancestors and descendants. To this we have to repeat the implications of *amae* relations. As long as Japanese people are to a large extent socialised to depend on the love and patience of others, and as long as they constantly seek to 'merge' with others, there is no doubt that Japanese people remain very strongly bonded.

The importance of harmony and the smooth running of social relations is also expressed in the idea of *kata* ('form' or 'model'). The idea of 'perfection' that I mentioned above is very much expressed in this term. One should always strive for excellence, be it in art, sports or professional life. The idea of *kata* contributes to a very strong disciplining of the individual subject: 'we see here not only the prioritisation of the *kata* over the free expression, and the prioritization of the role over the individual, we even see the taming and forced withering of the individual personality' (Henshall, 1999, p. 153).

Let us conclude by combining what we have learned about Japanese other-directedness, relationalism and contextualism with social control theory. In Japanese culture individuals are socialized to be very sensitive and aware of the wishes of others. They are socialized to become dependent on the support of other people. They are socialized to obliterate the individual self for the (presumed) best of the collective group. But we have to add: those principles are primarily related to their *uchi* world. In the *soto* world the Japanese can behave more 'out of control', as seen with Western eyes (their behaviour on public transport is an often-mentioned example). When Japanese people seem to conform in their *soto* world, that has to be explained with their 'representative role'. Since the individual person always represents his family, his ancestors and his descendants, she/he will have an attachment and a commitment to her/his fellows that will function as a very strong social control. If social control theory has something important to say concerning crime preventing 'factors', then Japanese society should be the best place to illustrate these principles. This is exactly the position of Braithwaite. Cultures based on a strong social bonding (where attachment and commitment to the family is the most important factor) are cultures that will both be able to minimize crime and at the same time reintegrate their offenders.[43,44]

If we stick to our description of crime as an action that offends the collective sentiments, then there is a very strong pressure in Japan not to participate in such behaviour. It would be more than strange if Japanese cultural characteristics like those presented above had no strong effect on the total amount of crime in this society. To put it another way: very much of sociological and criminological theory would be declared 'invalid' if the basic socio-cultural characteristics of Japanese society had no crime preventive effect. However, I immediately rush to add that these characteristics might be very controversial as basic ideals, and some of these characteristics might even *trigger* some types of crime.

Japan is a hierarchical and patriarchal society

A. General description

I have described Japan as a social-conservative society.[45] Most character-isations of Japanese society have been the subject of rather polarised debates. However, there seems to be broad agreement in describing Japan as a hierarchical society. Singer (1989, p. 330) compares daily life in Japan with a diplomatic cocktail party at which most guests are military attachés, and argues that hierarchical order pervades every nook and cranny of this society. Benedict (1967) supports his description:

> Any attempt to understand the Japanese society must begin with their version of what it means to 'take ones's proper station'. Their reliance upon order and hierarchy and our faith in freedom and equality are poles apart and it is hard for us to give hierarchy its just due as a possible social mechanism. Japan's confidence in hierarchy is basic in her whole notion of man's relation to his fellow man and of man's relation to the State and it is only by describing some of their national institutions like the family, the State, religious and economic life that it is possible for us to understand their view (p. 30).

The Confucian legacy has been conducive to securing hierarchical principles that still have a strong influence in Japan. Hofstede and Bond (1988) describe Confucianism by way of four dimensions, and the first they mention is that *the stability of society is based on unequal relationships between people.* According to this ideology there are five basic vertical relationships to be aware of: between ruler and subject, between father and son, between older and younger brother, between husband and wife, and between older friend and younger friend. These relationships are all based on a hierarchical principle where the subordinate has to accept the authority of the superior. In return she/he can anticipate protection and consideration.

Throughout its history Japan has been a class and a caste society. When Nakane (1970) decided to undertake a *structural* (not a cultural or historical) analysis of Japanese society, she made hierarchy the main topic of her book. 'The working of what I call the *vertical principle in* Japanese society is the theme of this book. In my view, the most characteristic feature of Japanese social organization arises from the single bond in social relationships: an individual or a group has always one single distinctive relation to the other' (p. x). It is the vertical relations that (according to this perspective) bind the different members of a group together, and rank is regarded as the basic social norm in Japan. This means that hierarchy is not limited only to class or gender relations, or to specific arenas like bureaucracy (where it is even more elaborate than in the West!), and company or organizational life. The principle of hierarchy permeates every aspect of Japanese culture, even in casual relationships. The master–disciple, senior–junior principle can be found at all levels and in all areas of Japanese life. As Resichauer (referred in Westermann and Burfeind, 1991) notes, 'it is as natural for a Japanese to shape his interpersonal relations in accordance with various levels of hierarchy as for an American to attempt to equalize his interpersonal relations despite differences of age and status' (p. 23).[46] Be it in the family, kindergarten, school, university, the sports clubs, or the company, the focus on status and ranking is a guiding principle. If Japanese culture is ambiguous in very many regards, there is very little ambiguity about hierarchy. In all situations where 'face' is important people have to pay attention to this principle.[47]

Why is hierarchy so fundamental for the smooth running of Japanese society? My answer would be: to safeguard the overarching principle of *wa* or harmony. Van Wolferen (1989) puts this very bluntly, when he argues that 'there can be no *wa* without hierarchy' (p. 329). It is hardly possible to decide to what extent Japanese (or any other) society is 'voluntarily' or 'forcefully' integrated. Analysis based on subjective versus objective data would probably be able to demonstrate both positions. The question what constitutes 'free will' in a society is probably as intractable in a commercialized Western as in a commercialized and 'Confucianized' Japanese society. In both types of society there are strong forces (commercial and religious to mention but two) counteracting anything like a 'free will'. However, to me there is little doubt that both manifest and latent power structures are the framework on which the Japanese *wa* hinges. In the polarised debate on Japan as a suppressing and authoritarian society, versus Japan as a 'synomic' or solidaristic (see Adler, 1983) society, I take the pragmatic stance that both can be right – on their respective premises. Socialization will be socialization to structures of values, and these structures are definitely not freely chosen. At the same time, there is a big difference between being socialized to submission versus empowerment. Even though the content of Japanese culture includes values like cautiousness and other-directedness, these values are all situated within a strong consciousness regarding high/low and outer/inner relations. These values are also reinforced by *fear* of not complying. With principles of group accountability and group responsibility there has not been much choice concerning alternative principles for social life. Consequently, I will argue that hierarchy is one of the instruments deliberately used by power elites in Japan to create the desired harmony in society. This means that there exists a 'hidden discipline' in Japanese society, even though some might argue that the power is only *partly* hidden.

The criteria for classifying within this hierarchical structure are very complicated, and ranking is used even between people of (seemingly) the same category. Individuals with identical qualifications will be differently ranged depending on age or sex. To manage this ranking one needs an elaborated language of distinctions, and Japanese language has a variety of expressions that indicate status and status differences. Within the general system called *keigo* (polite language) one has different sub-categories which give each individual a chance to express all types of nuances concerning position and status: The *sonkeigo* raises the level of an addressee, *kenjogo* lowers the level of the speaker, while *teineigo* raises the general level of the speech (Hendry, 1993, p. 52). The tradition with adding 'san' or 'kun' to a surname (only for men!) reveals if you are talking to an older or younger man. It is the status relations, the site for conversation, the gender of those involved, etc. that decide which language is applied. The structure is very complicated, and even for native Japanese it can sometimes be hard to choose the 'correct' expressions.[48]

Nevertheless, an obvious effect of this polite language is that everyone is keenly sensitive with respect to how other people must be addressed.

To master fully the ranking system and the polite language one has to know the importance of concepts like *sempai* (senior)/*kohai* (junior), and *oyabun* (parent)/*kobun* (child). Every Japanese person is involved in such vertical relations, where the junior or child has to show respect, gratitude, obedience and loyalty to the senior or parent. The existence of this vertical structure must be analysed against a background of the *amae*-relations, which I presented earlier. From early childhood people are socialized into dependency relations with other people, and the *oyabun/kobun* or *sempai/kohai* ties are only a kind of formalization of these early bonds. Even though this structure obviously implies status differences and distinctions between superior and subordinate, one should warn against equating subordinate with inferior. It should also be added that the role of superior implies obligations with respect to friendship, guidance, support and confidence.

The meaning of all these hierarchical relations can be traced in a multitude of everyday life situations; how deep people bow to whom, the way they use their voice towards persons of different status, in which order personal cards are exchanged, and how people are physically placed in the room. This system of ranking is learnt in childhood, and is typically found in schools: 'The children make their relative position within the group quite clear in the language they use to one another and by the terms they use to refer to one another. A senior is a sempai, a junior kohai, and behaviour is adjusted accordingly' (Hendry, 1993, p. 124). This can be seen when a school soccer team travels to an away game. The back seat in the bus will always be reserved for the eldest pupils. The youngest must sit next to the door. Or to take Nakane's (1970) example, for students who are mountain climbing it is a matter of course that the youngest students carry the heaviest sacks, it is the youngest that have to put up the tents, while the eldest will be the first to take food when the meal is ready (and prepared by the youngest!). In a company one can determine ranking from where in the room people have their desks: the junior will be placed near the exit, while the superior will sit furthest from this position. In meetings it would be unthinkable that a person sitting next to the door would raise her/his voice. People of a subordinate status would never start laughing, or laugh louder than one with a higher position, and they would definitely not take the chance of expressing opposing views to a senior person. The network of norms dictating correct behaviour in all those and comparable situations are infinite. It takes a lot of skill to master all those contextual principles, and this, in turn, confers considerable power on people who have full control of *keigo*. As an example, Hendry (1993) tells about a headmistress of a kindergarten, who ran her establishment primarily through the most polite language: 'it was impeccably polite, and it kept everyone not only in their place, but constantly on their toes' (pp. 161–2).

If we apply a perspective of power, much could be said about the organic and functional ways of thinking that underlie the hierarchical principle. However, in this connection it is important to stress the importance of this principle for the chances deviance will occur: the person who eventually quits the authority and leadership of his *sempai*, will soon receive the label of *'ippiki okam'* (lonely wolf). Such a person will automatically be ostracized from the group, and will be excluded from a lot of social relations.

It is very easy, looking through Western glasses, to make rapid and simplified conclusions about the vertical principles in Japan. Without reducing this to cultural relativism it is important to underline that we must avoid equating hierarchy with authoritarianism. The power of the leader will always be limited by the demand for group consensus. A leader who tries to force his will upon the group, will lose sympathy and co-operation. The principle of 'belly communication' applies strongly to a leader. As already mentioned, the superior principle in Japan is *wa* or the harmony of the group, and it is expected from any senior that he (and it is almost always a he) perceives the atmosphere and the wishes among his subordinates. Vogel (1979) argues in this connection that decisions in Japan are much more a result of bottom up than of top down processes (p. 143), and Benedict (1967, p. 38) emphasizes that the Japanese do not learn to appreciate random authority but a common loyalty.[49] Benjamin (1997) presents the same perspective in an analysis of Japanese elementary school. What she in her first encounter with the school felt as the arbitrary imposition of power, gradually became rather an 'expression of a concern for fairness and equality of opportunity' (p. 24). The principle of hierarchy contributes to both stability and rigidity in Japanese society. It also contributes to an extremely strong social control where ranking has been described as 'the principle controlling factor of social relations in Japan' (Nakane, 1970, p. 29). In Japan of today it is obviously the women who pay the highest price for this system. Both at home and at work women are at all levels subordinate to men, and this lower position is also expressed in the language. 'Japanese is a sexist language, differentiation between male and female vocabulary, expressions, and accents. The male language is supposed to be coarse, crude and aggressive, while the female language is expected to be soft, polite, and submissive' (Sugimoto, 1997, p. 7).[50]

Patriarchy can be defined as a 'male hierarchical ordering of society' (Eisenstein, referred to in Wolf and Wallace, 1991, p. 96), or a system where 'male power controls women in family and community life' (Sugimoto, 1997, p. 150). In other words, patriarchy is the gendered dimension of hierarchy. I have already concluded that Japanese society is hierarchical. Is it 'male' as well?[51,52] Let us look first at the arguments supporting the patriarchal perspective on Japan.

An overview of Japan's economic and social statistics reveals that compared to most Western countries (but with many reservations) women in Japanese society are lagging behind. Regarding employment situation and wages, social benefits system, control of the female body (contraception/abortion), and even regarding some formal regulations, feminists in Japan can regard most of their Western sisters with jealousy (White, 1992, Sugimoto, 1997, Henshall, 1999, Kalland, 1988, *Feministisk perspektiv*, 1998, McGregor, 1996, McVeigh, 1997). I will give three illustrations concerning Japan as a patriarchal society: religious tradition, the institutional framework of the household, and the gendered Japanese language.

It has been argued that in the earlier period of Japanese history women had a high status in the society (Clifford, 1976, Henshall, 1999). Until the eighth or ninth century Japan had a matrilineal family system concerning marriage. It was the husband who had to move in with his wife's family. However, to draw the conclusion (as Clifford, 1976 does) that 'women were prominent in the early Japanese period' (p. 125), and that 'they had both a recognized and an established authority in society' (p. 126), is probably to simplify a rather complex picture. If we study the role played by religion in Japanese society one might be tempted to draw a more careful conclusion. According to the religious belief of native Shinto, women have been considered impure (connected with physiological dimensions, blood, and menstruation). On the other hand, the woman is also the one who gives life, and this has contributed to giving her a quite prominent position within Shinto mythology. Within Taoism, Buddhism, and Confucianism ('imported' from China to Japan 500 AD) women have a more unambiguous position; they are very subordinate. In *Taoism* the positive (and male!) principle of *yang* is contrasted with the negative (and female!) principle of *yin*. The male dimension is associated with life, light, purity and the holy, while the female dimension is linked to death, darkness, impurity and the profane

(Kalland, 1988, p. 104). In *Buddhism* the woman is one who tempts the man and prevents the man from reaching Nirvana (which *she* cannot attain as a woman. She will first have to be re-born as a man). According to some Buddhist sects, women were regarded as fundamentally evil and incapable of salvation (Henshall, 1999, p.11).[53] *Confucian* philosophers used to regard women as less gifted than the man. Consequently, her position was subordinate to that of men. In traditional Confucian teaching the husband was to be regarded as 'Heaven', and the woman would invoke the wrath of Heaven if she disobeyed her husband.

In short, it seems that 'these various factors of Buddhism, Confucianism, some aspects of Shinto, and militarism each played a significant part in the decline of women's status in Japan. Of these it was probably a combination of Buddhism and Confucianism that struck the most damaging blows' (Henshall, 1999, p. 12).

Women in Japan are supposed to give full priority to the family. This is not only an ideological reality, induced through the socialization process. It is also clearly signalled through the *institutional framework* of the Japanese family (*ie*). In Japan each household is enrolled in a special registration system (*koseki*) that contains all types of data concerning the household. Sugimoto (1997) regards this system as an integral part of a more widespread control system, since any 'stains' in *koseki* will have a negative effect on all the members of the household. Consequently, this system is a powerful deterrent against deviant behaviour. Women especially suffer under this system. The information contained in the *koseki* registration might easily ostracize those who do not fit into the male-dominated conventional family structure. 'Thus, the understanding of gender relations in Japan requires an in-depth knowledge of the working of the family registration system, which affects all Japanese at every turn of their lives, functioning as an often invisible, but highly effective, way of maintaining patriarchal order' (*op. cit.*, p. 142).

Japanese *language* is not only hierarchical; it is also patriarchal and consequently gendered. Of course, this is not a unique Japanese phenomenon, but there are nevertheless significant differences. In the Japanese language, women are described (and even defined) in more clearly gendered ways than will be found in the West. But also, the existence of a specific 'female language' makes Japan different from most Western countries. Women are supposed to use more careful and polite formulations than men, they have to avoid certain words (that men can use), and they have to employ a special tone of voice. From early childhood the girls are taught this polite, reserved and submissive language (Endo, 1998, p. 28).

The Japanese word for 'woman' (*onna*) has a strong and often negative sexual connotation. The term *onna* can replace words like prostitute or mistress. The expression *otokomasari* means to be superior to the man, and this term has an unambiguous meaning. A person labelled in this way is definitely not very feminine, which women are supposed to be. *Shokuba no hana* is an expression used to describe young female employees. Directly translated this means 'office flowers', and signifies the role women are expected to play in the company: as decorations that will brighten the environment. But, like a flower, the female worker is also supposed to have a short life. After a short period in full bloom, they are expected to wither away (i.e. return to the home to take care of their children).

Of course, modernization has meant gender changes in Japan. In the beginning of the 1990s some 50 per cent of Japanese women participated in the paid workforce. Legal, material and cultural changes have opened new possibilities for Japanese women. But as indicated earlier, traditional values also have a strong position in present-day Japanese society. To a much larger extent than in the West, social lives are lived within a pre-modern cultural setting. This fact is strongly expressed in Jolivet's book: *Japan: The childless society? The crisis of motherhood.* A main focus in this book is the extraordinary pressure Japanese women feel in fulfilling their roles as 'good' mothers in a modernized world. The general ideology, not least as told in the enormous amount of books about child raising, is for the woman to stay at home, to be self-sacrificing, enduring, and to put up with her situation. The other part of this ideology is the expected role of the husband. He is supposed to give all his time and energy to the company ('the good husband is healthy and absent', White, 1978, p. 151), and husbands who play an active role at home are often regarded as lazy and will lose their chances of advancement. If a man spends time with his family, this will be defined in Japan as if he is offering a service. Jolivet gives strong evidence concerning isolation, loneliness and uncertainty among Japanese housewives. With a non-existent father (37.5 per cent of fathers say they have no daily contact with their children and, on average, they see their children no more than eight minutes a day), with strong pressure on giving the children a successful education, and with the ideology of 'silent suffering' (no complaints), many mothers live in a situation of isolation and depression.

From an outside position, it might be argued that women's situation is gradually improving. But the picture is ambiguous. Increased participation in paid work was possible only as long as the economy was growing. With the burst of the economy bubble women have been the first to suffer (Olson, 1998). Increased commercialism has also had a negative effect on women. The 'sexification' of Japanese society has created new challenges and difficulties for Japanese women. Today, the birth rate is 1.4 – one of the lowest in the world. The expression 'bellies on strike' (Jolivet) might also be a sign of increasing problems of being woman in modern Japan. According to Olson (1998) 'traditional appraisals have not changed very much. Women are still regarded as second-class citizens, and their due place is in the home' (p. 24).

With regard to ambiguity in interpreting women's place in Japanese society, what is the other story that might be told? White (1987) has warned against Western ethnocentrism concerning our understanding of gender questions in Japan: 'We must refrain from imposing our values on the lives of women in other cultures. What represents limited opportunity in the views of one society – the apparent restriction of women to the sphere of the home – may actually represent a source of self-enhancing productivity in another' (p. 159). This, of course, might be interpreted as an argument in defence of complete cultural relativism. I shall not go into that debate. However, White's main argument follows this logical structure: Japanese women (and she is primarily talking about middle-class women) have an important, autonomous and highly valued position in society. She has full charge of the family domain (including cooking and cleaning), manages the husband's salary and is in charge of the family budget (the purchase of all clothing and equipment), is responsible for the upbringing of the children, and represents the family in local activities (neighbourhood meetings, etc.). But even more importantly there is (according to White) a national consensus that Japan's most important resource is its children. Consequently, job number one is that carried out by those who raise the children. It is not the work she does cooking and cleaning that defines her role. Neither is it her role as subservient or sexually available housewife that is important. It is by her mothering that a Japanese woman gains her important social status in society. From this perspective it follows that 'Japanese women perceive their work as wives and mothers as important because it is socially valued' (*op. cit.*, p. 153).

In a later work White (1992) admits that this conclusion reports only part of the picture. With regard to gender relations, women have recently become more critical about their position in Japanese society. The new role that women have been achieving has a huge potential for changing more basic Japanese structures because they are in a position to launch a powerful critique of Japan as a modern capitalist society. This will 'threaten valued aspects of family life.' Their actions 'may effectively call into question not just women's lot, but the basis of society itself' (p. 81).[54]

From this it seems that, once again, the presentation of Japanese society is one of ambiguity. To a large extent, different conclusions are an expression of different value premises. While Swedish feminists (with a Western perspective) describe the situation of Japanese women in a clearly negative way (see *Feministisk perspektiv*, 1998), Fukuyama (2000), writing from a male communitarian point of view, draws completely contradictory conclusions. His evaluation is based on the view that women with small children should stay at home (a viewpoint, he argues, with which a majority of Japanese women agrees). Fukuyama predicts increasing social problems if the government encourages more women to join the labour market.

The important question is what relevance patriarchal and hierarchal structures have for the level of crime in Japanese society. Let's try to answer that question.

B. *Discussion*

From a structural-functionalistic perspective, one might argue that hierarchy – under given circumstances – will contribute to social order in a society. Social integration might be attained in three different ways: via common values to which everybody subscribes (a Durkheimian/ Parsonian perspective); via the rational identification of complementary individual interests (a Lockeian perspective); or via the use of power or force (a Hobbesian perspective) (see Wrong, 1994, p. 34). In relation to those three ideal types, hierarchy is primarily an expression of power (even though the two other dimensions might be involved as well). 'Power' in this sense does not necessarily mean active exercise of physical power, but a relation between people based on a Weberian concept of power: the ability to have your interests realized, in spite of opposition. In this way, the relevance of hierarchy to crime prevention is closely linked to the question of social control.

If we make a distinction between internal social control (i.e. implanted through the socialization process) and external social control (i.e. all kinds of social sanctioning via rewards and punishments to attain conformity), then one could argue as set out below.

The Japanese are systematically socialized into dependence relations with other people (cf. *amae*). The individual meets society with a baggage of values that invites dependence and makes it not only legitimate, but also desirable to be in a subordinate position. From early childhood one learns to appreciate being taken care of by others. With this ballast the individual is confronted with a structure that totally encircles the whole life cycle. The need to be loved and taken care of (socialization, internal control) fits neatly with the lord–subject, master–disciple, *oyabun–kobun*, *sempai–kohai* principle (structure, external control) that is the basis of the *iemoto*. Through their socialization the Japanese will meet hierarchical structures in ways where they will 'willingly' accept (even wish for) vertical relations. In this way the need for open coercion will be minimized. Social order is created in a subtle way, first through the *amae* ideology, and next, safeguarded by hierarchical structures that totally encapsulate the individual.

In this way power is systematically embedded in social relations. The basic orientation of the social order permeates every aspect of society, far beyond the limits of the institutionalized group. Much of Japanese life is regulated via the ranking order. Of course, these structural aspects of Japanese culture must be regarded as functional in relation to the superior aim of harmony. Hierarchy and patriarchy are means of safeguarding men and women from revolting against situations that – in a perspective of justice – might otherwise call for action.

From what I have presented in this section it seems that 'communitaristic' arguments about other-directedness and solidarity as crime preventive aspects of Japanese society have to be supplemented with more critical perspectives. Social control based on vertical power relations seems to be an important characteristic of a crime preventive social structure. For hundreds of years Japanese society has been based on obedience to authorities. The organizing principles within every cell of the society are aimed at attaining conformity and harmony. This influence seeps through every section of Japanese society.[55]

Even more than men, women are supposed to submit to authority.[56] Through the socialization process girls are taught to find their subordinate place, not only in society in general, but also in relation to dual relations with men. While every Japanese citizen is ordered in social networks to a far larger extent than is found in the West, with women this is even stronger. Following my interpretation of crime (as being a strike against the community committed by 'outsiders'), people in complex dependency relations (cf. Hirschi's (1969) four 'bondings') are less likely to deviate. In Japan this applies to an even greater extent to women. If crime is regarded as an offence against an authority that transcends individual sentiments and interests (see Anleu, 1999, p. 48), then it is very improbable that women in Japan will offend. Both because of the way they are socialized and because of their structural position in society, they are internally and externally controlled in ways that make the predatory types of crime we are focusing on a very unlikely alternative. As Braithwaite (1991) notes, patriarchy is structurally humiliating. In Japan, reactions of shame and guilt will more often be the outcome of dominion than rage.

Japan is a defensive shame culture

It is time to pull together main ideas. My conclusion will be that Japanese society can be described as a *defensive culture* and that this defensiveness goes a long way to explain its low crime rates. There are three restrictions to this statement. First, Japanese are governed by a situational ethic. Their morality follows what we might call 'the principle of the inverted refrigerator: creating warmth inside by keeping a cold outside. As a rule, warm, intimate relationships are maintained only among group members, and the group closes its doors to outsiders' (Andrews *et al.*, 1996, p. 117). Events related to 'external' situations (i.e. actions that are not connected to shame, and that are directed against out-group members) are not included in this description. Japanese warfare behaviour is an illustration. Secondly, I am not saying that 'defensive' is tantamount to 'non-coercive'. Finally, I am not (on this occasion) commenting on the power structure which attends this defensive culture.

As mentioned earlier, crime is both a 'wilful' (intentional) act as well as an 'effect' of causal determinants. I would like to underline that whatever the 'structural flow' surrounding the criminal action, in order to define something as 'criminal' there must be an agency. If people 'choose' (with degrees of deliberation) to breach normative restrictions, they must neutralise social control mechanisms (and this is so even if we apply a strain perspective). Those control mechanisms can principally be of two kinds: internal and external. Through the socialization process individuals will internalize norms and values and they will learn social expectations in ways that create a 'desire' to conform to collective standards. Social norms will become an integral part of the individual's personality (superego). The external control is about different forms of social sanctioning that the individual will meet from the environment. The social context will induce conformity via overt or subtle pressures. To commit a criminal act the individual has to 'break through' internal and external control mechanisms. In other words, criminal acts can be committed a) when the shell of inhibition (superego) that according to Freud surrounded the primitive impulses of the 'id' is either weak or neutralized, and b) when the different types of (external) social controls have become devalued.

From my point of view Japan can be described as a defensive culture, both because of the way people are socialized (internal control), and because the social structure surrounding the individual (external control) to a large extent induces conformity, consensus-orientation, and consequently defensive actions. Before I sum up these two perspectives, let me briefly recall that the overarching value in Japanese society is harmony. Originally a value imposed by authoritarian leaders to create control over its citizens (which, of course, still might be true), Japanese people are indoctrinated in the belief that 'happiness is to be found in the valleys'. Harmony is attained by 'finding one's place in the shadow of a big tree'. Society in total is to attain harmony through sacrifice of individual and self-promotional values. In this way, harmony is a question of controlling individual urges, inclinations and, on occasion, rights.

Re. external control

As we have noticed, the presentation of self in everyday life in Japan is a complicated matter. Life in Japan is highly ritualized with a specific 'ethnomorality of etiquette', and with a specific 'policy of politeness' (McVeigh, 1997, p. 10). *Seken* (or the others) watches everything one does. *Seken* is a kind of imagined community with an enormous normative power concerning correct behaviour:

> As an intermediate network, *seken* makes its presence felt in the minds of many Japanese as the largest unit of social interaction which does not imply blood relations. In reference to *seken*'s censuring functions, it is often said that if one deviates from social norms, *seken* will not accept one. If one does something shameful, one will not be able to face *seken* (Sugimoto, 1997, p. 255).

Seken is a strong and omnipresent censor in the everyday life of ordinary Japanese citizens, and could be described as the common denominator for what we referred to as the 'Japanese common will'. What Dennis Wrong ('all of us are prisoners of the gaze of the other') and J. P. Sartre ('hell is other people') have observed within a Western frame of reference is even truer in Japan. It is hardly a coincidence that the Japanese word for 'the public' (*hitome*) directly translated means 'peoples' eyes'. Neither is it a coincidence that one very much used saying in Japan is 'a nail that sticks out will be hammered down'. This means that one should perhaps not only speak about 'the significant' and 'the generalized other' in Japan, but also operate within a concept of a 'monolithic other'. A Japanese person always represents one group or another rather than himself, and she/he will always be linked to other people in a vertical dependency. This is why shame plays a very important role in how people behave. One has to avoid being *seken banare* (eccentric, different), one should avoid being *medatsu* (spectacular, conspicuous), and one should not be *seken shirazu* (ignorant of etiquette). And of course, one should not do anything that might disturb the harmony of the relationship of which one is a part.

In Japan one can say that form is more important than content, or even that form replaces content. The functionality of the group (what I have called 'group utility') is more important than individual freedom. Functionality will in this connection be synonymous with harmony. Confrontation must be avoided, and 'conflicts of individual opinions must be subdued and resolved for the good of all the members of the group.' (Shelley, 1997, p. 142). The concept of *nemawashi* is especially well known in politics and business. This word means literally 'to dig around the roots of a tree prior to transplanting, thus making the uprooting and movement much easier' (*Keys to Japanese Heart and Soul*, p. 129). This term is used in a figurative sense to describe the careful inquiries one makes to avoid confrontations or conflicts with other people. As most Western businessmen have experienced this is a rather time-consuming process, but more important to the Japanese is that this safeguards harmony.

Regimentation and etiquette are means to attain the goals for the common good. Consequently, correct behaviour is measured more by form than content. Or, as McVeigh (1997) formulates it, 'morality is expressed through manners. This is because hierarchy and in/out group status are grammatically embedded in the Japanese language' (p. 53). In this way one can speak of a 'sociolinguistic choreography' in Japan which is far more detailed, and which has a far wider function than in the West. If we stick to the Goffmann (1958) terminology concerning the playing of roles, we could say that the Japanese are performing their roles with much more attention and alertness than their Western counterparts. The Japanese concept *komaru* indicates this. The word means worried or dissatisfied, but connotes feeling embarrassed, clumsy, confused or not knowing what to do. It is much easier to find oneself in such situations in Japan than in most Western countries. While in the West self respect is defined as holding on to your rights, in Japan it means that you should not create any problems for other people. Rather, the individual should play down his or her own person, abilities, and assets. Modesty is very important. This is also expressed in the term *enryo* or reserve: One should never accept gifts, or food served at a party, without showing polite hesitation. An offer to help someone has to be put forward many times before it can eventually be accepted. The extensive use of apology in Japan also represents a good illustration of the importance of *seken* and *enryo*.

As another expression of defensive aspects of Japanese culture, I have referred to different scholarly descriptions of Japan as a 'wrapping culture' (Hendry, 1993, 1999, Ben-Ari, Moeran and Valentine, 1990). Whether in language, architecture, home decoration, dress, it is all about covering oneself up. In a culture where one should not express things directly, where one should wrap things up, the body also becomes a meaningful icon. The elaborate respectful language in Japan is described as a form to hide one's true feelings. *Keigo* is, like nicely wrapped gifts, a basic expression of respect towards those one is addressing (cf. rituals of greetings, rituals of serving, the use of white gloves, etc.). In other words, the Japanese do not only wrap up physical objects, but also themselves physically and emotionally. This is in accordance with what I noted earlier: the self must be hidden. The language is carefully adjusted to this need.

One might ask, to what extent are the Japanese unique regarding characteristics like timidity, reservedness, and modesty? I would argue strongly that the consistency and omnipresence of these values makes Japan unique among industrialized countries. These defensive dimensions of Japanese society are best articulated by Singer (1973). In a chapter called 'The mists of concealment' he argues that for the Japanese the 'first and last urge is to lead a life unseen by others'. He calls Japan a 'walled island hidden by clouds' and describes Japanese literature as characterised by 'hints and intimations'. The 'law of laws' in Japan is that 'in every gesture of daily life, in the style of conversation, in the proper form of giving a present, the main concern, it seems, is how to wrap up things, ideas, feelings' (p. 45). Their daily life is always administered within a network of walls and fences that give them a safe place to hide. These walls may be linguistic, physical, normative, or ceremonial; they may be taboos, etiquette, and rituals. These all contribute to place the individual inside 'a wall of inscrutability and silence which allows him to live the life he likes best, shy reserved, self-centred' (*op. cit.*, p. 46).

This may sound inconsistent with what I have argued previously. Since Japanese people live their lives under an extreme degree of visibility and transparent control, how can I argue that everything in Japanese society is wrapped up? This only appears to be a contradiction. What the Japanese do wrap up is their individual self, their true feelings, their *honne*. Everything that might disclose a multitude of opinions and diverse attitudes will threaten the basic harmony in society. Conse-quently, that is what is hidden. Thoughts as well as actions (verbal as well as physical) have to be non-offensive. On the other hand, the outer behaviour of each individual is very visible, strictly regimented, and under the (outer) control of the *seken* and the (inner) internalized knowledge that one always is representing a wider collective. Japan is a society of watching eyes and with so many visibility mechanisms that van Wolferen (1989) has defined this phenomenon as the 'inescapable embrace'. In this way one can talk about Japanese society both as being transparent (physical behaviour) and as being wrapped and defensive (individual attitudes and actions).

Re. internal control

After a few years of freedom, the Japanese child is in a mild, but never-theless very firm way, folded into society. Singer (1973) gives this harsh description of the development from childhood to adulthood:

> As the years grow in number a network of constraints begins to be woven around these divine tyrants [i.e. the children, D.L.]. As the child grows into a youth and then into a young man, the demands of society strengthen their hold on him, slowly and with increasing severity. When the student graduates from his university he is like a tree enclosed within a hard and colourless bark. A mask has been growing on him, made out of discipline, tradition, self-restraint and diffidence (p. 31).

There is not much room for ambiguity in this presentation, and I think Singer neglects some other important aspects: *omoiyari*, or empathy is one important ingredient in the socialization process in Japan. If a Japan-ese person was to select between the heart or the brain as a guide in contact with other human beings, she/he would clearly choose the heart. It is not the spoken word from the reflective brain, but the unspoken silence from the cautious heart that is appreciated when someone needs support. Sympathy with others is rather offered in the way of quiet support than reassuring words. Shelley (1997) adds to Singer's description that

> when a Japanese encounters differences of opinion between himself and another, he will first try to put himself in the shoes of the person disagreeing with him and see how the other person would feel. He will try to empathise with that person. It is through such searching

for the feelings of others that the Japanese understand their differences and resolve them' (p. 144).

The principle of *kenson* (modesty) is another expression of defensiveness and cautiousness that supplements Singer's description. The basic principle of patience in the Confucian teaching is but one aspect of this modesty. On most occasions the individual would rather hide his difference than market his talents. Sugimoto's (1997) 'mind correctness' is a good expression of this.

Anthropologists studying exchange theory (in general) or 'gift relationships' (in particular) have a rich empirical crop to harvest in Japan. As we all know, there is a huge potential for power built into donations of presents. In Japan such obligations are very scaring, and they consequently have detailed binding norms of reciprocity. This contributes towards making the individual very sensitive toward one's fellows and strengthens the cautiousness in interacting with other people. Let us add to all this the importance of keeping face (*kao*). This is learned the hard way through early socialization. It is a rather commonplace experience to see Japanese women use ridicule of their children as a method to make them conform. In this way the fear of shame is brought into the life of every Japanese child as a tough reality. Of course, this fear will further increase tendencies that make people defensive in their everyday interaction. Finally, the world of *amae, ninjo* and *giri* is generating social relationships where people make themselves objects rather than subjects. According to Doi, (1976), to emphasize *ninjo* is the same as affirming *amae*, while emphasizing *giri* means that one binds human beings in a dependent relationship. This aspect of the socialization process also aims at bringing the child in a waiting and *re*-active position.

Not surprisingly, the basic value premise for this socialisation is the principle of harmony. How is this portrayed? First of all, it is rendered by instilling an anxious and even fearful attitude in the child. The criminological relevance of this defensiveness becomes evident if we return to the perspective launched by Gottfredsson and Hirschi (1990). According to these scholars

> people who lack self-control will tend to be impulsive, insensitive, physical (as opposed to mental), risk-taking, short-sighted, and non-verbal, and they will tend therefore to engage in criminal and analogous acts. Since these traits can be identified prior to the age of responsibility for crime, since there is considerable tendency for

these traits to come together in the same people, and since the traits tend to persist through life, it seems reasonable to consider them as comprising a stable construct useful in the explanation of crime (pp. 90–1).

From this perspective it is low self-control, which in turn reflects ineffective child-rearing, that leads some people to engage in criminal and analogous acts. Even though I think these authors are more descriptive than explanatory in their way of interpreting crime, I think their linking of sociological variables (like their four 'bonding dimensions') to a micro perspective (internal control) gives us important tools with which to understand conformity in Japanese society. Komiya (1999) confirms this perspective in his own analysis of low crime rates in Japan: 'the Japanese have succeeded in internalizing the forces restraining people from committing crime; they are cautious, patient and punctual. They are not adventuresome, risk-taking, short-sighted, self-centred, and responsive to tangible stimuli in the immediate environment' (p. 385).

I have defined crime as an outsiders' strike against society. Criminality is about 'acting out'; it is about 'letting go'; and it is about eliminating filters of control (inside and outside the individual). This being so, it should be more clear why we should have reason to (*a priori*) expect that Japan should really be a low-crime nation. These are the main points in this connection:

> *We have seen that the socialization process in Japan stresses the importance and the legitimacy of being dependent (cf.* amae *relations). Both as a child, but also as an adult, one is stimulated to take the role of an object of others' love and control. But objects do not act, and they definitely do not act aggressively. Objects are reactive, but 'they' do not actively take initiatives. Objects adapt, they do not challenge.*

> *We have seen that Japanese culture obliterates the self. Obliterated selves will be afraid of acting in general. In particular, they will be even more afraid of acting contrary to the common will.*

> *We have seen that the Confucian values encourage cautiousness, belly communication, polite hesitation, and seeking the best for the group rather than for the individual.*

> *We have seen that the Japanese always represent a wider collective. One must not bring shame to the* iemoto *of which one is a member, and the consciousness of this is deeply internalized. Even one's ancestors are included in this obligation to other people.*

In short, what we have seen is that in Japanese socialization the values instilled are quite opposite to what Gottfredson and Hirschi describe as the 'prototypical criminal'. The characteristics of Japanese culture that have been brought forth on the preceding pages show that Japanese people are systematically socialized into, and live their lives within, a very *defensive* culture.

The criminological relevance of being a defensive culture is very tellingly illustrated in the Semai culture. The Semai people live in Malaysia and are known to be a culture completely without violent crimes. In an attempt to explain the absence of violent crime in this culture, Moss (1997) presents this very interesting argument:

> The ability of the Semai to prevent violent crime appears to be significantly aided by a form of violence prevention that criminological theory has not yet addressed. The Semai, that is, appear to have universally socialized their members to react to potentially violent situations (i.e. frustrating stimuli) with a fear response that inhibits them from committing violent criminal acts (p. 177).

What Moss reports is a culture where the supreme moral values are avoidance of danger. The Semai regard the individual as helpless in a world with many types of danger. This threatening outer world makes it important to stick together and to be well aware of how dependent each individual is on her/his family and friends. In this regard the Semai people have a basic collectivistic culture and they have a fundamental other-directedness in their way of behaving. Moss also reports that the Semai people on all occasions try to avoid conflicts (or *hal*) since this will lead to destructive splits in the community. In their socialisation they are taught to be sensitive to what others might think and feel so that they can maintain a situation of harmony in society: 'From a social control perspective, the ability of the Semai to develop an extremely high level of attachment to their community may be viewed as a function of their extremely high level of sensitivity to others' (p. 186).

There are obviously a lot of similarities between the Semai culture and what I have written about Japan. The important common denominator seems to be *defensiveness*. Semai children are consciously made dependent on their mothers and this is achieved by teaching them about the fears in the outer world. Compare this to what Vogel (quoted in Creighton, 1990) writes about the socialization of children in Japan. In Japan 'it is assumed that the child will naturally want to be close to his mother and will be afraid to be alone. The mother deals with such fears not by assuring the child that there is nothing to be afraid of, but by remaining with him. The implicit attitude seems to be that the mother agrees that the outside is frightening, but that while she is there she will protect the child against all outside dangers' (p. 300). The same perspective is presented in *Japan* (1985, p. 134). The mother teaches the child that it is only the family that will give protection against a dangerous outer world. A basic uncertainty and dependence is thereby implanted in the children, and this will as a further consequence lead to a defensive and reserved way of behaving.

A final way of confirming the importance of the 'internal control' perspective is to recall what I earlier referred to about Japanese citizens living abroad. Even when disconnected from their native environment and from the cultural hegemony of Japanese society, they seem to preserve the conformal and law-abiding way of behaving. When Japanese Americans were asked to answer the question 'Why is it that Japanese Americans rarely if ever violate the law?', the respondents systematically referred to 'the moral values instilled in us by our parents', to the fact that 'our immigrant parents instilled in us children respect for authority', and to the fact that 'we were brought up, taught to be honest, respect our elders, work hard and do what's right' (from Thornton and Endo, 1992, p. 23).

In conclusion: a culture that in most respects cultivates attentive and reserved behaviour will most probably not have a high potential for 'acting out'. In Japan, no one should be hurt and no one must lose face. This invites behaviour that will be the opposite of the 'low self control' Gottfredson and Hirschi write about in their theory of crime. And this is definitely a culture that strongly contrasts with a Western culture, which could rather be characterized by words such as narcissistic and acting out.

5
Look to Japan?

Introduction

I started this book by asking two main questions:

1. *Why is it that Japan, a modern and urbanized society, appears to a large extent to have succeeded in combating (predatory) crimes during the period 1950–85?*
2. *Is there anything to be learned from the Japanese case concerning the Western crime paradox (increasing affluence and increasing crime despite increasing crime policy)?*

As I argued in Chapter 1, the 'war against crime' in Western countries has been a failure. In my view, this is because the question, 'what is the problem?' (Bacchi, 1999) has been wrongly framed. Too often politicians and social scientists have searched for 'preventive measures' as if crime could be understood as a kind of virus problem and be solved by some kind of interventive social technique. If one could only find the source of contamination it would be an easy task to abolish crime. Preventing crime and preventing contagious health problems seemed to be one and the same type of problem. In both cases it has been out of the question to define the core of the problem as a *value conflict*. Health problems and crime problems both seemed to call for some kind of social engineering programmes. Consequently, preventing crime did not represent a challenge to the main political priorities in Western countries. It did not represent a challenge to value priorities in these societies. Even though it was admitted that rapid social change could represent a possible challenge to social integration in society, this problem was not regarded as antagonistic. Even though important aspects of the value foundation in the economic system seemed contrary to values propagated for the socio-cultural system, this contradiction was not regarded as irreconcilable. With insight from criminologists and social planners it was taken for granted that an individualistic, competitive, and efficiency-oriented value system in the market place could proceed at great speed without destroying the social web in society. The crime problem was supposed to be solved by means of well-informed strategies prepared by social science experts.

An alternative way of answering the question 'what is the (crime) problem?' would be a more 'politicized' approach, in which crime is regarded as the final consequence of conflicting aims and values in society. The rhetoric of 'crime prevention' and the promise of 'giving social values first priority' (Leonardsen, 1993) might alternatively be critically analysed in the light of other important political aims and values. This way of addressing the complicated matter of understanding social problems has been illustrated by George and Wilding (1979). In discussing the failure of the welfare state to achieve its fundamental aims within health services, education, social security, and housing, they focus on the paradox of continuing inequalities in modern Britain. Why is it that inequality in the provision of health care has survived, that poverty lingers, that inequalities of opportunity within the educational system remain, and that homelessness is still prevalent? While the commonest explanations are given in terms of shortages of resources or administrative weaknesses, George and Wilding address more fundamental reasons for the failure of social policies to achieve their aims:

> If it is to flourish, any economic system both requires and generates a particular value system. Capitalism is no exception. It depends on and fosters the development of an ethic of self-help, freedom, individualism, competition and achievement – the classical liberal values.
>
> Such a value system, which is required for the successful operation of a capitalist economy, is in clear opposition to the values needed to underpin a successful public welfare system. If such a system is to flourish, the stress on the virtue of self-help must be replaced by stress on the need to help others. Individualism must be replaced by a concern for the community at large; competition by co-operation; achievement must be defined in social and communal rather than in individual terms – values which are socialist rather than liberal. The economic system and the welfare system, therefore, require and depend on quite different value systems. Conflict between economic and social purposes and between liberal and socialist values is therefore

inherent in capitalist society. Wilensky and Lebeaux describe America's response to the human problems of industrialism as 'a constant moving compromise between the values of security and humanitarianism on the one hand, and individual initiative and self reliance in the competitive order on the other'. This captures the heart of the problem (p. 118).

This focus on value conflicts captures not only the heart of the mentioned welfare problems, but also the heart of the crime problem in Western countries. The socially well-integrated, low-crime society presupposes a value foundation which runs counter to the imperative values in the economic system. In modern capitalistic societies economists have gradually reached a position where they have been able to put forward ultimate demands for a well-functioning economy. These demands have more and more been regarded as imperatives which any nation involved in the global economy must obey,[1] no matter what social consequences they produce. However, experts on the socio-cultural system have not been in a position to make 'ultimate demands' in a comparable way. As we have seen in Chapter 3, sociologists will argue that not only the economy, but also the socio-cultural system has prerequisites that have to be taken care of to avoid a breakdown. The law of 'the survival of the fittest' in the market place has serious negative implications for the socio-cultural system which, over time, will experience serious problems in absorbing unwanted reverberations. This way of answering the 'what is the problem' question accords with the perspective I have called 'the sociology of worry'. One of the logical results of the mentioned value conflict has been an increase in predatory crimes committed by marginal and expelled groups. In this perspective this type of crime has been the (more or less) necessary concomitant to a Western type of modernization.

So we turn our eyes to Japan. The interesting question is, does this country teach us another lesson? Does Japan represent a 'deviant case' where a capitalist market society has been tamed by strong socio-cultural forces? Is Japan a society where the hegemonic influence goes in the opposite direction of what we see in Western countries, i.e. from the socio-cultural to the economic system? Is Japan a society that demonstrates that the economic system might be manipulated to a much larger extent than we, in the West, appreciate, and that social solidarity can be maintained in spite of a demanding economic system? Is Japan a society where crime prevention has succeeded as a result of socio-cultural arrangements? If the answer to these questions is in the affirmative, what kind of socio-cultural 'mechanisms' are we talking about concerning Japan? Is it mainly at the ideological/normative level, or is it at the structural/ organizational level that Japan diverges from Western countries?

To address these questions it might be useful to recall the following perspectives:

Crime is a social construction (a social constructivist perspective)

Before crime can appear as a social phenomenon someone in an authoritative position will have to have labelled certain actions as criminal. Societies will vary as to what extent they use legal prohibitions/ prescriptions to regulate social behaviour. The more a society uses legal mechanisms to attain social control, the more crime (*ceteris paribus*) this society will experience. Little crime in Japan could be the simple reflex of this phenomenon. This perspective has been sufficiently elaborated in Chapter 2 and will not be repeated here.

Crime is the result of social exclusion and an accompanying loss of belonging (a structural–deterministic perspective)

People carrying out more than just coincidental criminal actions will most probably have a very loose connection to binding social networks among law-abiding citizens. As a consequence, mechanisms of social control preventing crime will be weak. Once an individual has been excluded from an established network, alternative deviant sub-cultural affiliations will contribute to maintain, support (rather than prevent), and legitimize (rather than condemn) law-breaking actions.

From a critical perspective crimes committed by excluded people could be defined as a 'conflict' or a 'contradiction' between incompatible values. It can be argued that it is difficult to safeguard basic social and existential needs for those having the experience of being squeezed from good company. People who are excluded from established society because they do not fit in with demands concerning efficiency, competition, success, etc., will develop alternative value structures, sometimes with criminal implications. Analytically speaking, crime (in this perspective) is caused by 'mechanical forces' operating on the individual from the outside. Crime is the likely result of structural conditions that make other options illusory.[2] Crime is a 'determined' re-action (rather than an act of volition) to incompatible demands on the individual.[3] This is the perspective of Bauman (1998), when he argues that it is the redundant non-consumer that is controlled by means of punishment. A redundant person is a threatening person because he/she is no longer bonded.

Crime is the result of individual choice and cultural values
(a volitional–cultural perspective)

Speaking formally and in legal terms, crime is an attack on society; it is a strike against democratically approved regulations committed by a responsible, reflecting individual. It is also a strike against a set of values that this society has consciously made and consciously agreed upon. While crime in the preceding perspective should be regarded as behaviour (i.e. non-intentional), crime in this perspective should be regarded as an act carried out by an individual aware of the deviance. No matter how extensive and arbitrary the labelling process has been, and no matter what forces of exclusion have been at work, crime is an expression of a choice based on individual and cultural values. This means that the criminal must subjectively be able to neutralize whatever moral impediments exist against the act. No matter what scruples of conscience the individual actor might have against committing crime, and no matter what conformist cultural values the individual is equipped with, this will have to be neutralized. Crime is an expression of agency directed against commonly accepted *values*. While the preceding perspective focuses on structural explanations, this perspective focuses on both an individual and a collective moral dimension (i.e. values transmitted in the socialization process as well as institutionalized cultural aspects). In this perspective one looks into acknowledged (at the individual and/or at the collective level) value parameters.[4]

With the discussion in Chapters 3 and 4 in mind, let me use this distinction between a structural and a volitional–cultural perspective on crime as the starting point for discussing how Japan and the West have during the last 50 years developed in widely different ways in both these regards. The differences concerning *structural* aspects I will link to the subtitle 'social exclusion', while the *cultural* dimension is linked to values transmitted in the socialization process and general collective norms.

Crime as the result of social exclusion

The main criminological message in this perspective is this:

It is difficult to control social groups that are marginalized, excluded or outside a tight group relationship.

From Durkheim to Hirschi it has been argued that people who are strongly bonded to legitimate social groups are unlikely to engage in deviant behaviour. Families, schools, neighbourhoods, voluntary organizations, etc. – these kinds of social networks will create close-knit relations that will protect the individual against the negative effects of social turbulence in modern society. Today, however, the life situation of (in particular) young people has been described as being 'set free' from these traditional networks. This means that they have been disembedded from important mechanisms of reciprocal obligations, especially in relation to work. More and more young people have come to live an autonomous life proximate to mainstream social relations; 'youth society' is loosely linked to 'productive society' (i.e. the society of work and reciprocal obligations). This situation has facilitated a life style characterized by inner-directed rather than other-directed behaviour. The less you are tied up in social networks the more you can focus on your own desires. Modern Western society has developed into a society with a myriad of particularistic interests, where the common good and the common interests have become more muted. According to Bauman (2000b) this has created a loss. In his book 'Missing Community' he describes 'community' as 'another word for paradise lost – but a paradise that we intensely wish we could return to; and this is why we so intensely search for the roads that can take us there' (p. 35). To a large extent, 'modern modernity' could be described as an *individualized* modernity, while the 'old' modernity (that classical sociology was writing about) was more of a *social* modernity. The loss of community in Western countries has led to a loss of social context that has left the individual in a vulnerable situation. Excluded people are loosely linked to social networks that exert a necessary social control, and they soon end in a situation of poverty.[5] In such a situation crime as an option becomes more likely. This perspective on crime is consistent with what Gilling and Barton (1997) refer to as 'the true causes of crime'.[6]

One way of characterizing excluded people could be to describe them as liberated people. Released from social bonding, obligations, expectations and demands from fellow human beings, they are free to do exactly what they want. Unfortunately, a large proportion of those liberated people, with – until now – an unprecedented freedom, do not experience themselves as empowered, as masterful people acting with a real influence and control of their own life situation. On the contrary, they very often find themselves in a situation of impotence. One can act, speak, and criticise freely, but one will nevertheless be more unable than ever to influence the agenda or the outcome of matters about which one cares. Modern (Western) society is a closed society or a society with very strong demands for certification before people are 'let in'. This hits the youth – and not a random sample of the youth! – especially hard. Consequently, modern (Western) society is a 'threshold society' where, in the last two decades, more and more people have been marginalized.

The modern period is in this way 'the great exclusion' (Jordan 1996). In the prosperous countries, the proportion of national income going to the worst-off has fallen, while numbers claiming social assistance have risen *everywhere except in Japan.* Jordan continues:

> In the 1980s, the New Right sought to dismantle barriers to 'flexibility' in exchanges between individual actors with a gung-ho optimism that this would make all but the seriously incompetent better off. In the 1990s, the debate has shifted; as millions have become poorer, unemployment has remained stubbornly high, crime rates have risen, and all kinds of other problems (homelessness, single parenthood, truancy, drug abuse, suicide) have multiplied, the focus has moved on to individual pathology. In the USA, the poor have become a target for remoralization through coercion; it is good populist politics to recommend 'orphanages' for the children of 'welfare mothers', so that the mothers can set to work for their keep (p. 3).

The serious worry linked to increasing social exclusion is echoed not only among 'radical' social scientists, but also (as we have seen) within the European Community, where social exclusion is defined as a major challenge to the member states. In other words, marginalization should not be mistaken for meaning a marginal phenomenon. Social exclusion, with accompanying problems related to social control, is today one of the most serious challenges to social integration in this part of the world.

High crime rates are the natural concomitant to this decay. Individuals excluded from the established community find their needs for belonging and safety satisfied among like-minded people. Such adaptation could be read with Merton (1968) as retreatism or as innovation. It could also be read (cf. 5.3) with Mesner and Rosenfeld (1994) as an increasingly narcissistic, hedonistic, irresponsible and un-solidary way of behaving. However, another way of interpreting this situation is to see it as the final outcome of a process I have described by the words '(individual) freedom gained, but (collective) community lost'. I think there are good arguments in support of such a conclusion, and I think the case of Japan confirms this interpretation. Let's first look at the general argument that links social exclusion and crime.

One important aspect of being marginalized or excluded is the weakening of what we could call ties of responsibility. Crime is typically an act of *ir*-responsibility. *Freedom/exclusion from responsibility* characterizes life conditions for people who are marginalized. Such a situation will easily confirm the common sense knowledge that there is often a very short distance between *exclusion from responsibility* and a *weakened sense of responsibility*. Or to put it this way; why should youth care about community values when they hardly count as an inclusive part of that community? One should not expect responsible actions from people who have imbibed little responsibility! This is the main thought behind the sentence above, underlining the difficulties of controlling excluded people.

Exclusion is experienced both from the economic (unemployment) and the socio-cultural (divorce, school drop out, etc.) system. Japan's uniqueness concerning crime might be related in part to a more inclusive employment and labour market system during the period discussed here (cf. Chapter 2). However, crime is primarily a *youth* phenomenon, which indicates that processes *before* one enters the labour market should be at the core of our analysis. Let me therefore elaborate a bit more on the loss of social control related to exclusion problems in the *socio-cultural* system.

Modern, highly differentiated societies are characterized by *segregation* (which is a type of exclusion) in at least two important regards: *roles* and *age*. To an ever-increasing extent young and adult people have been separated from each other, and to an ever-increasing extent we live our lives in specialized and time limited secondary groups. The consequence of this segregation has been limitations of the informal social control that we exercise every day in routine interaction with each other. If focus is on informal social control, role specialized interaction is less effective than interaction between 'whole persons'. Social control is more effective in primary groups than in secondary groups. This is the lesson we have been taught from sociology. The important question for us is: is Japan different from Western countries in this regard?

As underlined in Chapter 4, Japan has to a large extent preserved traditional social structures during a time of huge social change, and this has to some degree compensated for the weakening of kinship and other primary group ties that accompany the modernization process. As underlined by Nakane (1970) 'certainly industrialization produces a new type of organization the formal structure of which may be closely akin to that found in modern western societies. However, this does not necessarily accord with changes in the informal structure, in which, as in the case of Japan, the traditional structure persists in large measure' (p. 8). Social relations in Japan are compartmentalized, but to a far less extent than in most Western countries. Japan has maintained structures of primary groups that have implications for informal social control. At least until the beginning of the 1990s Japanese people interacted with each other more as 'whole persons' than is usual in Western societies.[7] Japan has been described as a society consisting of millions of small 'cells', or as a society that has maintained a pattern of small villages even within the big cities. As Singer (1973) observes, 'Japan is a nation far more populous than Great Britain or France: but the structure and the political physiognomy of the country have retained the characteristics of a small group of men, characteristics such as are likely to arise from neighbourhood, kinship, or teamwork' (p. 75). This means that social adhesives like transparency/visibility and reciprocity have survived into modern times – at least more so than most western societies can report. In this type of society, where each citizen is structurally related to a myriad of different groups, the fear of shame (for good and bad) will operate as an efficient crime moderator.

Modern societies are characterized not only by role differentiation, but also by differentiation regarding *age*. Young people have gradually been excluded from full participation in productive life. The proportion of our lifetime spent as wage labourers has been dramatically decreased in the postwar period. Not only in relation to the economic system, but also in relation to the socio-cultural system, modern societies have come to separate the population into age-specific groups. An implication of this has been the removal of adult role models from the lifeworld of new generations. As we know, we do not have an inborn capacity to become adults. It has to be learned – *in close contact with adults!* With the systematic segregation into more or less homogenous age societies – in nursery schools, in schools, in leisure time activities, etc. there is a lack of sufficient intimate, primary contact with adult role models. This has consequences for youth socialization. While we know that informal social control is more effective in age-integrated than in age-segregated groups, this pattern of social life organization will have consequences for the amount of deviant behaviour.

An important aspect of this age-segregated society is the *withdrawal of social responsibilities* from the younger generation. Once upon a time (but not very long ago!) young people were important contributors to society, with clearly defined tasks and responsibilities – both within the sphere of production and in the sphere of reproduction. Today, young people have less productive and reproductive value. In our type of high tech society we consequently prefer to place young people into different types of 'as it were'-societies, where it is the adults who are in charge and who take the full responsibility for the current activities. The younger generation is only on a short-term visit to the adult world and, in return, the adults are visiting the children's and the youths' world primarily as (responsible) organizers and (controlling) spectators. This way of organizing social life is hardly compatible with preparing young people to take responsibility and giving them a chance to learn about adult roles. People who are set free have few reciprocal obligations structurally built into their everyday lives. They have few institutional arrangements that – as a matter of course – make them morally responsible people in relation to their fellows (Christie, 1971, Bruun and Christie, 1985, Magnussen, 1983). The question is whether Japan is very different from Western societies in this regard.[8]

In fact, Japan is at least as age-segregated as the West. As I have already reported, children in Japan spend extremely little time with their fathers. In nurseries, schools, as well as in organized leisure time activities, there is probably a lower adult–child ratio in Japan than in most Western societies. Participation in productive life is postponed just as long as here. Children and adults in Japan are not participating in each other's worlds any more than they do in western societies. However, Japanese culture has been more determined to 'compensate' the negative effects of segregation. I have already referred to the way Japanese school children are *made responsible* by having to clean their own school,[9] and even teaching responsibilities can be 'delegated'. Benjamin (1997) reports with surprise how school children (even first graders!) take responsibility if their teacher is absent. It is not common in Japan for the children to get a substitute teacher if their ordinary teacher is away for a couple of days, but this does not seem to create much trouble or noise. These days the Japanese government is presenting a (controversial!) plan to force all students to perform community service. The education reform bill will require children of elementary and junior high school age to spend two weeks doing community service during the course of their education (see *Mainichi Daily News*, 14 February 2001). Even though corresponding ideas during the latter years have also been presented in Western countries they are more easily turned down since they run counter to some of our basic liberal values. Social integration by way of obligatory instructions is alien to the idea that it is by maximizing the individual self-interest we should attain the collective good. On the other hand, if we open up to the possibility that the opposite logic might be valid, namely that pursuit of the social good is what best contributes to the satisfaction of self-interest, then it is a bit more difficult to reject at least the idea behind the mentioned proposal. But more important than specific cases like this is the way children in Japan are made *socially and morally responsible* via the penetrating system of *giri* and *ninjo* (the system of reciprocal social obligations), and via the important principles of *iemoto*.

Also at a very early stage of life children get acquainted with the positive connotations of *amaeru*, or the importance of involving oneself into emotional relations of dependency.[10] As a consequence, Japanese citizens will usually be embedded in social relations where awareness of the needs of other people (within your group context!) is of paramount importance – in spite of a structural segregation. This awareness is linked to the age dimension. As we have seen, senior–junior (*sempai–kohai*) relations penetrate the entirety of Japanese society. Even though there exists a structural segregation between age groups in Japan in much the same way as in the Western world, this does not have a corresponding *mental* (or cognitive) variation. On the contrary, while age is a very important distinctional category in Japan, the young and old are tightly interlinked mentally.[11]

Sennett (1998) has pointed out that social bonds are the final result of a feeling of reciprocal dependence between people. In Western societies dependence has more and more come to be regarded as something negative, even shameful. This has definitely not contributed towards creating strong and tight relations between people. In Japan this is very different. Gibney (referred to in Dale, 1986) comments that Japanese society in a strange way has realized the 'emotional edition' of the Marxist economic slogan 'from each according to his abilities, to each according to his amae needs' (p. 147). As long as people participate and do what they are expected to do, they can presume upon the indulgence of near-related people. When the Japanese psychiatrist Doi (1976, 1985) stayed for some years in the US in the 1950s, he observed that Americans did not show the same consideration and sensitivity towards others as the Japanese did. As a matter of fact, he described the contrast between those two countries with the term 'culture shock'. In the US the main ideology was expressed in the saying 'the Lord helps those who help themselves'. In Japan one could trust that the group would supply necessary help. Quite tellingly, Doi reports that the American ideology of self-help made his days in America very lonely. In my view there is little doubt that the Japanese preoccupation with *nigen kankei* (personal relations) in its manifold versions has persevered through the process of modernization and its compartmentalizations: it has countered the disintegrating effects of rapid economic and technological change.

As pointed out in Chapter 4, these fundamental differences between the US (as the prototype of Western countries) and Japan are highly relevant criminologically. For the Japanese it is very difficult to transcend the group and act without regard to the group. Even though the younger generation is as physically segregated from elder generations in Japan as in the West, they are far less *mentally* segregated. Young people are socialized into a cultural codex where they are painfully aware of this reality: the individual is close to non-existent. Consequently, there is a permanent fear of bringing shame on the group which is your cognitive reference point. The pressure from the life-giving group fellowship provides a strong incentive to tow the line. In the West, in contrast, one looks down on individuals who are too emotionally dependent on others. If Hirschi (1969) is right in underlining the importance of 'attachment' among people to avoid crime, then it should be evident that Japanese society all through the period we are studying has been structured in ways that has been crime preventive. To the extent that a person does not care about the expectations of other people she/he is free to deviate. If there is one thing we can ascertain, it has to be that Japanese people are extremely sensitive to the opinion of others. They do not only feel ashamed when breaking social norms, they even feel ashamed when doing something on their own. In other words, even if age segregation in Japan might appear to be structurally very much the same as in the West, there are strong 'ligatures' that very much counteract the disintegrating effects of this type of segregation. There is reason to believe that this contributes to inoculate against law-breaking actions. Or to express it otherwise: Japanese people experience (i.e. their subjective feeling) far less social exclusion than do Westerners.

These final observations, underlining not only the structural but also the cultural characteristics of Japanese society, bring us further into the perspective of crime as an action within a normative context.

Crime as the result of cultural values and individual choice

The main criminological message in this perspective is:

Inner-directed individuals with little self-control who live in compliant cultures will more easily engage in criminal acts than self-controlled and other-directed individuals living in more strict cultures.

While the preceding perspective – focusing on structural aspects – is in the spirit of Durkheim, this one adds a Weberian dimension: social life should be understood not only in causal terms, but also as an expression of meaningful actions. Crime must be understood as a *chosen* alternative. However, this choice is made within a specific normative context or culture. This implies that our concept of culture has a 'double' content. As discussed in Chapter 4, culture is both 'a human-made part of the environment', influencing the individual from 'the outside', and it is 'the software of the mind', operating as a compass for navigating in a complex environment. In the first meaning of the concept, 'culture' should be regarded as what Triandis (*op. cit.*) calls 'standard operating procedures, ways of doing things that have been internalized to such an extent that people do not argue about them' (p. 16). In this sense culture is something 'taken for granted' and on which the individual rarely reflects. The value content of the socialization process could be an illustration of this paradigmatic framework in which every human being is enveloped. In the second meaning, 'culture' implies a reflective dimension where each individual is something more than a 'cultural dope' – the individual is carrying out actions that will ultimately have to be accounted for. This distinction is important for identifying Japanese uniqueness concerning crime. But first, let me present some characteristics (ideal types!) concerning content of values in Western culture towards the end of the twentieth century.

While the years after the Second World War naturally called for co-operation, moderation and a personal ethic demanding reservation and caution, quite a few scholars will argue that the twentieth century ended in hedonism and individualism. The liberal cultivation and worship of the individual turned into its travesty. What started as a process of liberation and emancipation ended in the 'culture of complaint.' While both children and adults once were taught – and practised – the blessings of delayed gratification, this was turned upside down before the end of the century. The affluent society has increasingly become the culture of instant gratification.

A typical expression of this is demonstrated in the Norwegian Government's appointment in 1998 of a committee called 'The Value Commission'. Its mandate was to create increased consciousness and reflection on values and ethical topics among citizens, to contribute to the support of positive communal values, and to foster personal responsibility. The appointment of this commission should be seen as a reflection of a general worry about increasing egoism and a general disintegration of norms. As commented in earlier chapters, the revival of the communitarian movement in Western countries is obviously a call for a new balance between individual and social needs – in favour of the latter. High crime rates are but one indicator of this feeling of increasing anomie.

No doubt, this growing social disorder in Western countries towards the end of the twentieth century can be defined as a cultural breakdown mirroring an ethical decay in society. As noted in earlier chapters, Fukuyama (1999) argues that it is the shift in values and ethical standards in the West that is at the centre of the 'Great Disruption', and it is the rise of moral individualism that has gradually undermined social order.

He explicitly supports conservative opinion against a general moral decline in the West. Similarly, scholars like Baumann (2000b), Dahrendorf (1985), von Wright (1994), Sennett (1998) and Hutton (1996) – to mention but a few – argue that altruism and the values of an inclusive society have been sacrificed on the altar of self-interest and individualism. In short, anomie is the concern of a great many sociologists today, particularly in reference to Western cultural tendencies.

This general description of narcissism and moral decay is mirrored within the social sciences. As indicated in Chapter 1, criminologists have shown a renewed interest in morality, and the notion of rational choice and the responsible criminal is once again on the agenda (cf. the title *The Reasoning Criminal* by Clarke and Cornish, 1986). Rather than looking at social and structural conditions surrounding the individual, attention has more and more been directed towards compliant cultures and sensation-seeking individuals. As a reflection of a self-centred and hedonistic culture, the criminal is doing nothing but seeking an immediate satisfaction of needs and delight (Gottfredson and Hirschi, 1990, Katz, 1988). Of course, if these satisfying actions imply cutting corners, this might represent a moral problem for the actor. But in a culture cultivating individual freedom and autonomy, and where self-control, adaptation and subordination have a dubious meaning, such considerations are weakened. According to this perspective, it is in the interaction between a compliant culture, on one side, and self-conscious individuals acting without too much thought for future consequences, on the other side, that we find the most important intake for understanding crime in modern society.

How does this description of modern western culture compare with Japan? What are the navigating parameters for the average Japanese citizen? What is the content of the cultural heritage in Japan compared to the values underpinning the socialization process in the West? What are the 'schedules of reinforcement' (Skinner, see Triandis, 1994, p. 16) that surround the individual in Japan? Or to put it another way: is Fukuyama (2000) right in arguing that 'Asian countries when they reached the same level of development as Britain or France have experienced very different levels of social dysfunction, which would indicate that it is culture rather than level of development that is responsible for the contrast' (p. 26)?

I have described Japan as a culture where the individual has been obliterated. Even though Japan these days is undergoing a period of social transformation,[12] compared to the worry about the loss of community in the West one should rather worry about 'the loss of the individual' in

Japan. If 'acting out' is a problem in Western countries, it is rather 'acting in' that best describes the parameters of acting in Japan.

If we recall my description of crime as 'conflict', it should be easy to imagine the criminological relevance of this moral codex. Both at the individual as well as at the collective level there are strong trajectories guiding the individual in the direction of conformity. People who experience unfair treatment, being squeezed or excluded, crowded, attacked (verbal or even physical), etc., should not fight back. The message of always seeking harmony (a moral imperative) together with the message of finding one's proper place means that crime as a strike against society is almost ruled out – with the exception, of course, of those who in despair of few 'outlets' for natural frustration 'hit blind'.[13]

It is the unique interconnection and unanimity between the collective normative regulations (the moral codex of society), and the values that are internalized in each individual through the socialization process, that I would like to emphasize. The guiding principles with which everyone is programmed, and that most social institutions confirm and reflect back, is to adapt, to submit, to do one's duty, and to avoid confrontations. These values both exist as a kind of ideological hegemony in society at large ('culture'), and as well are transmitted through the socialization process.

Sticking to my analytical distinction between structural and value-based explanations of crime, we should now (with support of Singer, 1973), be able to sum up the two previous sections in the following conclusion:

Little crime because of social or organizational structures   In spite of being a modernized and urbanized society, Japan is still a society of primary groups. What Singer (1973) calls 'the law of small numbers' is a telling expression of this. 'The smooth flux of ordinary Japanese life has in the past been secured not because of, but in spite of, the vast machinery built upon Western models: its true strength does not reside in the rationalized perfection of its mammoth organizations, but in the dense tissue of small society relationships supporting those vast superstructures and infusing their living substance into the framework of the Leviathan' (p. 82). This social structure of a small-scale society within a mastodon society, making people visible and reciprocally dependent, should (according to mainstream sociology) operate in a crime preventive way in itself.

Little crime because of the dominating values at the collective level ('ideological hegemony')   In spite of being a modernized and urbanized society, Japan is still a society where principles of self-sacrifice are cultivated throughout society, no matter the class, region or sex. If crime is about *breaking* and *challenging* broadly accepted social values, life in Japanese society is about *conformity* and *adaptation* to such broadly accepted values. The pressure from the 'Japanese spirit' is severe and ubiquitous. Members of Japanese society become members of a 'mythical body', and to this body the individual 'sacrifices his life and thought in order to receive his true self' (Singer, 1973, p. 35). While in the West modern society can be described as a 'plurality of life-worlds' with continuously changing values (Berger, Berger and Kellner, 1973, p. 62), individuals in Japan live in life-worlds that are more or less unified and deeply-rooted in history. In this society there are few sanctuaries for outsiders.

Little crime because of values transmitted through the socialization process
In spite of being a modernized and urbanized society, Japan is still a society founded on 'traditional' values, and different agents of socialization convey very much the same message. Even though Japanese children enjoy an enormous freedom (more than in the West), gradually 'a network of constraints begins to be woven around these divine tyrants', and before adult age 'a mask has been growing on him, made out of discipline, tradition, self-restraint and diffidence' (Singer, 1973, p. 31). 'Outer' normative regulation is not sufficient to make people comply unless those ethical principles are internalized in the personality of each individual (as 'conscience' or 'reason'). In Japan the *social* codex of harmony is mirrored in a *personal* codex of reserve and defensiveness. If crime is an action of 'acting out', then Japanese culture is definitely not a crime prone culture.

From my point of view, it is the unique combination of these three perspectives that gives us the main clue to understand why Japan – until the 1990s – has been able to contradict traditional textbooks in criminology. I have summed up this discussion in Table 5.1, and added to the Japanese and the Western model my idea of the Utopian society with the aim of little crime.[14]

One final question remains: does the Japanese model represent an acceptable way of creating social integration in a capitalist society? If yes, is it possible to 'import' some Japanese principles or patterns of thinking to Western societies? Let me finally approach these questions.

Is there a lesson to be learnt from Japan?

Japan teaches us a lesson that is fundamentally different from (what at least might be interpreted as) the deterministic message presented by

Table 5.1 The Western, the Japanese and the Utopian society in a criminological perspective

		The West (Anomia)	Japan (Hypernomia)	Utopia (Synnomia)
Structural perspective	Economic system	Marginalisation → freedom from responsibility → weakened sense of responsibility	A more inclusive labour market	An inclusive labour market
	Sociocultural system	Segregation into a) roles → b) age categories weakened informal social control, and fewer adult role models	Segregation, but a) more *whole persons* b) counteracted by *giri/on*	Strengthen primary groups Young people participate *together* with adults
Value perspective		Freedom from collective obligations Individualism Independence Narcissism Inner-directedness Sensation seeking	Collective obligations are superior Collectivism Dependence (*amae*) Group narcissism Other-directedness Submissions	Autonomous individuals *and* self-reflection as *social* participating human beings

George and Wilding above (value conflicts render impossible the realisation of basic welfare measures). I agree with these authors concerning the indicated value conflict between economic and socio-cultural values. However, even if a capitalist market society is based on a value system that in a fundamental way challenges social integration, this influence should – as Japan illustrates – not be described in 'absolutist' or deterministic terms. The almost nomothetic perspective implied in George's and Wilding's analysis should be modified in confrontation with Japanese culture and society. In the postwar period Japan has in a unique way combined one set of values in the economic system (modernisation and rapid change) with another set of values in the socio-cultural system (traditionalism, stability and social interdependence). Furthermore, I think that those authors are trapped in an ethnocentric fallacy when they delimit the alternative to liberal ideology to be 'socialist' values. As I documented in Chapter 1, authors like Dore, Fukuyama, Vogel, Berger,

Hofstede and Bond, all underline that *Confucian* values, stressing common purposes and social solidarity, have to a large extent (and up until the 1990s) succeeded in getting the upper hand in Japanese society. These are the values that, in combination with 'primary group' principles of social organization, seem to have hampered raw capitalism in Japan.[15] Even though economic interests have a strong position in Japan, these interests have had to adapt to other, socio-cultural, considerations. To a much larger extent than we see in the West, communitarian values have made an impact on the way the economy is run. This has taken place without any 'socialist' experiment (cf. Berger, 1987, pp. 156–7: 'The East Asian evidence falsifies the proposition that successful development cannot occur in a condition of dependency upon the international capitalist system'. 'East Asia, to put it bluntly, is bad news for Marxists'). As long as we end our analysis in 1985, it can be argued that socio-cultural values have affected the economic system in Japan in a much more penetrating way than in the West (with important reservations, for example regarding welfare security). Even though Japanese capitalism could be described as extremely competitive, putting insatiable demands on its labourers,[16] this has taken place within a frame where the (hierarchically organized!) collective best has been given priority. I rush to remind of my critical remarks regarding power structures, paternalism, and democratic deficit. As Young (1999, p. 194) emphasizes, we must not forget that virtues like deference for authority, stoic acceptance of unfairness, sacrifice to the will of others, unthinking obedience both in wider society and in the family, often come together with values such as trust, honour and respect. However, as long as we delimit our focus to a kind of functionalist, 'descriptive', sociological analysis, the conclusion seems to be that Japan has developed a capitalist market society that includes a broader set of values and more intimate social structures than we find in our ideal type of a Western society. To the extent that a feeling of *belonging* and a certain amount of *predictability* represent essential values for integrating people in a social web, then the Confucian ideology, embedded in a tight network of primary groups, has been a very important contribution to realize those values. In effect, this unique blending of social and normative structures seems to have made Japan a low-crime nation (remember my definition of crime!). In essential ways Japanese society and Japanese culture is qualitatively different from what I have called Western societies. Consequently, so far we can conclude that, yes, there is a lesson to be learnt from Japan, and, yes, 'culture' seems to be an important dimension with a 'relative autonomy' that has been underestimated in criminology.[17]

The conclusion that there is a lesson to be learnt from Japan is not the same as saying that this gives the West direction to follow Japan or that it should have *policy* implications for Western countries. To say that Japan is holding up a mirror for other cultures is something different from saying that what we see should have consequences for how we design *our* societies. Let's pursue that topic a little bit further (and in this context I disregard the complex question 'if cultures can learn and deliberately change'). In this final discussion the structural and the value-oriented level will gradually merge.

Western style modernization has been accompanied by structural changes that have left the individual in a vulnerable situation. For those with sufficient personal and network-based resources this development can be described in positive, even in emancipating terms. The increased freedom to choose should in many ways be recognized as a step forward in the civilizing process. However, the weakening of primary group structures has impaired social bonding and predictability. With few and badly developed 'compensatory forces' to this development an increasing number of people have found themselves in a situation of exclusion. Admission to an important structural arrangement like the labour market has been hampered for more and more people while, simultaneously, stable membership in social institutions within the socio-cultural system has crumbled. This is the unpleasant side of Western style modernization.

Japan has undergone much of the same structural change as the West. An extensive geographical mobility has undermined traditional primary group structures – as in the West (even though the extended family group has lingered on for a longer period, and even though long-lasting working relationships are much more common in Japan). However, what I have called 'compensatory forces' are built into Japanese society. Even if turbulence and change have negatively affected families and neighbourhoods, Japanese society has retained 'functional equivalents' to shrinking social institutions. Organizational structures like *iemoto, han, batsu, sempai/kohai, oyabun/kobun*, represent a structural framework that gives most people a feeling of belonging. This belonging is not primarily something one makes oneself deserving of, but rather something that is positionally conditioned. This does not mean that each individual has a carte blanche membership in a diversity of primary groups in Japan (cf. the risk of experiencing ostracism from the group if one fails to accept the rules and the social etiquette). However, compared to Western societies, each Japanese citizen has a relatively elaborate social network that protects against potentially anomic processes.[18]

Is there something to be learnt for Western societies in this 'structural' regard (in the meaning of organizing principles)? It is hardly possible, and surely not desirable, to adapt the vertical principle as a baseline for organizing social life. As Nakane (1970) stresses, the Japanese have a tendency to create a difference even among individuals sharing identical qualifications. Vertical orientation is overwhelmingly ascendant in this society and this, of course, is very much in contradiction to Western egalitarian and libertarian principles. Creating a sense of belonging by way of implanting new types of senior–junior relationships among people is not compatible with other widely held values in our culture. However, if we return to our Western societies, I think it is very important to be aware of how seemingly autonomous forces in the economic system these days undermine basic prerequisites for 'institutions of belonging'. When Habermas (1973) talks about how the economic system 'invades' the socio-cultural system in the West, it is essential to see how this applies not only to mentality structures (an 'economic man'-way of thinking), but also to institutional structures. It is not only our values and norms that are affected by the economic rationality but also our institutional arrangements. As noted in Chapter 1, the Nordic welfare state probably functioned for a long time as a powerful preventive force in the wake of a turbulent modernization process. It is reasonable to argue that the comparatively little crime in the Nordic countries is partly due to a collectively financed support of basic welfare institutions, and the universalistic ideology on which this model is based. The more a 'pure' market logic is allowed to force its way through, the stronger the forces of exclusion, and the more one can expect an increase in crime. The less we are willing to support (not only economically) and protect important social institutions like the family, the neighbourhood, voluntary organizations, etc., the less we should expect of social harmony. And the less we should expect to be able to prevent crime through different types of relief measures. During a period of turbulence and rapid social change the Keynesian welfare state model was (until the 1970s) to a large extent a guarantee for safeguarding social network functions.[19]

Japanese society is very far from deserving the label of being a welfare state. Nevertheless, crime prevention has been taken very seriously at the organizational level. From top to bottom, from Government to neighbourhoods, the Japanese have elaborated a network of institutional arrangements that are geared towards preventing crime. A lot could be said about this as a system of social control. Both its historical origin and its current operation invite criticism. Nevertheless, we must also avoid pouring the baby out with the bath water. If Western societies really want to attack the crime problem this will mean that they have to be willing to think twice about the true meaning of individual liberation and freedom. Living in a society implies (functionally) the necessity of integrating particulars into an overarching unity, and (volitionally) the willingness of each 'particular' to give up (to some extent) short-sighted, egoistic interests in favour of the common good. Saying things like this typically echoes the classical debate on individual freedom and collective suppression. As is well known, authoritarian regimes and authoritarian leaders (like, for example, Mussolini) have on many occasions misused the argument of 'the collective best' to suppress people illegitimately. Also, we should remember the warnings explicitly expressed by Erich Fromm. In his famous book *Escape from freedom* (1941) he pointed out that a man who is unable to stand the challenges of freedom will most probably seek refuge under an authoritarian system. Therefore, the 'good society' is most of all dependent on autonomous individuals who know their rights, who have the courage to fight for these rights, and who possess the knowledge and the wisdom that make them able to identify hegemonic and suppressive forces in society.

However, I think the danger for Western societies today is at the other extreme. The liberalistic ideology that more and more percolates into the economic and also into the socio-cultural system is clearly on a collision course with basic community structures. Societies that disregard the importance of relatively stable face-to-face groups as the basic foundation for all types of social life – economic life included – have a poor chance of surviving. Societies that disregard the close interrelationship between organizing principles and prerequisites for establishing a 'moral society' based on trust, have paved the way for crumbling processes. Taking individual freedom from the group as a premise for how to build our society, it is important to be aware of the danger that this freedom is challenged by a kind of 'survival of the fittest' ideology. Many authors have pointed out the paradox that unprecedented freedom in Western societies seems to have come together with unprecedented impotence (cf. what I have called the 'threshold society'). The 'liberal market society' boasts of giving the consumer 'freedom to choose', but this freedom is more formal than real (Klein, 2000). The liberal political democracy boasts of empowering people from below, but this is hardly what people experience on election day. The atomized individual, with enfeebled obligations to the group is not as free as she/he might think.

Even if such a message might sound alien today, my sociology tells me that the submission of man to society can also be regarded as an important condition for her/his liberation. This is the sociology of solidarity, so eloquently expressed by Durkheim:

> The individual submits to society, and this submission is the condition of his liberation. For man freedom consists in deliverance from blind, unthinking physical forces; he achieves this by opposing against them the great and intelligent force of society, under whose protection he shelters. By putting himself under the wing of society, he makes himself also, to a certain extent, dependent on it. But this is a liberating dependence; there is no contradiction in this.[20]

From a criminological point of view, I think this Edmund Burke-inspired argument[21] should be considered seriously. In these times of liberalism and an almost unfettered cultivation of individual freedom we need to be reminded of a perspective saying that social obligations, and attention paid to collective interests, also might be regarded as an emancipatory force for the individual. And we need to be reminded of a perspective saying that 'a chain is no stronger than its weakest link'. It is the quality of life among those at the bottom of society that decides the quality of the whole society. The gradual withdrawal of public responsibility from important welfare functions might of course be described in terms of liberation from the omnipresent Leviathan, but it is hardly a good strategy for safeguarding collective networks that include and protect those in need. As Baumann (2000b) points out, it is not true to say that the public sphere is threatening the private. It is the other way around. 'Society is now primarily the condition which individuals strongly need, yet badly miss – in their vain and frustrating struggle to reforge their *de jure* status into the genuine autonomy and capacity for self-assertion' (pp. 40–1). Structures of stable primary groups and occasions for collective identity-building are 'articles' in short supply in Western society. To have a feeling of belonging is first of all about being an integral part of a group that is based on principles of solidarity and that possesses a collective identity. However, the soil establishing this type of social networks has been severely reduced in Western modernity. With the strong hegemony that the economic profession possess today, it is important to recall the stock of knowledge that sociology has acquired through the years. As Skirbekk (1999) emphasizes, 'sociologists can say a lot about what kind of groups will be important for creating moral societies. This will be the lasting and surveyable groups where the members will have the options of many-sided identification as well as getting the confidence that might follow from reciprocal control, in one word: *primary groups'* (p. 219). Without these types of structures it will be impossible to cultivate the set of values that I presented in Chapter 1 as the basic prerequisites for the socio-cultural system. After many years with a one-dimensional economic hegemony, the time should be ripe for 'the sociology of primary groups and collective celebrations' as a corrective force of information to governing elites – at least if we want to take the broadly accepted idea of 'preventive politics' seriously. There is no short way to attain a society in social balance. There are no preventive measures that will have any lasting effect on social integration unless the basic premises are present. This is the message that – after years and years of preventive programmes all over the Western world – should be declared crisp and clean. Or, in the words of Currie (1989):

> Criminologists and criminal justice practitioners can play a very important part in that struggle by pointing out continually the many links between the problems that confront us daily and the larger forces that shape them; between economic violence and interpersonal violence; between the erosion of communal life and livelihood and the deterioration and distortion of individual personality. We cannot concern ourselves only with the 'downstream' consequences of the systematic abuse and neglect of the social environment; we must be bold enough to look unflinchingly at the source (p. 23)

Does this mean that Japan *does* teach Western societies a lesson that should have some consequences? Yes, I think there is good reason to argue that we have forgotten some important *collective prerequisites* for individual welfare, both at the structural and at the cultural/normative level. Baumann (2000b:20) carries Durkheim's argument above one step further, arguing that there is no way for the individual to pursue a genuine liberation but to submit to society and to follow the given norms: 'Freedom cannot be gained against society,' he argues. Group controlled routines and obligations can spare us from agonies and can create predictability in life that might *increase* rather than decrease freedom. Baumann (*op. cit.*) gives a presentation of the positive aspects of predictability that I would like to refer to in full, since this description also has direct reference to Japanese society:

> thanks to the monotony and regularity of recommended, enforceable and in-drilled modes of conduct, humans know how to proceed most

of the time and seldom find themselves in a situation with no road markings attached, such situations in which decisions are to be taken on their own responsibility and without the reassuring knowledge of their consequences, making each move pregnant with risks difficult to calculate. The absence, or mere unclarity of norms – anomie – is the worst lot which may occur to people as they struggle to cope with their like-tasks. Norms enable as they disable; anomie augurs disablement pure and simple. Once the troops of normative regulation vacate the battlefields of life, only doubt and fear are left (pp. 20–1).

In this regard it is important to underline the unique interplay in Japan between principles of social organization and the substantial cultural content, between social structure and normative codex. From a perspective of social integration the transformation from primary to secondary groups, and from primary to secondary control in the West is fundamental to understand *structural/organizational* changes with relevance to crime development. As elaborated in Chapter 3, essential structural conditions for informal social control are easily undermined as modernization and urbanization escalate. This does not mean that modern cities should be described *in toto* as alienated and anomic 'settlements' with no social webs and no social solidarity. As Giddens (1990) underlines, 'the idea of the decline of community has been effectively criticised in the light of empirical research into city neighbourhoods . . . Thus in criticising Louis Wirth's interpretation of the anonymous nature of urban life, Claude Fischer has sought to show that modern cities provide the means of generating new forms of communal life, largely unavailable in pre-modern settings' (p. 116). However, this kind of empirical research does not falsify the broad documentation of inner city decay, of ghettos of poverty, unemployment and social exclusion, etc. Rather, they remind us to avoid biased one-sidedness where all nuances disappear. In spite of flourishing social life and documentation of lively community life in most Western cities, this does not exclude a perspective arguing that in the West these changes have not been completely compensated by alternative primary group structures. Neither have these changes been compensated by powerful 're-moralizing' interventions. Community values like solidarity and other-directedness have to some extent vanished together with stable face-to-face relationships. Regarding both social structures and codex for behaving, this has been different in Japan. Cultural values and structures of organization constitute a kind of organic whole that bind the community together (but remember: not without strong elements of power relations).

While the West might suffer from anomie, Japan might perhaps best be described by the term 'Hypernomia' (Dahrendorf, 1985). There is a lot to bear out an assertion that the Japanese are 'over-socialized', and that this over-socialization is a functional requirement for the harmony of the group. Having pointed out this I would say that Japanese citizens pay too high a price for safeguarding social harmony. While there is good reason to believe that the 'abolishment of the individual' is one (among many) cause(s) of low crime rates in Japan, I nevertheless find it difficult to recommend Japan as a model to copy in this regard. Even though a lot could be said about this, let me limit my argument to the question of *democracy*.

A society based on discipline, dependence and blind loyalty to the group (be it the family, the company or the state) will easily suffer with regard to basic values in an open discursive society. Deliberation is one such basic value, and Japanese culture is too repressive and too consensus- and harmony-seeking to safeguard this fundamental principle. Sugimoto (1997) describes the Japanese society with the label 'friendly authoritarianism', while Foote (1992) talks about 'benevolent paternalism'. Japan might well be described as an integrated society, but in that case we may also talk about a forced integration with strong elements of what Marcuse (1965) called 'repressive tolerance'. Japan is often mentioned as a typical consensus culture. I think such a description could be defended only if one adds that the established consensus is based on hegemonic relations of power, strongly influenced by Confucian hierarchical and patriarchal ideology. Henshall (1999) argues convincingly that the negative Japanese attitude to the Western-style independent individual 'has significant bearing on Japanese perceptions of democracy and individual rights' (p. 148). Dale (1986) is even stronger in his critique of Japan in this regard, saying that 'every inch of self-assertion by the individual is contested as threatening the hegemonic reach and authority for the corporate, national ideal' (p. 22). No doubt, Japan is founded on an extreme model of harmony, and this harmony is imposed from above rather than generated from below. To use a phrase from Linton, the cultural pattern that moulds the attitudes and feelings of the individual '... comes to the individual like suits of ready-made clothes' (quoted in Guneriussen, 1988). The actions that the individual undertakes should be read as the realisation of normative claims on action that are carried through *only* because they have been internalized. This situation can easily represent a danger for democracy.[22]

In my imagined Utopia I would – at the individual level – create a society that stimulates autonomous and masterful individuals. As we have seen, Japanese culture is very much about the negation of these ideals. Japanese children are said to have little self-confidence and to be rather fearful (see Jolivet, 1993, p. 43). I think Braithwaite (1989) is too superficial on this problem when he 'rejects any pejorative connotation of dependence as threatening individual autonomy' (p. 100). Japanese society is based on a social conservative/Confucian ideology, and important aspects of this ideology are not very conducive to basic civil and political rights and liberties (cf. Belsey, 1986). Braithwaite omits some really controversial aspects of Japanese society, primarily those related to political and individual self-determination. He is soft on the obvious dangers of omnipresent groupism. Sanger (referred to in Triandis, 1995) reports a telling case about a 13-year-old boy who died because of bullying (called *ijime*). *Ijime* occurs when people do not fit in. This 13-year-old boy's error was speaking standard Japanese instead of the local dialect. According to the regional newspaper the father of the boy had studied in Tokyo, and this contributed towards setting the boy apart. Even for Japanese people living abroad this group pressure can be extreme. In New Zealand a Japanese student was roughly attacked by three other Japanese youths. The reason was that 'the victim was known as a rebel and that the three attackers had taken it upon themselves to make him recognize that his behaviour was unacceptable if he was to fit back into Japanese society' (*The Dominion*, 30 April 1999). Futaba (1984) shows that costs related to Japanese harmony include not only the political sphere but also 'the powers of the police, the rights of suspects in criminal cases, the treatment of members of radical dissenting groups, and the administration of punishment, including capital punishment' (p. 1). When all attention is paid to harmony and social integration in a society, one must be extremely aware of hegemonic, structural and ideological power relations. Collectivism can emancipate, but it can definitely also suppress. Criminologists in particular should be aware of such challenges and the reason has to be made explicit: *we have to remember that low crime is not all there is to the Good Society*! Little crime *might* be an expression of harmony and social integration in a society, but it *could* as well indicate something negative about that society. This would be a far too simple conclusion in the case of Japan, but since much of my argument on the preceding pages has been based on a kind of functionalist sociological perspective I would like to add a few reminders:

> The much-celebrated Japanese friendliness might be described as a Janus-faced friendliness. If you are an insider you will definitely

experience the best of Japanese care and warmth. Outsiders, on the other hand, will describe the Japanese in a much less flattering way.

Caplan and Dubro (1986) remind us that the Japanese can be just as devious and corruptible as Western people. They do not co-operate very much with the National Tax Agency, and bribery is rampant (McCormack, 1996, McGregor, 1996). Hidaka (1984), supplements this critical perspective by saying that 'economism has destroyed the fabric of relations between human beings. People rarely use yardstick other than profit and loss' (p. 73).

According to Takahashi (1991, p. 2) more than 30,000 white collar workers die every year due to exhaustion from long working hours (called *'karoshi'*).

The description of Japan as a low-crime society needs fundamental corrections if we include white-collar crime, organized crime, and crime in the private sphere in our discussion.

The loss of individual freedom should alert us to the possibility that there may be a relationship between low crime and intolerance. Hopefully, the preceding pages have given the reader an opportunity to draw conclusions her/himself. In this book the focus of interest has been on *social integrative forces* in Japanese society, and with that as the starting point a Durkeheimian and structural-functionalist perspective has dominated. However, it is not always true that you can tell the quality of the tree (Japanese society) by its fruit (little crime).

Where does this take us? Which aspects of Japanese culture should be of inspiration to Western culture? Since I have argued that crime prevention in the West is not primarily about social engineering programmes but rather about principles of social life, what are these principles that should be of interest for the crime-ridden West?

One basic question is whether we can agree upon the important statement from Durkheim (1952) that, 'the more weakened the groups to which the individual belongs, the less he depends on them, the more he consequently depends only on himself and recognises no other rules of conduct than what are founded on his private interests' (p. 209). I think most criminologists would agree that a low-crime society has to create social conditions that make people important to each other. In the same degree as social control is important to make people obey common rules, it is important that individuals are linked to a web of social networks. In this connection I agree with the communitarian movement in the West: we will have to re-invent those meso level institutions that create belonging and responsibility (i.e. neighbourhood and voluntary organizations). It is at the level between the individual and the wider collectivity that the fight against disintegration has to be led – a perspective that very much echoes Durkheim's plea made more than one hundred years ago. However, today that would be a much more radical demand than Western societies might be able to cope with. What I mean by this is that before we discuss 'the *sociology* of integration' we have to discuss 'the *economy* of integration'. From my point of view, this demand would mean creating both a more (economic) egalitarian and a more participating culture than we have today. It would also mean creating a society where altruistic values are revitalized through non-economic institutions (Chamlin and Cochran, 1997, Messner and Rosenfeld, 1994). As discussed above, crime control is primarily about bringing people into responsible positions in society. This is not easy in a modern high-tech society. But as long as this topic only is discussed as a 'technical' (cf. social engineering) question, this will be like ordering more of the same ineffective medicine. Crime has first and foremost to be discussed as a political question as to what we offer those of no use to an ever more demanding society (Christie, 2000, Taylor, 1990, 1998, Hagan, 1994). We will not be able to fight crime unless we are able to integrate youth 'materially' into society. Today the young are – and they *know* it! – of no use until they have passed 25 years of age. This is the case in the West as well as in Japan. However, as we have seen, Japan has socially integrative mechanisms that compensate for this. They also have a way of socializing people (which I have criticized) that promotes a 'crime preventive' way of being. The reason why I argue that preventing crime implies a 'radical' policy in the West is simply that participation of youth in today's high tech society demands organizational, legal and economic changes.

But then, youth participation in society is not only a question of rights, but also about responsibilities in relation to a wider collectivity. And in this regard Japan might be an interesting model for the West. This demands a discussion about how to lead our culture from a unilateral to a reciprocal perspective. Marshall (1950) presents the development of modern society as a gradual expansion of individual rights, from civil rights, via political to social rights. This, of course, has been important as well as proper. But at the same time I recognize Etzioni's (1994) description of a major aspect of contemporary American civic culture: 'a strong sense of entitlement – that is, a demand that the community provide more services and strongly uphold rights – coupled with a rather weak sense of obligation to the local and national community' (p. 3). This observation is exactly what I mean by missing reciprocity. Modern society puts few moral restrictions on the younger generation where obligations in relation to *collective interests* are in focus. In Western societies a traditional strategy to improve the situation for young people has been to demand more and better leisure activities. That might possibly be an acceptable idea. But a more important strategy would be to give society back to the young! If irresponsibility from young people is a main problem in the West, then there is no other way but to make them responsible.[23] But this has to be done not in a fictitious but a real way. Instead of discussing what kind of activities we could supply young people, we should ask what kind of jobs should be done – by the young. If young people don't get both the right and the responsibility to participate in our society we will (as Baumann (1998) has pointed out) continue to experience that the superfluous will have to be regulated by way of punishment.

In Japan, it is – at least to a larger extent than in the West – a matter of course that current tasks are integrated into general activities – not taken care of by a caretaker. To me, it is a huge paradox that we do not manage to bring young people into binding work relations in our community. There are plenty of jobs to be done, but a shortage of organizing models that meet this challenge. In my first point above, my message was to create a society where we do not give people good *material* reasons to break with the fellowship of other people. My second message is to create a society where we do not give people good 'social' reasons to break with this fellowship. We are then talking about a society where taking care of others' interests becomes more important than taking care of one's own interests. We are talking about a society where the inverted market mechanism will have as important a role as the ordinary one. We are talking about a society where people do not only have individual identities but group identities as well (and opportunities to have them continually confirmed!). We are talking about a society where the essence of such collective identities is systematically embedded into society. We are talking about a society with a group-founded morality. And not least, we are talking about a society where honour means a lot, and where it is shameful to break with the community.

In such a society the ties between people would be so tightly knit that each single individual would be 'morally relevant' to each other. But it has to be underlined that shame would not be a moralizing activity exercised as a compensation for losing fellowship. It would rather be a latent function of exactly such a fellowship. If anyone would argue that this means to dispose of the individual in favour of the group, I would choose an answer in the spirit of Rousseau: When everybody gives her/himself to everybody else, she/he gives her/himself to no one in particular. It is exactly through the participation in a collective group that each can find her/his moral identity. And it is primarily through a multitude of dependence relations that independence can be achieved. Or, in the words of Guneriussen (1999), 'even to become an autonomous individual depends on non-individual preconditions: well functioning communities and social institutions' (p. 37). I guess the society we are talking about in this connection is what Adler (1983) calls 'Synnomia', a concept closely related to Durkheimian 'social solidarity.'

The objections are obvious: a shame culture of this type does not pay attention to crime as *conflict*. This collectivistic way of thinking will easily become a dangerous weapon in the hands of 'the establishment' (as it has been in Japan). Furthermore, one could argue that the 'shame-inspired' perspective presented above might trigger a 'blaming the victim' attitude. An established drug related crime culture (which represents a significant part of all crime in the West) could fall outside the reach of a shame culture. In addition, it might be difficult to realize, and it might even be precarious to realize these ideas in a globalized and 'creolized' society. There would be a danger that repressive social control might be ignited and that it might kill precious diversity.

I admit that there is a danger of increased intolerance and of new excluding mechanisms in such a society. However, today I am more afraid of the repressive formal control described as the 'gulagisation' of the West (Christie, 2000) than of the moralizing and informal control that works through honour- or shame-mechanisms. I support Dahrendorf (1985) when he says that, 'once the Hobbesian problem of order arises, the solution tends to be Hobbesian as well' (p. 6). Today it is the liberals who must carry the burden of proof: to show that sociology is wrong when it teaches 'without brother/sisterhood, no society; without society, no freedom!' No doubt, we will return to the question of how a shame culture (or, as I would prefer to call it, an honour culture) could be created without being exclusionary. In this regard we might learn something from Japan. It is hardly a coincidence that the wolf in the adventure of 'Little Red Riding Hood' in Western culture has to pay with his life, while in the Japanese version the wolf has to apologize, and then is forgiven. But that is another adventure!

Notes

Preface

1 de Mente (1992, p. 17), Davies and Jansz (1990, p. 267), Shelley (1997, p. 100).
2 My experience of Japanese people being very friendly towards strangers is contradictory to what others have observed. The Japanese friendliness is first and foremost related to their inner circle, and it could be argued that it is more form than genuine content. Also, one should of course not jump to any conclusions after just a few days' experience. One of the guidebooks for Japanese visitors points out that 'it is these people who stay a short time, go home, and spread myths about Japan being a mystical Shangri-La, full of happy, happy people...'. I will return to this topic later.

1. The Western welfare paradox. Or: why is Japan an interesting case?

1 I use the concept 'the West/Western countries' as an ideal type (i.e. something that does not exist in reality, but which is constructed to purify some characteristics that help us simplify a complex reality). Of course, these countries do not in many ways represent a monolithic unity. What Japan shows us is that there is much more space for political autonomy within a capitalistic economy than we used to think within a Western context. As Berger (1987) argues (note: before 1990!), 'the East Asian evidence falsifies the idea that a high degree of state intervention in the economy is incompatible with successful capitalist development' (p. 158). The distinction between three types of welfare states (the liberal, residual one, the conservative, corporative one, and the social democratic, distributive one, Titmuss, 1974, Esping-Andersen, 1990) is precisely an expression of this fact. The Nordic, social democratic model should, until the 1970s, clearly be described as a strongly interventionist state that, like Japan, in many ways defined political and social integrative preconditions for economic development. Before the liberalisation of international free market trade gained momentum in the 1970s, one could really say that these countries followed (in a broad sense) a preventive and social integrative policy. In this regard, the Nordic countries represented, like Japan, an interesting case for studying how solidaristic values could 'compete' in a capitalist market economy. However, during the last 30 years it has become more and more meaningful to operate with 'the West' as one unifying concept (even though there still are huge internal variations).
2 Since the early 1990s both Japan and the West have registered contradictory changes: increasing (registered!) crime in Japan (especially since the early 1990s), and decreasing crime in the West (also from the early 1990s). These interesting changes will not be discussed in this book (see Leonardsen, in print).

3 Cf. for example Buendia (1989): 'In addition to the obvious material and other benefits it brings, economic development generates massive urbanization and social and occupational changes that can erode the cohesiveness of traditional societies. One result is that in many societies economic growth correlates to increasing crime rates. The phenomenon is global in scope touching the lives of most of the world's largest cities' (cover page).

4 Let me from the very start of this book make one statement explicit: I am well aware of the blessings of modernity, but this is not the topic of the present book. For a brief overview of optimistic and pessimistic perspectives on the modernisation process, see Hirschmann, (1986).

5 Much the same perspective is presented by Lea (2002): 'It is widely admitted that criminal justice systems are highly inefficient at controlling the level of crime. There is a constant search to discover "what works", if indeed anything does, and a constant fear that "nothing works" either in policing or penal policy' (p. 184).

6 Another aspect of this phenomenon is the paradox expressed by Clifford (1976): 'One of the absurdities of modern times has been the flow of "experts" from countries with more crime to countries with less to show them how to organize their police, courts, and correctional services' (p. 174). Or Braithwaite (1989): 'Third World criminal justice professionals are accustomed to discreet jokes about American criminologists being funded as UN consultants, or by some other form of foreign aid, to communicate words of wisdom to countries that manage their crime problems much more effectively than the United States. There are reasons for fearing that such foreign aid exports not only American criminology, but may risk also the export of American crime rates' (p. 6). Indeed, a rather depressive perspective concerning a professionally based preventive policy!

7 It has been argued that at the end of both the nineteenth and the twentieth centuries one could register an increase in pessimistic and even doomsday inspired literature ('fin de siècle' literature: see Alexander, 1995).

8 Cf. Cohen (1996), referring to Handelman and to Sterling: 'All serious accounts suggest that the emerging crime problem is real enough' (p. 8), and Young (1999): 'Crime has moved from the rare, the abnormal, the offence of the marginal and the stranger, to a commonplace part of the texture of everyday life: it occupies the family, the heartland of liberal democratic society as well as extending its anxiety into all areas of the city' (p. 30).

9 Baumann (2000a) gives this version of the problem: 'Community defined by its closely watched borders rather than its contents; "defence community" translated as the hiring of armed gatekeepers to control the entry; stalker and prowler promoted to the rank of public enemy number one; paring public areas down to "defensible" enclaves with selective access; separation in lieu of the negotiation of life in common, rounded up by the criminalization of residual difference – these are the principal dimensions of the current evolution of urban life' (p. 94).

10 Crime has definitely become a challenge to public economy. For governments who would like to offer tax reliefs, the crime problem has become a main obstacle. According to Buendia (1989), between 4 and 7 per cent of GNP is lost to crime or spent in prevention/repression of crime. This figure increases to 10–20 per cent of the annual national budget in some third world countries.

11 This type of typification easily invites new discussions: are not organizations like EU, WTO and IMF neo-liberal constructions more than instruments for international 'planning'? Should not neo-conservative advocates be grouped together with communitarians rather than with the neo-liberals? Is the focus on value conflicts characteristic only for the left? The answer to these questions has to be: 'it depends on': depending on specific countries we are talking about, depending on within what context we apply our concepts, and depending on how these different concepts are operationalized, we will reach different conclusions. However, for my analytical purpose I do believe this typification is meaningful.

12 Or to put it this way: I have given a supporting answer to Fukuyama's (2000) rhetoric question: 'Are capitalist societies destined to become materially wealthier but morally poorer as times goes on? Is the very ruthlessness and impersonality of markets undermining our social connectedness and teaching us that only money, not values, matters? Is modern capitalism destined to undermine its own moral basis, and thereby bring about its own collapse?' (p. 249).

13 According to Currie (1998) the market society is one 'in which the pursuit of private gain increasingly becomes the organising principle in all areas of social life' and in which 'all other principles of social or institutional organisation become eroded or subordinated to the overarching one of private gain' (p. 138).

14 Currie (1989) gives a good illustration of what I mean by regarding crime problems as value problems: 'By the time my own daughter is my age, toward the end of the second decade of the twenty-first century, we may hope to have fostered some comparable changes in aspects of American culture that now may seem to set in stone: the degree of social deprivation and inequality we tolerate; the amount of violence we consider normal and acceptable in the course of child rearing or of marriage; the level of access to social and health services we deem the minimum responsibility of civilized society; the relative importance of private gain and of cooperative endeavour as esteemed personal motives, or of private economic "choice" versus the stability and socializing competence of communities and families' (p. 22–3).

15 This does not mean that nothing can be done to mitigate negative impacts of one set of value priorities, but it does mean that one has to calculate with considerable 'externalities' (as economists call it) whichever way one chooses to prioritize.

16 As Dore (1987) says: 'Send a British parliamentary delegation to Japan and the result is like the Rashomon film: versions of the story so unlike that they appear to be set in different countries. Right-wing MPs come back full of praise for a system whole-heartedly devoted to free enterprise competition, for unions which cooperate with management, for a society which accepts the discipline of the market, ...' (p. 3).

17 Dore (1986, 1987) is one of the scholars who has most consistently confirmed the picture of Japanese capitalism as unique. Writing before the burst of the bubble economy, Dore asks how Japan can compete in an international free market economy when this country seems to give such a strong priority to moral and communal values. Dore adopts Harvey Liebenstein's concept of 'x-efficiency' to explain this apparent paradox. According to Dore there are

two kinds of efficiency. One is focusing what economists call allocative or accounting efficiency. This is the efficiency we are well acquainted with in the West and which is about getting a maximum profit from all your investments. The main idea is to pursue a narrow economic and profit-oriented perspective and avoid considerations that might not work with these principles. In short, these are the principles proclaimed within traditional liberalistic philosophy with a strong belief in the invisible hand of the market, and where governmental (or any other) intervention should be minimized. Within such a system the rationality of the economic system will definitely determine the development within the socio-cultural system. The price will be registered as a broad variety of welfare problems.

18   However, he rapidly adds that, 'the cross-national evidence on individuating modernity is strong enough to make one very sceptical about the ability of these societies to continue on their merry course of happy "groupism"' (p. 170).

2.   Is Japan really a low-crime nation?

1   For an illustration, see Wallerstein (1995).

2   Cf. Clifford (1976) who comments the uniqueness of the Japanese crime figures in this way: 'There has been a great deal of scepticism among the criminological pundits both at home and abroad, not only about the reliability of the figures, but about their *true meaning*' (italics added, p. 1). Benjamin (1997, p. 67) argues correspondingly that we should not assume that our Western concept of 'group' has the same meaning for the Japanese people.

3   The best illustration of the emicist position in relation to Japan will be found in the so-called *nihonjinron* debate. In this debate emicists have strongly argued for the uniqueness of Japanese culture, and that this is a culture that strangers never will be able to grasp fully (see Dale, 1986).

4   Finch (2000) discusses this in an article about *Homicide in Contemporary Japan*. He underlines for example that the statistics for homicide in Japan include *attempts*. What further complicates our analysis is the changing of crime categories within one and the same country over time. In Japan, parricide (*sonzokusatsu*) was abolished in 1995.

5   This should not be interpreted as a genuine harmony between the police and the citizens. As Komiya (1999) argues, 'the Japanese regard law as an instrument of constraint used by the government to control the people. This legal consciousness is probably derived from the foreign origin of much of Japanese law (p. 372). Also, it is important to remember the critical research on the police referred to by Steinhoff (1993). He points out (with reference to Katzenstein and Tsujinaka) that security considerations extend into many aspects of police work. There was a substantial growth of security policing in Japan from the 1960s (when crime rates started dropping!) and, while many authors have underlined the co-operative aspects of police practices in Japan, one should not under-communicate the surveillance and subtle coercion that is implicit in the neighbourhood policing system.

6 Ames (quoted in Araki, 1988) argued in his doctoral dissertation that 'the Japanese have long believed that the primary responsibility for social control lies with the community and that citizens must discipline themselves to maintain order. Japanese society, in effect, polices itself' (p. 1034).

7 Article 1 of the Offenders' Rehabilitation Law proclaims that, 'all the people are required to render help according to their position and ability, to accomplish the objective mentioned in the preceding paragraph' (quoted in Clifford, 1976, p. 100).

8 Triandis (1994) gives us this illustration: 'There is much tightness in Japan about crossing against red lights and jaywalking. My friend John Adamopoulos was chased for two blocks by an angry Japanese who saw him cross against a red light on a deserted street' (p. 163).

9 Thornton continues: 'Instead, the public prosecutor often calls in not only the offender but also family members, neighbours, and even workplace superiors. All are given admonitions so that they will understand their responsibility for supervising the offender in order for prosecution to be suspended' (p. 30).

10 The further elaboration on these points are found in the Penal Code, Article 57, and reads:
'The court must pay special attention to the following factors:

(i) The personal history, habits and hereditary factors of the criminal,
(ii) The intensity of the determination of will to commit of the criminal,
(iii) Whether the motive was blameworthy or tolerable in view of morality such as loyalty to the Emperor (*chu*) and filial piety (*ko*) or in view of the public interest,
(iv) Whether the offence was committed under fear, surprise, excitement, embarrassment, provocation, threat, mass psychology or some other similar causes,
(v) Whether the offence was committed either by abusing the position of ascendant, guardian, teacher, employer, or another superior position, or by disdaining (the position of these superiors),
(vi) Whether the means employed in the offence were cruel or whether they were cunning or crafty,
(vii) Whether the planned offence was of a large scale and how far-reaching was danger or damage created by the offence,
(viii) Whether the criminal has repented of the offence and whether he has made efforts to mitigate the physical damage which was caused by his offence by such means as paying damages' (quoted from Tanaka, 1976, p. 316).

11 Westermann and Burfeind (1991) comment that even *within* the US the criminal law – an area left to state control – will vary from state to state (p. 62).

12 Nevertheless, the following quote from Kaplan and Dublo (1986) should warn us against defining away the assertions of extensive bribery as 'culture': 'How corrupt, then is Japan? Anthropologist Befu jokes that to really enforce law, the Japanese government would have to create a huge Department of Bribery Investigations. So pervasive is its use that virtually every contemporary Japanese politician has had some brush with the nation's postwar bribery law at one point in his career' (p. 166).

13   However, MacFarlane (1995) reports that 'many local studies bear out the absence of crime' (p. 370). The only study they refer to themselves is one from Kamo village where official records revealed no serious crime during the period 1934–45.

14   Rex Shelley is a Eurasian, brought up in Malaysia and Singapore. He has written a reference book on Japan and a book on Japanese business style. He has also translated many Japanese short stories, a novel, traditional folk tales and modern Japanese poetry.

15   De Mente has had intimate contact with the Japanese society since 1949, has worked for the Japan Travel Bureau, has been editor of several major publications in Japan, and has written more than a dozen books on Japan, its culture, and language. When he published his guidebook on Japan he was senior editor of *Far East Traveller Magazine* in Tokyo.

16   Bazemore (1998) argues that the root of crime is community *conflict* and disharmony. Consequently, 'justice cannot be achieved by a government war on crime but rather by peacemaking and dispute resolution' (p. 786).

17   The term *yakuza* means the three numbers 8, 9, and 3. In traditional gambling these figures formed a useless combination.

18   The yakuza is described both as embedded in and excluded from society. Jacob Raz, who spent a year living with the yakuza, comments: 'yakuza declare themselves Japanese, very Japanese, while at the same time being both excluded from Japanese society, and excluding that society' (quoted in Henshall, 1999, p. 67).

19   This perspective has been typical in Marxist inspired criminology (see Taylor, 1998). In 1842 Marx himself wrote on the theft of wood lying on the floor of the forest by local workers.

20   For an overview, see Adler (1983), Chapter 13.

21   For a short summary of research claiming there is a causal link between crime and unemployment, see Watts (1996b). Watts himself, however, denies such a claim.

22   See for example, Currie (1989) argues in much the same way: 'We must reduce inequality and social impoverishment . . . Evidence continues to grow from both cross-national and domestic studies, that violent crime is generated by extremes of inequality, especially when coupled with excessive mobility and the fragmentation of community and family life' (p. 16). According to Christiansen (1974) 'most of the older European studies of the relationship between the economic structure and criminality supported the opinion that there was a direct connection between simple economic factors and various forms of crime, first of all property crimes and particularly theft, but also crimes of violence in which abuse of alcohol played a part' (p. 3). He adds that recent criminology has given more nuanced conclusions. Heiland, Shelley and Katoh (1992) conclude: 'Taking an historical perspective, we find at the beginning of the modernization process a close link between poverty and crime' (p. 6). Also Faulkner *et al.* (1996) support the conclusion that criminal offending is associated with relative inequality and poverty.

23   Fukuyama obviously forgets theories about relative deprivation. As cited in Guneriussen (1988, p. 270) black people from low status groups increase

their criminal activity in times of economic prosperity because of a feeling of relative deprivation.

24 Cf. Taylor (1998) when he criticises American criminology for loss of theoretical ambition in their research on this topic: 'Particularly in the United States, there is a voluminous literature investigating the statistical relationships between different aspects of "the economy" (especially unemployment) and crime, in which "the economy" has no greater significance than any other variable that could have been chosen (for example, levels of police presence, the severity of local magisterial sentences and so on). In some respects, the work in this tradition is a twentieth-century variant of the kind of statistical investigation that was widely undertaken during the nineteenth century, in different European societies into patterns of crime – for example, in relation to the business cycle or to consumer prices' (p. xix).

25 Lea (2002, p. 118) refers similarly to a major British report on poverty and social exclusion published in the mid-1990s: 'Regardless of any moral argumentation or feelings of altruism, *everyone shares* an interest in the cohesiveness of society. As the gap between rich and poor grows, the problems of the marginalized groups which are being left behind rebound on the more comfortable majority. Just as in the last century it was in the interests of all to introduce public health measures to combat the spread of infectious diseases fostered by poverty, so in this century it is in the interests of all to remove the factors which are fostering the social diseases of drugs, crime, political extremism and social unrest' (italics by Lea).

26 To illustrate my point of view, let me use the following analogy: traffic accidents in a society are closely linked to physical characteristics of the road. Mutatis mutandi, roads covered with ice and snow will experience more accidents than roads with a dry surface. How the cars are 'situated' on the roads will (naturally) affect the frequency of accidents.

How people are situated in society will in a comparable way affect the amount of crime 'accidents'. In a society with a high degree of poverty/unemployment/inequality some are better situated into the socio-material structure than others. As a fish in the water is confident with this substrate, most middle-class people occupying a fairly safe position in the labour market will be confident with 'their' substrate. In short, they know how to take advantage of the socio-material structure in which they are enclosed.

3. Why has modernization in the west been synonymous with increased crime? Is rapid social change synonymous with loss of moral sentiments and loss of community?

1 At this point I am not going into a debate on *decreasing* crime rates in the 1990s. However, there is little reason to regard this change as an expression of successful interventionist political action.

2 Or in condensed form expressed by Lea (1999): '... from the last quarter of the twentieth century modernity has moved into a new type of crisis. The

dominant forces have been fragmentation and a weakening of the type of social structure that underpinned the social relations of crime control' (p. 22).

3 Cf. Cohen (1989) who stresses that cultures should not be regarded as 'blind' reactors or adapters to structural changes, but active creators. Currie (1989) supports such a perspective: 'There are those who think deliberate cultural change is difficult, if not impossible; who invoke the idea of cultural rigidity as a way of downplaying altogether the possibility of conscious social change' (Jencks, Currie, and Herrnstein 1988). But that approach betrays a narrow and static view of culture. After all, in the last generation alone we've seen several major – even epochal – normative changes in American society: in the way we think about the social role of women, or about relationship to the natural environment; increasingly, too, in the way we think about health and nutrition. On all of these planes, as a culture, we are very different than when I was growing up (p. 22).

4 One might of course question the relevance of discussing those broad historical perspectives to our topic about crime prevention. It is for example a very relevant objection to argue that crime in the West has not increased steadily since the dawn of modern society. Rather, rapid increase in crime is mainly a post-Second World War phenomenon. Consequently, we must avoid any simple bi-lateral cause–effect analysis between modernization and crime. Do not those general sociological perspectives represent a too general approach to our topic? Also, one could argue that Japan has not deserved the status as a low-crime nation all through modern time. Both in the 1930s and a few years after the end of the Second World War Japan experienced 'aberrant' periods in this regard (i.e. increasing crime), and – as a matter of course – the cultural dimension was the same in those periods. Consequently, it is far too simple to give the impression of some kind of mechanical and deterministic link between crime and modern times. I accept those critical remarks. However, this does not exclude the relevance of broad historical perspectives to understand the more fundamental crime-producing forces in society. We cannot argue that Confucianism or a special group structure will prevent crime, no matter what other social conditions exist, much the same as we cannot argue that modernization will produce crime, no matter what other parameters exist. Internal differences between Western countries concerning crime are of course an important reminder to our analysis. But I have to repeat my starting point for discussing crime: my focus is not micro-level analysis, and it is definitely not a search for instrumental strategies for crime prevention. On the contrary, I want to discuss crime at a broad societal and cultural level. I want to analyse deep structural and cultural dimensions as frame-setting premises for the crime pattern in a society. In such a perspective I will argue that classical sociology and broad historical perspectives should have a strong say in modern debates on social disintegration. If crime prevention is less about techniques of social engineering and more about basic cultural, normative and social organizing principles, then we have to be aware of our own historical heritage. If we really want to attack the crime problem, we might have to be willing to attack some of our cherished values, as well as some of our organizing principles in

modern society. As we shall see, this has special relevance to the Western way of dealing with youth.

5 As I will show later, for example Durkheim wrote about how different social structures gave different premises for the development of what he called 'moral tightness' in society.

6 Elias (1994) is another spokesman of increasing civilisation as a fruit of modernity.

7 Elster (1989) identifies two concepts of disorder, one being 'lack of predictability', the other being 'absence of cooperation' (which compares to loss of belonging/loosening of social bonds).

8 According to Kant this 'increasing rationalisation' is also about differentiation. Kant operates with three types of rationalities: the theoretical (which addresses itself to the question of 'truth'), the practical (concerning 'the good'), and the aesthetical (concerning 'the beautiful'). With the differentiation process our consciousness becomes 'departimentalised and decentralised' and we will operate with different rationalities within different systems.

9 For an elaboration on the topic micro–macro and individual vs aggregate level analysis, see Mouzelis (1995).

10 The central author writing about how relations between people within primary groups constitute the primary foundation for social integration in society, is Cooley. It is in and through the face-to-face relations in the primary group that the individual develops qualities like ability to feel loyalty, justice and freedom. It is within stable primary groups that the individual has a chance to develop a stable and consistent self. The perspectives developed by Cooley (cf. his famous concept of the 'looking-glass self') have strong affinity with the perspectives in Mead's 'Mind, self and society' (which is no surprise since they worked at the same university and knew each other very well).

11 From this perspective some authors have drawn a simplistic (as I see it) conclusion that crime will be much more habitual in cities than in rural areas (less differentiated). I will return to this discussion later.

12 The assumption that social development from traditional to modern society is a linear process has been criticized by many scholars. Especially if we focus on the family institution in the West the idea of a unilinear movement away from interdependency should be challenged (Braithwaite, 1993, p. 12).

13 Cf. Kumar (1983) quoting Polanyi: 'The idea of a self-adjusting market implied a stark utopia. Such an institution could not exist for any length of time without annihilating the human and natural substance of society; it would have physically destroyed man and transformed his surroundings into a wilderness' (p. 153).

14 By ligatures Dahrendorf means a type of deeper bond that links people together.

15 Anomie is for Durkheim a social condition where the norms that govern people's behaviour have lost their validity.

16 Young (1999) gives us an important reminder at this point:

It is an axiom of conservative social commentators that the unravelling of the rigours and disciplines of culture and everyday life will automatically release the dangerous anti-social creature that exists just beneath the patina of civilization. In this instance to celebrate self-expression makes matters even worse: first you weaken the culture then you actually exhort the individuals to do their own thing! In this book I have argued the reverse of this: *true*, deferential, unreflecting discipline is necessary if order is to be maintained in an unequal world; *true* the rise of individualism helps the cataracts of conformity fall away and the individual is likely to be mightily discontented with what he or she sees; *very true* that this may well cause a rise in crime, disorder and disagreement, but *false*, that this is a product of human nature and the only thing to do is "realistically" put up with the world ['we have made our society and we must live with it', Wilson notes gloomily: p. 249]. For the growth of individualism and the greater reflexivity of the human actor offers great promises as well as the pitfalls and perils of late modernity' (p. 194).

17 In the works of Simmel (1959) it is a central topic how modernity means a development from simple to complex ways of organizing society. As a consequence this will produce an effect where people develop a more distanced way of relating to each other, and even to themselves.

18 Cf. Lockwood's (1999) concept of 'unbridled consumerism'.

19 However, the psychological concept 'anomia' relates to the individual level. See McClosky amd Schaar, 1965.

20 'To be sure, the biological fact of the helplessness of human infants at birth and for some time afterward necessitates a long period of nearly total dependence on parental, or at least adult, nurturance and protection. Infantile dependence is a precondition for both habituation to life with others and extensive learning from them, but the very absence of instinctive dispositions, including inborn social response, is the cause of the dependence, that is, endows it with critical survival value in evolutionary terms' (Wrong, 1994, p. 2).

21 I have to repeat that what I have presented above is a biased presentation of the sociology of social change. The social impacts of modernization should be described in terms of ambivalence rather than in terms of unanimity. As Kumar (1983) expresses, 'at the very outset of the capitalistic era therefore we find a fundamental ambivalence and anxiety about the capacity of the capitalistic system to fulfil the goals variously set for it' (p. 150). However, my intention has not been to give a balanced presentation on this topic, but rather to 'purify' the most important negative social aspects.

I also have to underline: a Durkheimian perspective that links modernity to social dissolution does not mean a glorification of 'traditional' societies. As Edgerton (1992) documents in *Sick Societies* it is important to challenge the myth of primitive harmony.

22 Cf. Etzioni (1991): 'Throughout human thought, from the Cynics to Karl Marx to Gary Becker, attempts have been made to deny the significance or autonomy of the moral dimension. In the neoclassical tradition little to no room is left for authentic altruism or other "pure" moral motivations' (p. 377). Watts (1996), discussing Braithwaite's moral theory about crime, claims that 'sociologists have all too often consistently refused the moral dimension' (p. 122).

23 I have to add here, in the words of Hirschman (1986): 'At mid-eighteenth century it became the conventional wisdom – Rousseau of course rebelled against it – that commerce was a civilising agent of considerable power and range' (p. 107). Hirschman goes on to quote Montesquieu ('Spirit of Laws'):

'It is almost a general rule that wherever manners are gentle there is commerce; and wherever there is commerce, manners are gentle (–). Commerce... polishes and softens barbaric ways as we can see every day' (p. 107).

24 The critique of the way the capitalistic market system functions is, of course, as old as capitalism itself. The works of Marx up to Keynes are reminders of this critique. Giddens (2000), in a reply to the critiques of 'the Third Way', clearly supports the idea that 'markets can't even function without a social and ethical framework – which they themselves cannot provide' (p. 33).

25 'As we take for granted the air we breathe, and what makes possible all our activities, so capitalism took for granted the atmosphere in which it operated, and which it had inherited from the past. It only discovered how essential it had been when the air became thin. In other words, capitalism has succeeded because it was not just capitalist' (1994, p. 343).

26 Cf. Horkheimer (referred in Hirschmann, 1986): '... the progress of subjective reason destroyed the theoretical basis of mythological, religious and rationalistic ideas (and yet) civilized society has up until now been living on the residue of these ideas' (p. 116).

27 Nygaard (1995) makes much the same point in summing up for sociology in general. He argues that for sociology it was importantly not only to say 'no collective without the individual', but more importantly, 'no individual without the collective' (p. 15). As I will show in Chapter 4 Japanese society is to a large extent based on such a philosophy, cf. Benjamin (1997): 'Children are not tricked, in some sense, into subordinating their own goals over an extended period of time to the interest of the group'; rather, they are put into situations where in order to satisfy their own needs, they must contribute to the efforts of others in the group' (p. 66).

28 Cf. Etzioni (1993) arguing that 'Americans – who have long been concerned with the deterioration of private and public morality, the decline of family, high crime rates, and the swelling of corruption in government, ...' (p. 2).

29 The assertion that there is an 'imbalance between rights and responsibilities' (Etzioni, 1993, p. 4) today is a main point in the communitarian movement. At this point they are echoing a general perspective from Charles Horton Cooley (1864–1929) who, in his writings stressed that the individual and his rights should not be regarded as the basic unit and starting point in modern society.

30 Hughes (1996) mentions both Aristotle's civic republicanism, Judaeo-Christian ideas of communion, utopian socialists and anarchists like Owen and Kropotkin, and the conservative sociological tradition of Toennies and Durkheim as the parentage.

31 Cf Etzioni's concept 'parenting deficit'.

32 Cf. John Stuart Mill: 'Except of matters of mere detail, there are perhaps no practical questions, even among those which approach nearest to the character of purely economical questions, which admit of being decided on economical premises alone' (quoted from Coughlin, 1991, p. 3).

33 By 'trust' Fukuyama (1995) means 'the unspoken and unwritten bond between fellow citizens that facilitates transactions, empowers individual creativity, and justifies collective action' (quoted from book flap). By the concept 'radius of trust' Fukuyama means how wide circles outside the individual trust is shown.

4. A Cultural, Sociological and Criminiological Description of Japanese Society

1 Hofstede and Bond (1988) argue that cross-cultural studies have shown that children learn patterns of cultural behaviour very early in life. They add that, 'Japanese male infants of 3 to 4 months are noisier than Japanese female infants of the same age, whereas in the United States the opposite is true' (p. 7).

2 Cf. Henshall: 'To many Westerners the Japanese do still seem a confusing people. They are both polite and impolite, self-effacing yet assertive, honourable yet duplicitous, and so on' (p. xx).

3 The wording of this heading is picked deliberately. I am *not* saying that Japan is a homogeneous society. I say it is a society with a high degree of continuity (over time) and consistency (across society). What is the difference?

I avoid using the term 'homogeneous' so as not to get involved in a running debate on Japanese uniqueness/the myth of Japanese uniqueness. For many decades Japan has been described, both by natives and by foreigners, as a unique culture encompassing every citizen. With regard to each of history, language, ethnicity and belief systems it has been stressed that Japanese people represent an extreme degree of homogeneity. In latter years this perspective has invited critical voices, saying that too much attention has been paid to exotic otherness (see Henshall, 1999, Sugimoto, 1994, Dale, 1986, Miyanaga, 1991, Stevens, 1997). These authors have all underlined Japan's internal variation, its social stratification, its diversity, its subcultures, and so on. In many ways I regard this discussion as rather futile. With no agreed yardstick for what is meant by a 'homogeneous culture' both sides will be right in their assertions.

An additional problem is the loss of distinction between an external (positivistic) and an internal (phenomenological) description of Japanese culture. Using the fact that some 90 per cent of Japanese define themselves as belonging to the middle class invites a conclusion that Japan is a very homogeneous society. When Clifford (1976) talks about the 'oneness of Japanese people' (p. 69), this is mainly about a subjective (collective) feeling among people. But if we use class or gender as analytical variables we might certainly be able to argue in favour of a heterogeneous thesis.

4 Durkheim argued that anomie and breakdown was not the typical result during revolutionary and collectively-led social changes.

5 A comparable evaluation is found in Clifford (1976): 'Japan has in many senses preserved this cohesion. It has grown economically and adapted socially to the change without abandoning the sinews of its national cohesion. There is an indefinable unity and addiction to older patterns of living that have been transferred to industrialization and urbanization. This means internal curiosity and limitation that does not suit everyone and drives many young Japanese abroad. But it satisfies a need that many Japanese abroad begin to feel as they miss the security of the old country' (pp. 173–4). And Numata (1999): 'This process of appropriation of 'the European', undertaken for instance within the framework of pragmatic educational reforms aiming at a scientific-technical modernization of Japan, hardly touched upon the cultural deep structures so that the European culture has remained largely foreign to the Japanese even until today' (p. 372).

6 We find much of the same perspective in Singer (1973): 'Among the social ties binding together unequals the patron–client relation was, and is likely to remain, in Japan by far the most important, all-pervading, of remarkable stability, and often of overriding strength' (pp. 84–5).

7 I would like to add at this point that the focus on harmony primarily applies to the *surface*. As correctly pointed out in one introductory text to Japan, many so-called Japan 'experts' tell the world about how much Japanese stress 'harmony'. However, 'the reality is that they push THE IMAGE OF harmony. What is beneath may be completely different' (http://japaninfo. esmartweb. com/FAQ-Primer.html).

8 Hofstede and Bond (1988) describe four characteristics as typical of Confucianism, the fourth being that 'virtue with regard to one's tasks in life consists of trying to acquire skills and education, working hard, not spending more than necessary, being patient, and persevering. Conspicuous consumption is taboo, as is loss of one's temper. Moderation is enjoyed in all things' (p. 8).

9 Ben-Ari (1997), supporting the argument of continuity of cultural practices in Japanese society, points out that these continuities very much are also *organizationally* produced and maintained. To my perspective of crime and social control he adds this interesting perspective: 'These patterns form part the processes of normalization of individuals (and families) that the Japanese state (like *any* state) has undertaken in the name of enhancing unity, stability, and economic progress. In this sense the coordinated and efficient use of people and resources, the discipline and control of teachers and the national standardization of preschool education form part of – or more correctly actualize – the macro forces of the state's penetration into individuals' lives' (p. 55).

10 McGregor (1996) warns against foreigners who too easily convey myths about Japan as a homogeneous and harmonious organism. 'Many foreigners take this largely undifferentiated Japanese message on board, and unwittingly turn themselves into a sterile echo chamber for what are truly the most conservative views of the Japanese power elite' (pp. 2–3).

11 Cf. Giddens (1991): 'In modern social life, the notion of lifestyle takes on a particular significance. The more tradition loses its hold, and the more daily life is reconstituted in terms of the dialectical interplay of the local and the global, the more individuals are forced to negotiate life style choices among a diversity of options' (p. 5).

12 In her in-depth study from a Japanese school, Benjamin (1997) remarks that 'there are no major contradictions between the lessons of school and those of life in Japan, and they are appropriate at all social and class levels' (p. 222).

13 It is interesting to note that Ben-Ari argues that 'the organizational model of care and education of preschools in Japan (as elsewhere in the industrialized world) looks towards, and is predicated on, many of the same kinds of premises as management techniques of industry and large scale organizations' (p. 50). In other words, Ben-Ari points to uniformity from pre-school to business life which represents an amazing perspective concerning the debate on how homogeneous Japanese culture really is. Also, Ben-Ari points out that the strict regulation of pre-schools cannot be understood apart from more general processes of social control in Japan.

14   There are important national variations to this picture: Japan experienced extraordinary strains because of the Nagasaki and Hiroshima catastrophe. In 1948, the number of orphans was estimated at 124,000, and there were many children living on the streets (see EAMM, 1996, p. 5).

15   Here are some typical expressions of this:

> Conflicts are permeated by a deeper consensus that is not really comparable with other, more pluralistic, societies . . . It is quite remarkable how the affairs of such a great nation of over 100 million people can sometimes be gleaned from the principles that inform a simple tribe. Perhaps Japan is more easily understood and explained as an example of a national tribe – a rare instance of the older tribal values and concepts being preserved into a modern industrial setting (Clifford, 1976, pp. 33–4).

> This unity of interests allied to the basic oneness of the Japanese people, carried them through their period of industrialization, gave them strength during the era of military expansion, and even provided the backbone to promote their post-War recovery and later economic success (*op. cit.,* p. 69).

> This racial and ethnic isolation has allowed the Japanese to develop a strong shared tradition. To be sure, it was a tradition that changed over the centuries as the ideas of Buddhism and Confucianism were introduced. But the new traditions, especially Confucianism's strong emphasis upon loyalty and fidelity, helped maintain a homogenous world view (Westermann and Burfeind, 1991, p. 37).

> One is the extraordinary homogeneity of thinking of the Japanese people. Typically, the Japanese take it for granted, almost unconsciously, that the people around them see things in the same light or have the same view as they do . . . The notion that all Japanese should think alike runs deep in their subconscious ideas . . . It is appalling the extent to which we accept things as self-evident. So unquestioningly, in fact, do we Japanese accept things as self-evident that we understand (at least we believe we understand) practically everything without any explanation or proof? This, I believe, is the peculiarity of the Japanese way of thinking (Tanaka, 1976, p. 296).

16   Cf: 'The state of de-regulation or anomie is thus further heightened by persons being less disciplined, precisely when they need more disciplining' (Durkheim, 1951, p. 254).

17   At this point, it is important to issue a warning. Value *consistency* should not be evaluated independently of value *content*. According to Sutherland's 'differential association theory' criminal behaviour is learned when individuals confront an excess of definitions favourable to law violation. This means that the question of *what kind of* value inconsistency we are talking about is important for the final outcome and direction of individual actions. A 'creolized' society is not necessarily a more crime-prone society. It may easily be a more conflict-ridden society, but a lot of other factors will intervene and determine the outcome of such conflicts (cf. Merton's (1968) typologies innovation, ritualism, retreatism and rebellion).

18 Even though critical comment has been made regarding the conception of Japan as a group-society (Befu, 1980a, 1980b), comparing to Western countries I have no hesitation in using this label.

19 Cf. Henshall, 1999: 'The rigidity of prescription in the Tokugawa period is still visible in the idea that everything has a proper form, known as a *kata* ('form' or 'model'). This is not a simple visual aesthetic: it has become a type of ideal to strive for in almost every aspect of behaviour. It is not the type of ideal that is far removed from everyday life, but an attainable one, a sort of 'functional ideal' that is very much normative' (p. 152). And: '[t]he *kata* is a major agent of social constraint and conformity. It is not just social order and stability in a political sense that is aided by it. Social relations, that means so much to the Japanese, are also made easier for the people involved if they know what to expect of others' (p. 153).

20 The tendency to focus on *functionality* is also found in the way the Japanese relate to religion. According to Nobuyuki (2000) the Japanese are polytheists (having a vast number of deities), and they have *efficacy* as their criterion of belief. People simply abandon gods that don't function. This has the further consequence that 'we Japanese find it hard to embrace ineffective morality, no matter how diligently we are taught it' (p. 59).

The name of *yakuza* to label organized crime can also be linked to the stress on group functionality in Japan. As we recall, the name *yakuza* means 8, 9, 3, which is synonymous to unuseful cards in a card game. The name *yakuza* signifies a group of individuals who are without any worth and, consequently, who are of no use to society.

21 In this regard Hsu follows the sociological (Mead-inspired) way of arguing: Man becomes man via interaction with other people. Or as Bruun and Christie (1985) conclude: 'a vast amount of observations, from the sciences on animals, children and adults right up to our own personal experiences, all point in a direction confirming that the cradle of mankind is other people' (p. 15).

22 Wrong (1994) reminds us that our ability to 'take the role of the other' (Mead), or our ability to handle 'reciprocity of perspectives' (Schutz) is basic for a discussion of social order as a problem of cognition of other selves.

23 We find much of the same way of thinking in Western philosophy about the social contract. According to Rousseau, the individual could calmly subjugate to the social contract or the common government since she/he thereby only subjugates to her/himself. We find the same line of argumentation both in Kant and Habermas.

24 *Asahi News* reported on 25 March 2001 that a ward government in Tokyo had withheld invitations for graduation ceremonies from people who refused to stand up and sing the national anthem. The argument was that such people set a bad example for children at school ceremonies.

25 Dale (1986) analyses this extinction of the self in a critical way. In his perspective 'every inch of autonomous self-assertion by the individual is contested as threatening the hegemonic reach and authority of the corporate, national ideal ... the *nihonjinron* vigorously deny the very possibility of individual, uniquely [sic] identity within Japan itself' (p. 22). Dale also refers to the psychiatrist Reynolds who argues that doctors define people who wish to be 'special' or different from other people as part of the neurosis itself, as something that should be treated.

26   This is how van Wolferen portrays the situation: 'The Japanese, especially in the cities, are constantly made to feel like subjects rather than citizens. They live in a cajoling and exhortative environment. They are continually warned about dangers, reminded of the proper way to do things, gently chided. Kawaji's nurses of the people have stayed on as permanent instructors. The loudspeakers on cruising police cars and on the bigger police boxes recall a worrisome mother; something is always *abunai*, dangerous. The hint of aggrievedness in the tone emphasizes further the likeness to a Japanese mother; people walking the streets are made to feel like potentially naughty children' (p. 186).

27   Cf. van Wolferen (1989): 'I once spent a Saturday afternoon with a small group of middle-aged housewives patrolling the streets on one of Tokyo's major entertainment districts. Their trained eyes would soon spot any teenagers from the suburbs, whom they would approach for questioning. The conversation usually ended with encouragement to return home on the next commuter train and avoid the temptations and traps awaiting innocent youth in the city. Encounters which in many Western countries would have resulted at least in foul language produced only bowed heads and muttered thanks for the advice given by the crime-prevention ladies' (p. 185).

28   Cf. van Wolferen: 'It is ironic that the only country in the world whose constitution deprives it of the right to wage war, whose official spokesmen seriously suggest that it can teach the world to love peace and which formally decries the use of military power, whenever and wherever and no matter whom it is resorted to, should so often remind one of a military organization. The flocks of high-school pupils dressed in black uniforms cut like those of Prussia at the turn of the century are just the surface. The emphasis on collective exercise; the drills continued for their own sake far beyond the point where skill ceases to improve; the social approval given to *gambaru* (not giving up, sticking with something beyond reason); the sentimental emphasis on the 'purity' of single-minded youthful exertions; the Spartan discipline in judo, karate, and aikido training; all these represent a militarized approach to social order' (p. 181).

29   At this point I have to warn against too simplistic conclusions as for a western 'emic' frame of reference. The authors remark themselves that their findings do not support those who argue that the extensive control relates to over-regulation or a repressive atmosphere in schools. They emphasise that school regulations are not enforced violently or blindly.

30   Shelley says further: 'Harmony is regarded as being a major attribute of being Japanese. The prefix *wa* is used to distinguish Japanese things from foreign things such as dress (*wafuku*, Japanese dress as opposed to western dress), paper, or food' (p. 142).

31   Cf. Westermann and Burfeind (1991): 'The Meiji government simply turned over the responsibility for the moral education of Japanese youth to the schools. The purpose of education became increasingly that of producing citizens who would be loyal to the emperor and obedient to his edicts' (p. 15).

32   Mori (1994, p. 23) maintains that children who have stayed for a period abroad together with their parents experience problems when returning to Japan because of lack of proper knowledge of *ningen kankei*. They are usually regarded as having become too individualistic.

33 However, referring to Henshall (1999), I would like to add that certain aspects of this relatedness have been exaggerated in the so-called *nihonjinron* debate. But even Henshall supplies this precaution with the following statement: 'There does seem to be some merit to the basic argument that in their interpersonal relationships Japanese do have a greater tendency than westerners to "merge" with others, to be interdependent rather than independent, to take the views of others into account and be less assertive of the self' (p. 149).

34 An interview with the Nobel Prize Winner in Chemistry, Hideki Shirakawa, gives a good illustration of Japanese caution. He underlined the importance of treating people with respect by saying: 'You should only say 20 per cent to 30 per cent of what you really want to say and you should be considerate of other people's feelings in forming good relations' (*Mainichi Daily News*, 13.10.00).

35 Nakane (1970) writes about how the fear of being ostracised from the group can be observed in everyday life: 'In particular, a junior takes every care to avoid any open confrontation with his superior. Such attempts lead to the point that a flatly negative form is rarely employed in conversation: one would prefer to be silent rather than utter words such as "no" or "I disagree". The avoidance of such open and bald negative expression is rooted in the fear that it might disrupt the harmony and order of the group, that it might hurt the feelings of a superior and that, in extreme circumstances, it could involve the risk of being cast out from the group as an undesirable member' (s. 35). Ezawa (1990), who was the leader of the 'Anti-Olympics People's Network' in Nagano, argues: 'The government and the corporations, in order to make the problematic Olympics the "will of the people", have created an atmosphere in which people who oppose the games are labelled *hikokumin*, or "non-citizens". This same mood, and same label, was used to isolate people who opposed the Japanese invasion of Asia during World War II' (pp. 57–8).

36 Cf. Ashby: 'Unlike American culture, which gives the greatest freedom to adults, Japanese culture allows the greatest latitude to those most innocent and least self-responsible, at the beginning and end of the life cycle' (*The Japan Times*, 2 February 2002).

37 A Japanese employee will normally prefer a considerate boss to higher wages.

38 This concept is related to another important concept in Japan: *ningensei*. In English, this means 'humanity' or 'human beingness' (se Goldman, 1994, p. 30). Goldman quotes Lebra's expression as for the importance of ningensei in this way: 'Ningensei orients Japanese to invest so much sensitivity, compulsiveness, circumspection, and refinement to the creation or maintenance of smooth and pleasant social relationships'.

39 Benedict (1967) refers to the following passage from Yoshio's book *When I was a child* from 1912: 'Let me give you my definition of two words: Murderer: one who assassinates some human flesh. Sneerer: one who assassinates other's SOUL and *heart*. Soul and heart are far dearer than the flesh, therefore sneering is the worst crime' (p. 112).

40 Shelley (1997) refers to another pair of concepts that are related to social reciprocity, namely *kashi* and *kari*. 'If Akamatsu Reiko does a favour for Murakami Tokiko, Murakami Tokiko automatically assumes an obligation to repay Amamatsu Reiko in the future. Both are aware of this. Akamatsu Reiko

is said to have *kashi* (literally, a loan) over Murakami Tokiko. Murakami Tokoiko in turn has *kari* (literally, a debt) to Akamatsu Reiko' (p. 147).

41 A man that does not know *giri* is defined as a 'miserable wretch' and will be ostracised by his fellows.

42 A typical expression by Durkheim in this regard would be this: 'Whether a person is of the highest or the lowest status, as long as he is operating in a network of interpersonal relationships, his behavior must also conform to the demands and expectations of other parties to the relationship. And this conformity requires that he restrain his behavior. He must control and modify his impulsive behavior to meet the definitions operating in the relationship' (here translated from Guneriussen, 1988, p. 272).

43 As I have already commented, I agree with Braithwaite concerning the social control, but I am more ambivalent as regards the reintegrative aspects of Japanese society.

44 I have to repeat that my analysis ends in 1985. Japanese society is rapidly changing. In the official publication *Japan Insight* one can today read (in a section analysing bullying) that, 'nuclear families are not interwoven into the generations of personal ties and human feelings that bound them together once in rural villages. On the one hand, they are able to live autonomous lives free of the network of relations, neighbors and friends who often pried into the personal lives of families'. Furthermore: 'They cannot rely on the type of network that existed in the old village. They often live in neighborhoods where they have only a nodding acquaintance with their neighbors. They assume a let-them-live-the-way-they-want attitude in regard to their neighbors. And they expect the same in return. When they must rely on someone, they usually contact relations living somewhere else, professional counsellors, teachers, city officials, or other people who are not their neighbors. Within the family, individuals maintain their own autonomous worlds. The children are just as adamant about maintaining their autonomy as their parents are. And the price children pay may be their feeling of isolation'. The article concludes that this situation 'once in a while' ends with suicide. (http:// jin.jcic.or.jp/insight/html/focus03/urban_middle/middle-class02.html)

   Japan Times (10.10.02) reports that 'relations among neighbors are weakening, and disinterest toward others is spreading even in local communities. An increase in juvenile delinquency mirrors the problems of adult society'.

45 Even though I have warned against applying western etic concepts, believing they can be given an emic interpretation, there are relatively few (but some!) objections to using 'hierarchy' as an emic term comparing Japan and the West.

46 It can of course be disputed how 'natural' this submission to seniors is experienced by the subordinates. *Asahi News* (14.3.2001) reported a scandal within the Police Department in Kanagawa. One of the officers told about how they had been hushing scandals up in order to protect their senior officers. Another officer complained that he and his colleagues were not appreciated when they gave up their weekends to work. 'We get blamed for all the failures, and our bosses get the credit for all the successful detective work', he reported.

47 Benedict (1967) shows us that even concerning international relations the Japanese used to think in hierarchical relations. Japan's participation in the

Second World War was legitimated by way of this argumentation: 'There was anarchy in the world as long as every nation had absolute sovereignty; it was necessary for her to fight to establish a hierarchy – under Japan, of course, since she alone represented a nation truly hierarchical from top to bottom and hence understood the necessity of taking "one's proper place"' (pp. 14–15).

48 Mori (1994) analyses the social problems that students experience returning to Japan from sojourns overseas. According to Mori, these students (called *ryugakusei*) 'violate the codes of behavior of Japanese society, especially the organizational culture of Japanese corporations. In other words, *ryugakusei* contaminate Japanese people by not readjusting to the society. It could even be said that *ryugakusei endanger* the moral foundation of Japanese society by undermining the organization of culture and practices of social relations in Japan' (p. 109).

49 Hsu (1975) maintains that 'the term paternalism is not often used in Japanese. It is definitely a Western term, but when it is used in Japan it is most appropriately translated as *onjo shugi*, or "kind treatment of employees"' (p. 203).

50 Let me in this connection also recall Giddens' (1984) reminder that 'structure' (or in our context, hierarchy) should not be regarded as synonymous to coercion. Structure will always imply both coercion *and* possibilities.

51 Again, we run into problems with emic and etic conecepts. Is 'gender equality' an emic concept?

52 Fukuyama (2000) argues that labour law in both Japan and Korea continues to treat men and women differently, but while 'in the West, this would be called gender discrimination; in Asia it is more often seen as an effort to protect women' (p. 132).

53 Cf. Henshall (1999), quoting to Prince Genji (c. 1004): 'If they were not fundamentally evil they would not have been born women at all' (p. 11).

54 A survey undertaken among several hundred Tokyo pupils entering elementary school in April 1998 showed that the top three professions boys would like to aim for were soccer player, baseball player and toy shop owner. For girls, bride topped the list, followed by piano instructor and florist. (Published at http://jin.jcic.or.jp/insight/html/focus05/a_women_growing_up/role_models01.html)

55 And 'the pre-eminence of authority implants in the Japanese a ready submissiveness, alongside fear and hostility. They are afraid to offer open opposition to authority and instead commit themselves to it...' (Nakane, 1970, p. 103).

56 This is how women's situation is presented in the book *Women and Travel* by Davies and Jansz (1990): 'Women in Japan are expected to take a subservient role. The renowned work ethic, the devotion to a company and a job, is greatly dependent on women's unpaid labour as housewives. Women are heavily discriminated against in the workplace and are often only taken on by companies as temporary, supplementary labour with less pay and none of the security and benefits available for full-time workers. It is also quite common for female employees to be pressurised to retire "voluntarily" when they reach thirty. Much the same level of discrimination has existed

in education and, until very recently, in almost all levels of government'
(pp. 267–8).

5. Look to Japan?

1 Powerful international organisations like 'The International Money Fund',
'The World Bank' and 'The World Trade Organisation' have typically put
these demands forward.

2 I emphasise once again that I am presenting an analytical, ideal type, of
explanation. Of course, most excluded people do not enter into criminal
careers.

3 In 'traditional' criminology this perspective would include the so-called
'control theories' (i.e. people do *not* commit crimes because they are held in
check or controlled by external forces). I have categorized this above as a (more
or less) deterministic perspective. I am well aware that control theories also
could be described as non-deterministic. Braithwaite (1989) argues that it is
'one of the attractive features of control theories that they do not conceive of
human beings as determined creatures' (p. 27). However, my 're-action'
perspective is more structural and less individually focused than traditional
control theory.

4 Cultural values, of course, have a 'double' status: they can be described as
'normative *structures*', and as such represent a given, deterministic status, and
they can be described as '*volitional* aggregates' (created by will and actively
interpreted and accommodated by each individual). However, for my discussion
of crime in a cross cultural perspective I want to focus on the human made and
humanly interpreted aspects of culture.

5 As for the seriousness and the extent of the exclusion problem Hutton (1996)
divides the British society into three groups: 30 per cent of the population
who he calls the 'disadvantaged' (i.e. unemployed or economically inactive),
30 per cent of the population who he labels 'the marginalized and the insecure'.
Finally, the third group (40 per cent of the population) is 'the privileged'
(i.e. the full time employees and the self-employed who have held their jobs
for over two years).

6 This is their formulation: 'For many decades there has been general acknowledgement of the links between crime and manifestations of social need such
as poverty, and the acceptance of a reformist agenda which seeks, therefore to
reduce crime by tackling these – the 'true causes' of crime, as it were' (p. 63).

7 Once again I would like to underline that Japan has undergone huge changes
the last 10–15 years. Increasing segregation between youth and adults is but
one of these changes. In an analysis published in a series called 'Japan
Insight', it is argued (under the headline 'Juvenile delinquency') that 'in
urban/suburban families, individuals often lead autonomous lives in separate
worlds. Teenagers when they are in their world sometimes get into difficulty
with the law' (http://jin.jcic.or.jp/insight/html/focus03/urban_middle/middle-
class02.html).

8 This argument that young people are excluded as productive or reproductive
contributors goes in tandem with the fact that the youth are also subjectified
as consumers or as targeted for the consumptive spectacle.

9 'Training children to take on responsibility in a group, for the group, is a legitimate task for schools in Japan, and cleaning is a major tool for teaching this. It's not part of a "hidden agenda"; it's part of the curriculum. It also encourages children to think of the school as theirs, as a place they each have a stake in' (Benjamin, 1997, p. 34).

10 Doi (1976) argues that both *giri* and *ninjo* have their roots deep in *amae*. He makes this distinction between those concepts: 'One might replace *amae* by the more abstract term "dependence", and say that *ninjo* welcomes dependence whereas *giri* binds human beings in a dependent relationship' (p. 35).

11 This is not to insist on any romantization or glorification of this kind of 'age embeddedness' in Japan. The coin has two sides. Complicated networks of social obligations definitely contribute to create an other-directed culture based on sensitivity and caution. However, as already documented, this description has to be supplemented with characteristics like regimentation, suppression, and the fear of losing the love of the group and significant others. Also, one should warn against confusing other-directedness with an *unconditional* altruism. As Nobuyuki (2000) points out, the Japanese 'are accustomed to a mutual aid system whereby one always gets back what one has paid in, as in the case of the pre-modern mutual assistance associations known as *ko*. Therefore people will not accept insurance systems (or pensions) that do not guarantee the eventual return of the equivalent of what one has paid in. People pay in to help themselves, not anyone who is in trouble' (p. 59). When I talk about Japanese other-directedness I am not saying anything about *motives* or *intentions* behind the observable actions. What I wrote in the section 'Japan is an other-directed, relational and contextual society' (Ch. 4) about Japanese morality should make such amplification understandable.

12 Cf. the subtitle *Emerging individualism in Japan* of Miyanaga's (1991) book *The creative edge*, or *Signs of a New Individualism* by Yamazaki, (1984). No doubt, Japan still represents a polar opposite to the West in this regard.

13 I would like to underline that this perspective might be under-communicated in my analysis. My interest has been in focusing on social conditions *preventing* crime, but obviously some of these conditions might *trigger* crime as well. The following case reports (randomly picked) illustrate this argument:

> On 7 April 2001, the police reported that a couple were arrested after allegedly trying to strangle their 22-year-old son because he wouldn't get a job (*Mainichi Daily News*, 8 April 2001).
>
> A former teacher who had been fired filed a lawsuit demanding 6 million yen from the school where she worked. The reason given by the school operator was that, as single woman, she set a poor example to the children (cf. pressure to conform to dominating values) (*Mainichi Daily News*, 28 March 2001).
>
> A man slaughtered his 19-year-old niece because he 'didn't like her lax attitude toward life' (*Mainichi Daily News*, 25 March 2001).
>
> A 17-year-old boy, who was charged with attempted murder by throwing a home-made bomb into a video shop, told the police that he did it because he was anxious about university entrance examinations and his

studies at the prefectural high school. Extreme pressure in school was what triggered the crime.

A police officer slew his female fellow officer and then took his own life because the lady had spurned him. The reason for this dreadful act (given by the head of the police department) was that 'it was an incident of unbearable shame' (*Mainichi Daily News*, 6 December 2000).

In October 2000 two youths were arrested for apparently beating a member of their gang to death after he tried to break from the group (*Mainichi Daily News*, 17 October 2000).

A 15-year-old boy killed three and injured three other members of a neighbouring family in a small community. Investigators quoted the boy as saying, 'about a week ago, my father accused me of peeping into the bathroom of the Iwasaki family's house and I developed a grudge against the family. Because members of the Iwasaki family gave me accusing looks, I decided to kill all of them'. The accusing looks represented obviously an unbearable shame to the boy. Also, the boy was afraid his father would detect that the boy had burgled the neighbour's house a week before (*The Daily Yomiuri*, 15 and 28 August 2000).

14   In addition to what has been presented in this final chapter, and to what is covered in Table 5.1, I will also refer to my discussion of the relevance of economic equality/low unemployment, as well as legislating practice as possible explaining variables to the paradox of little crime in Japan. My conclusion in this regard was that these dimensions could not be excluded, but that they certainly are of far less importance than the other dimensions.

15   McGregor (1996) quotes Richard Koo, of the Nomura Research Institute in Tokyo, saying, 'in such a society [as Japan, DL], it is difficult to say and do something which may disturb harmony. Such moves as sacking workers, viewed as mere business decisions elsewhere, in Japan take on cultural and social overtones' (pp. 3–4).

16   'Companies extract lengthy, even slavish, service from their employees, . . .' (McGregor, 1996, p. 5).

17   Braithwaite (1989, pp. 111–18, referring to Wilson and Herrnstein) gives a good historical illustration of the independent role of 'culture' in explaining crime by pointing to the experiences during the Victorian era. There was a strong decline in crime in this period, and this happened in spite of massive urbanization, immigration and a widening gulf between the classes. What else other than cultural values could explain this paradox? See also Fukuyama (2000, p. 268).

18   The other side of this story is, of course, the hardship for those who, in spite of inclusiveness, fall outside the established group structure. The status of 'outsider' is probably harder to live with in Japan than in a Western country. Cf. Stevens (1997): *On the margins of Japanese society*.

19   This perspective goes contrary to some of the critiques of the modern welfare state. Especially the conservative communitarians (but also some scholars from the 'left') argue that the omnipotent welfare state itself has contributed both to disable people and to weaken social bonding among them. Fukuyama (2000) argues that the Scandinavian welfare model has contributed to the rapid increase in divorces in these countries, because it has made it easier for women to break up from unsatisfactory relationships.

20 From *Sociologie et philsophie* (1924), here quoted from Bauman: *Liquid modernity* (2000), p. 20.

21 Edmund Burke is in the science of political philosophy often regarded as the 'founding father' of Conservatism.

22 I admit that this way of arguing may be accused of being ethnocentric. I discussed in Chapter 2 the difference between 'emic' concepts (which are specific to a particular culture) and 'etic' concepts (applicable to all cultures). *Democracy* means something different in Japan than in the West. Riesman points out that, 'people refer to organizations as "undemocratic" if there is no harmony or consensus. Thus, democracy and politics would seem anti-thetical' (referred in Nakane, 1970, p. 143). In Japan 'democracy' refers more to a form of relationship than to politics. However, this important difference does not change my basic premises for being sceptical about the Japanese political democracy. Cf. Etzioni (1994, p. 159) who argues that those who are committed to democracy, individual rights, and mutual respect will find little comfort in Japan.

23 Cf. Murray's (referred to in Bauman, 2000a) nostalgic comment: 'What filled an event with satisfaction is that *you* did it ... with a substantial responsibility resting on *your* shoulders, with a substantial amount of the good thing being *your* contribution' (p. 19).

References

Adler, F. (1983) *Nations Not Obsessed With Crime*. Rothman & co.

Alexander, J. F. (1995) *Fin de Siécle Social Theory*. Verso.

Andrews, A. A. *et al.* (1996) *Keys to the Japanese Heart and Soul*. Kodansha International Ltd.

Anleu, S. L. R. (1999) *Deviance, Conformity and Control*. Longman.

Araki, N. (1988) 'The Role of The Police In Japanese society'. In *Law and Society Review*, vol. 22, no. 5.

Arimoto, M. (1995) 'Japanese educational System Improving Ongoing Practice in Schools'. In *School Effectiveness and School Improvement*, vol. 6, no. 4.

Asahi News, 10.03.2001.

Asahi News, 25.03.2001.

Ashkenazi, M. (1991) 'Traditional Small Group Organization and Cultural Modelling in Modern Japan'. In *Human Organization*, vol. 50, no. 4.

Bacchi, C. L. (1999) *Women, Policy and Politics*. Sage Publications.

Balvig, F. and B. Kyvsgaard (1986) *Kriminalitet og ungdom*. København: Borgen.

Bauman, Z. (1998) *Globaliseringen og dens menneskelige konsekvenser*. Vidarforlaget.

Bauman, Z. (2000a) *Liquid Modernity*. Polity Press.

Bauman, Z. (2000b) *Savnet fellesskap*. Oslo: Cappelen Akademisk Forlag.

Bazemore, G. (1998) 'Restorative Justice and Earned Redemption'. In *American Behavioral Scientist*, no. 6.

Becker, C. B. (1986) 'Reasons for The Lack of Argumentation and Debate in The Far East'. In *International Journal of Intercultural Relations*, vol. 10.

Becker, C. B. (1988) 'Report From Japan: Causes and Controls of Crime in Japan'. In *Journal of Criminal Justice*, vol. 16.

Befu, H. A. (1980a) 'A Critique of The Group Model of Japanese Society'. In *Social Analysis*, vol. 5/6.

Befu, H. A. (1980b) 'The Group Model of Japanese Society and An Alternative'. In *Rice University Studies*. Rice University.

Befu, H. A. (1989) 'The Emic-Etic Distinction and Its Significance for Japanese Studies'. In Y. Sugimoto, Y. and R. Mouer (eds) *Constructs for Understanding Japan*. London.

Belsey, A. (1986) 'The New right, Social Order and Civil Liberties'. In R. Levitas (ed.): *The Ideology of The New Right*. Polity Press.

Ben-Ari, E., B. Moeran and J. Valentine (eds) (1990) *Unwrapping Japan*. Manchester University Press.

Ben-Ari, E. (1997) *Japanese Childcare. An Interpretative Study of Culture and Organization*. Kegan Paul.

Bendle, M. F. (1999) 'The Death of The Sociology of Deviance? In *Journal of Sociology*, March, vol. 35.

Benedict, R. (1967) *The Chrysanthemum and the Sword*. Routledge & Kegan Paul.

Benjamin, G. R. (1997) *Japanese Lessons. A Year in a Japanese School Through the Eyes of an American Anthropologist and Her Children*. New York University Press.

Ben-Yehuda, N. (1992) 'Criminalization and Devianization as Properties of The Social Order'. In *The Sociological Review*, no. 1.

Berger, P. L., B. Berger, and H. Kellner (1973) *The Homeless Mind*. Vintage Books.

Berger, P. L. and T. Luckmann (1966) *The Social Construction of Reality*. Penguin Books.

Berger, P. L. (1987) *The Capitalist Revolution. Fifty Propositions about Prosperity, Equality, and Liberty*. Gower.

Bestor, T. C. (1989) *Neighborhood Tokyo*. Kodansha International.

Bosanquet, N. (1983) *After The New Right*. Heinemann.

Braithwaite, J. (1989) *Crime, Shame and Re-integration*. Cambridge University Press.

Braithwaite, J. (1991) 'Poverty, Power, White-Collar Crime and The Paradoxes of Criminological Theory'. In *The Australian and New Zealand Journal of Criminology*, vol. 24.

Braithwaite, J. (1993) 'Shame and Modernity'. In *The British Journal of Criminology*, vol. 33, no. 1.

Bruun, K. and N. Christie (1985) *Den gode fiende*. Universitetsforlaget.

Buendia, H. G. (ed.) (1989) *Urban Crime: Global Trends and Policies*. The United Nations University.

Chamlin, M. B. and J. K. Cochran (1997) 'Shame, Altruism and Crime'. In *Criminology*, vol. 35. No. 2.

Christiansen, K. O. (1974) 'Industrialization, Urbanization and Crime'. In *United Nations Asia and Far East Institute For The Prevention of Crime and The Treatment of Offenders*, vol. 8.

Christie, N. (1991) *Hvis skolen ikke fantes*. Universitetsforlaget.

Christie, N. (1975) *Hvor tett et samfunn?* Ejler/Universitetsforlaget.

Christie, N. (2000) *Crime Control as Industry*. Routledge.

Clifford, W. (1976) *Crime Control in Japan*. Lexington Books.

Clifford, W. (1980) *Why Is It Safer to Live in Tokyo?* Australian Institute of Criminology, Canberra.

Cohen, A. P. (1989) *The Symbolic Construction of Community*. Routledge.

Cohen, S. (1996) 'Crime and Politics: Spot the Difference'. In *The British Journal of Sociology*, vol. 1.

Coleman, C. and J. Moynikan, (1996) *Understanding Crime Data*. Open University Press.

Cornish, D. B. and R. V. Clarke (eds) (1986) *The Reasoning Criminal. Rational Choice Perspectives on Offending*. Springer-Verlag.

Coughlin, R. (ed.) (1991) *Morality, Rationality and Efficiency. New Perspectives in Socio-Economics*. M.E. Sharpe.

Crawford, A. (1998) *Crime, Prevention and Community Safety*. Longman.

Creighton, M. R. (1990) 'Revisiting shame and guilt cultures: A forty-year pilgrimage'. In *Ethos: Journal of the Society for Psychological Anthropology*, no. 3.

Currie, E. (1989) 'Confronting Crime. Looking Toward the Twenty-First Century'. In *Justice Quarterly*, vol. 6, no. 1, March.

Currie, E. (1998) 'Crime and market society: lessons form the United States'. In P. Walton and J. Young (eds) *The New Criminology Revisited*. MacMillan, now Palgrave Macmillan.

Dahrendorf, R. (1985) *Law and Order*. Stevens & Sons, London.

Dale, P. N. (1986) *The Myth of Japanese Uniqueness*. Croom Helm and Nissan Institute for Japanese Studies, University of Oxford.

Davies, M. and Jansz, N. (eds) (1990) *Women travel. Adventures, Advice and Experience.* Rough Guides Ltd.

De Mente, B. (1992) *Discovering Cultural Japan.* NTC Publishing Books.

Die Zeit, no. 51/1999.

Doi, T. (1976) *The Anatomy of Dependence.* Kodansha International.

Doi, T. (1985). *The Anatomy of Self.* Kodansha International.

Dominion, 30.04.1999.

Dore, R. (1986) *Flexible Rigidities. Industrial Policy and Structural Adjustment in The Japanese Economy 1970–80.* London: The Athlone Press.

Dore, R. (1987) *Taking Japan Seriously. A Confucian Perspective on Leading Economic Issues.* London: The Athlone Press.

Durkheim, E. (1952) *Suicide: A Study in Sociology.* London: Routledge & Kegan Paul.

Durkheim, E. (1964) *The Division of Labour in Society.* The Free Press.

EAMM (1996) *The Japanese Experience in Social Security.* East Asian Ministerial Meeting on Caring Societies. December 5.

Edgerton, R. (1992) *Sick Societies.* Free Press.

Elias, N. (1994) *The Civilizing Process.* Blackwell.

Elias, N. and E. Dunning (1986) *Quest for Excitement: Sport and Leisure in The Civilizing Process.* Oxford: Basil Blackwell.

Elster, J. (1989) *The Cement of Society. A study of Social Order.* Cambridge University Press.

Endo, O. (1998) 'Språket speglar synen på könen'. In *Feministisk Perspektiv. Kvinnans dubbla roller. Tema: Japan*, no. 1.

Eriksen, T. H. (1994) *Kulturelle veikryss: essays om kreolisering.* Universitetsforlaget.

Esping-Andersen, G. (1990) *The Three Worlds of Welfare Capitalism.* Cambridge: Polity Press.

Esping-Andersen, G. (1997) 'Hybrid or Unique? The Japanese Welfare State Between Europe and America'. In *Journal of European Social Policy*, vol. 7 (3). Sage Publications.

Etzioni, A. (1988) *The Moral Dimension. Toward a New Economics.* The Free Press.

Etzioni, A. (1991) 'The Moral Dimension in Policy Analysis. In R. M. Coughlin (ed.) *Morality, Rationality, and Efficiency.* M.E. Sharpe.

Etzioni, A. (1994) *The Spirit of Community. The Reinvention of American Society.* Simon & Schuster.

Ezawa, M. (1990) 'Levelling Nagano to Lure the Olympics'. In *AMPO Japan-Asia Quarterly Review*, vol. 22, nos 2–3.

Fagan, J. and R. B. Freeman (1999) 'Crime and Work'. In *Crime and Justice. A Review of Research*, vol. 25.

Faulkner, D., Hough M. and Halpern, D. (1996) 'Crime and Criminal Justice'. In D. S. Halpern *Options for Britain: A Strategic Policy Review.* Aldershot.

Feministiskt Perspektiv (1998). 'Kvinnans dubbla roller'. Tema: Japan, no. 1.

Fenwick, C. R. (1985) 'Culture, Philosophy and Crime: The Japanese Experience', *International Journal of Comparative and Applied Criminal Justice*, vol. 9, no. 1.

Field, N. (1996) 'Foreword'. In McCormack *The Emptiness of Japanese Affluence.* M.E. Sharpe.

Finch, A. (2001) 'Homicide in Contemporary Japan'. In *British Journal of Criminology*, vol. 41, no. 2.

Foljanty-Jost, G. and M. Metzler (2003) 'Juvenile Delinquency in Japan: a Self-preventing Prophecy. In *Social Science Japan*, no. 25, February.

Foote, D. H. (1992) 'The Benevolent Paternalism of Japanese Criminal Justice'. In *California Law Review*, no. 2.

Friedman, M. and Friedman, R. (1980) *Free to Choose*. Harmondsworth: Penguin.

Freudenburg, W. F. (1986) 'The Density of Acquaintanceship: An Overlooked Variable in Community Research?' In *American Journal of Sociology*, vol. 92.

Fujimoto, T. (1994) *Crime Problems in Japan*. Chuo University Press.

Fukuyama, F. (1995) *Trust*. The Free Press.

Fukuyama, F. (2000) *The Great Disruption*. Profile books.

Futaba, I. (1984) 'Crime, Confession and Control in Contemporary Japan'. *Law in Context*.

Garfinkel, E. (1967) *Studies in Ethnomethodology*. Prentice-Hall.

Garland, D. (1996) 'The Limits of The Sovereign State'. In *British Journal of Criminology*, vol. 36, no. 4.

Gelsthorpe, L. and A. Morrison (1990) *Feminist Perspectives in Criminology*. Open University Press.

George, V. and Wilding, P. (1976) *Ideology and Social Welfare*. Routledge.

Giddens, A. (1984) *The Constitution of Society: Outline of a Theory of Structuration*. University of California Press.

Giddens, A. (1990) *The Consequences of Modernity*. Polity Press.

Giddens, A. (1991) *Modernity and Self-Identity. Self and Society in the Late Modern Age*. Polity Press.

Giddens, A. (2000) *The Third Way and its Critics*. Polity Press.

Gilling, D. and A. Barton 'Crime Prevention and Community Safety'. In *Critical Social Policy*, vol. 17 (3).

Goffman, E. (1958) *The Presentation of Self in Everyday Life*. University of Edinburgh.

Gold, R. L. (1985) *Ranching, Mining, and the Human Impact of Natural Resource Development*. Transaction Books.

Goldman, A. (1994) 'The Centrality of Ningensei to Japanese Negotiating and Interpersonal Relationships: Implications for U.S.–Japanese Communication', *International Journal of Intercultural Relations*, no. 1.

Gottfredson, M. R. and Hirschi, T. (1990) *A General Theory of Crime*, Stanford University Press.

Gould, A. (1993) *Capitalist Welfare Systems: A Comparison of Japan, Britain and Sweden*. Longman.

Guneriussen, W. (1988) *Tvang og autonomi*. University of Tromsø.

Guneriussen, W. (1999) *Å forstå det moderne*. Tano Aschehoug.

Habermas, J. (1976) *Legitimation Crisis*. Heinemann.

Hagan, J. (1994) 'Crime, Inequality and Efficiency'. In A. Glyn and D. Miliband *Paying for Inequality*, Rivers Oram Press.

Haley, J. (1998) 'Apology and Pardon. Learning from Japan'. *American Behavioral Scientist*, vol. 41, no. 6.

Hechter, M. and S. Kanzawa (1993) 'Group Solidarity and Social Order in Japan'. *Journal of Theoretical Politics* 5 (4).

Heiland, H. G., L. I. Shelley and H. Katoh (1992) (eds) *Crime and Control in Comparative Perspectives*. Walter de Gruyter.

Hendry, J. (1993) *Wrapping Culture. Politeness, Presentation and Power in Japan and Other Societies*. Clarendon Press.

Hendry, J. (1999) *An Anthropologist in Japan*. Routledge.

Henshall, K. G. (1999) Dimensions of Japanese Society. MacMillan Press, now Palgrave Macmillan.

Hidaka, R. (1980) *The Price of Affluence. Dilemmas of Contemporary Japan.* Kodansha International.

Hiroshi, K. (1997) *The Inscrutable Japanese.* Kodansha International.

Hirsch, F. (1976) *Social Limits to Growth.* Harvard University Press.

Hirschi, T. (1969) *Causes of Delinquency.* University of California Press.

Hirschmann, A. O. (1986) *Rival Views of Market Society. And Other Recent Essays.* Viking Penguin.

Hobsbawm, E. (1994) *The Age of Extremes.* Michael Joseph.

Hofstede, G. (1998) 'A Case For Comparing Apples With Oranges'. In *International Journal of Comparative Sociology,* no. 1.

Hofstede, G. and M. H. Bond (1988) *The Confucius Connection – From Cultural Roots to Economic Growth.* In American Management Association, vol. 4.

Høigård, C. (1997) 'Hva er kriminologi?' In Høigård and L. Finstad *Kriminologi.* Pax.

Hsu, F. L. K. (1975) *Iemoto: The Heart of Japan.* Halsted Press.

Hunter, A. (1974) *Symbolic Communities.* The University of Chicago Press.

Huntington, S. P. (1993) 'The Clash of Civilizations?' *Foreign Affairs,* no. 3.

Hutton, W. (1996) *The State We're In.* Vintage.

Illich, I. (1973) *Tools For Conviviality.* Fontana/Collins.

Illich, I. (ed.) (1977) *Disabling Professions.* Marion Boyars.

Ito, K. (1993) 'Research On the Fear of Crime: Perceptions and Realities of Crime in Japan', *Crime and Delinquency,* vol. 39, no. 3.

Ito, M. (1998) 'The Status of the Individual in Japanese Religions: Implications for Japan's Collectivistic Social Values', *Social Compass,* no. 45.

"Japan" (1985) *Time-Life,* translated by Isak Rogde, Gyldendal.

Japan Echo, vol. 15, Special Issue, 1988, vol. 24, no. 2, 1997, vol. 15, Special Issue, 1998, vol. 25, no. 3, 1998, vol. 27, no. 5, 2000.

Japan Government. http://jin.jcic.or.jp.

Japan Insight. 'The Urban Middle-Class Society. Middle-Class Anxieties'. http://jin.jcic.or.jp/insight/html/focus03/urban_middle/middle–class02.html

Japan Times, 09.05.2000.

Japan Times, 20.12.2000.

Japan Times, 02.02.2002.

Japanese Culture: A Primer for Newcomers. http://japaninfo.esmartweb.com/FAQ-Primer.html.

Jolivet, M. (1993) *Japan: The Childless Society? The Crisis of Motherhood.* Routledge.

Jordan, B. (1996) *A Theory of Poverty and Social Exclusion.* Polity Press.

Kalland, A. (1986) *Japan bak fasaden,* Cappelen.

Kalland, A. (1988) 'Kvinner i det moderne Japan'. In *Orientens kvinner. Kvinnenes kulturhistorie,* K. Vogt, K. Gundersen and S. Lie (eds), Universitetsforlaget.

Kaplan, D. E. and A. Dubro (1986) *Yakuza. The Explosive Account of Japan's Criminal Underworld.* Addison-Wesley Publishing Company.

Katz, R. (1998) 'What Japan Teaches Us Now'. *The American Prospect.* September–October.

Kawai, H. (1998) 'A Buddhist Remedy'. *The Unesco Courier: A Window Open on the World,* no. 2.

Kersten, J. (1993) 'Street Youths, *Bosozoku,* and *Yakuza*: Subculture Formation and Societal Reactions in Japan', *Crime and Delinquency,* vol. 39, no. 3.

Kitamura, T. *et al.* (1999) 'Frequencies of Child Abuse in Japan: Hidden but Prevalent Crime', *International Journal of Offender Therapy and Comparative Criminology,* 43 (1).

Klein, N. (2000) *No Logo*. Flamingo.

Komiya, N. (1999) 'A Cultural Study of The Low Crime Rate in Japan'. In *The British Journal of Criminology*, vol. 39, no.3.

Kühne, H. (1994) 'Comparison in Good and Bad: Criminality in Japan and Germany'. *Forensic Science International*, no. 69.

Kumar (1983) 'Pre-Capitalist And Non-Capitalist Factors In The Development of Capitalism: Fred Hirsch And Joseph Schumpeter'. In A. Ellis and K. Kumar *Dilemmas of Liberal Democracies*. Tavistock Publications.

Kyvsgaard, B. (1991) 'Fald I Boerne- og ungdomskriminaliteten: mulige forklaringer. In *Nordisk tidsskrift for kriminalvidenskab*, no. 1. København.

Ladbrook, D. A. (1988) 'Why are Crime Rates Higher in Urban Than in Rural Areas? Evidence From Japan'. In *Australian and NZ Journal of Criminology*, no. 21.

Lasch, C. (1979) *The Culture of Narcissism – American Life in an Age of Diminishing Expectations*. W. W. Norton & Company.

Lea, J. (2002) *Crime and modernity*. Sage Publications.

Leonardsen, D. (1993) *Rammer for velferdspolitikken*. Skrifter, ODH, no. 79.

Leonardsen, D. (1996) *Den sosiale konstruksjon av OL. Om lokalbefolkningens møte med en mega-begivenhet*. HIL, no. 9.

Leonardsen, D. (1998) *Community Lost or Freedom Gained?* HIL, no. 30.

Leonardsen, D. (2002) 'The Impossible Case of Japan'. In *Australian and New Zealand Journal of Criminology*, vol. 35, no. 2.

Leonardsen, D. (forthcoming) *Crime in Japan – a Lesson for Western Societies?*

Leonardsen, D. (in print) 'Crime in Japan – a lesson for criminological theory?'

Levine, D. N. (1985) *The Flight From Ambiguity: Essays in Social and Cultural Theory*. University of Chicago Press.

Levitas, R. (ed.) (1986) *The Ideology of The New Right*. Polity Press.

Levitas, R. (1996) 'The Concept of Social Exclusion and the New Durkheimian Hegemony'. *Critical Social Policy*, vol. 16 (1).

Lincoln, E. J. (1998) 'Japan's Financial Mess'. *Foreign Affairs*, no. 3.

Lockwood, D. (1964) 'Social Integration and System Integration'. In G. K. Zollschan and W. Hirsch (eds): *Explorations in Social Change*. Routledge.

Lockwood, D. (1999) 'Civic Integration And Social Cohesion'. In Gough and Olofsson *Capitalism and Social Cohesion*. MacMillan Press/St. Martin's Press.

McCann, H. J. (1998) *The Works of Agency. On Human Action, Will, and Freedom*. Cornell University Press.

McClosky, H. and Schaar, J. H. (1965) 'Psychological Dimensions of Anomie'. In *American Sociological Review*, vol. 30.

McCormack, G. (1996) *The Emptiness of Japanese Affluence*. M.E. Sharpe.

MacFarlane, A. (1995) 'Law and Custom in Japan: some comparative reflections'. *Continuity and Change*, 10 (3).

McGregor, R. (1996) *Japan Swings*. Allen & Unwin.

McVeigh, B. J. (1997) *Life in a Japanese Women's College*. Routledge.

Magnussen, F. (1983) *Om å bli voksen*. Universitetsforlaget.

Mainichi Daily News, 13.10.2000.

Mainichi Daily News, 17.10.2000.

Mainichi Daily News, 06.12.2000.

Mainichi Daily News, 07.12.2000.

218   *References*

Mainichi Daily News, 14.02.2001.
Mainichi Daily News, 25.03.2001.
Mainichi Daily News, 08.04.2001.
Marcuse, H. (1965) 'Repressiv toleranse'. In Marcuse *et al. Om toleranse.* Pax.
Marshall, T. H. (1950) *Citizenship, Social Class and Other Essays.* Cambridge University Press.
Massaro, T. M. (1997) 'The Meanings of Shame'. In *Psychology, Public Policy and Law,* vol. 4, no. 4.
Merton, R. K. (1968) *Social Theory and Social Structure.* N. Y.
Mieko, Y. (1999) 'Domestic Violence: Japan's 'Hidden Crime'. In *Japan Quarterly,* no. 3.
Miyanaga, K. (1991) *The Creative Edge. Emerging Individualism in Japan.* Transaction Publishers.
Moeran, B. and J. Valentine (1990) 'Unwrapping Japan: Society and Culture in Anthropological Perspective. In Ben-Ari *et al.*
Mori, S. (1994) *The Social Problems of Students Returning to Japan from Sojourns Overseas: A Social Constructionist Study.* Dissertation. University of California, Santa Cruz.
Morrison, A. (1987) *Women and Criminal Justice.* Basil Blackwell.
Moss, G. (1997) 'Explaining the Absence of Violent Crime Among the Semai of Malaysia. Is Criminological Theory up to the Task?' *Journal of Criminal Justice,* vol. 25, no. 3.
Miyanaga, K. (1991) *The Creative Edge: Emerging Individualism in Japan.* New Brunswick: Transaction Publishers.
Miyazawa, S. (1992) *Policing in Japan.* NY Press.
Mozelis, N. (1995) *Sociological Theory. What Went Wrong?* Routledge.
Nafstad, P. (undated) *Den klassiske sosiologien og det moderne samfunn.* Lillehammer College.
Nakane, C. (1970) *Japanese Society.* University of California Press.
Neapolitan, J. L. (1996) 'Cross-national Crime Data: Some Unaddressed Problems'. *Journal of Crime and Justice,* no. 19.
Neapolitan, J. L. (1999) 'A Comparative Analysis of Nations with Low and High Levels of Violent Crime'. *Journal of Criminal Justice,* vol. 27, no. 3.
Newman, G. R. (ed.) (1980) *Crime and Deviance. A Comparative Perspective.* Sage Publications.
Newsweek, 21.02.00.
Nobuyuki, K. (2000) 'Call for a Return to Popular Morality'. In *Japan Echo,* June.
Nosco, P. (1998) 'The Religious Dimensions of Confucianism'. In *Japan. Philosophy East and West: A Quarterly of Comparative Philosophy,* no. 1.
Numata, H. (1999) 'Das Europäische als das Vertraute und das Fremde in der Japanischen Kultur'. In Z.f.Päd., 45, no. 3.
Nygaard, T. (1995) *Den lille sosiologiboka.* Oslo: Universitetsforlaget.
Offe, K. (1984) *Contradictions of the Welfare State* (ed. J. Keane). The MIT press.
Olaussen, L. P. (1996a) 'Kriminalstatistikk og virkelighet'. Politihøgskolen, PHS Småskrifter 1996: 1.
Olaussen, L. P. (1996b) 'Kriminalstatistikk som målestokk for kriminalitetsutviklingen'. Institute of Criminology, Stensilserien, no. 85.
Olofsson, G. (1999) 'Embeddedness and Integration'. In Gough and Olofsson (eds) *Capitalism and Social Cohesion.* MacMillan Press/St.Maritin's Press.

Olson (1998) 'Splittrad kvinnorörelse'. In *Feministiskt Perspektiv. Kvinnans dubbla rolle. Tema: Japan*, no. 1.

Park, R. E. (1952) *Human Communities*. Glencoe, Free Press.

Parker, L. C. (1987) *The Japanese Police System Today. An American Perspective*. Kodansha International.

Parsons, T. (1951) *The Social System*. Glencoe, The Free Press.

Peak, L. (1989) 'Learning to Become Part of the Group: The Japanese Child's Transition to Preschool Life'. *The Journal of Japanese Studies*, 15.

Pfohl, S. J. (1994) *Images of Deviance and Social Control*. McGraw-Hill.

Polanyi, K. (1944) *The Great Transformation*. Beacon Press.

Rasmussen, J. (1996) *Sosialisering og læring i det refleksivt moderne*. Cappelen.

Riesman, D. (1961) *The Lonely Crowd: a study of the changing American character*. With N. Glazer and R. Denney. Yale University Press.

Rohlen, T. P. (1989) 'Order in Japanese Society: Attachment, Authority and Routine'. *Journal of Japanese Studies*. 15 (1).

Rosenfeld, R. and S. F. Mesner (1994) 'Crime and the American Dream'. In *Advances in Criminological Theory* 6 (1), pp. 159–81.

Sano, K. (1995) 'Japanese Mentality and Behaviour – Based on Indigenous Japanese Culture'. *Acta Neurochirurgica*, no. 132.

Saunders, P. (1981) *Social Theory and the Urban Question*. Hutchinson University Press.

Schneider, H. J. (1992) 'Crime and Its Contol in Japan and in The Federal Republic of Germany', *International Journal of Offender Therapy and Comparative Criminology*. 36 (4).

Schutz, A. and T. Luckmann (1974) *The Structures of Life-World*. Heinemann.

Sennett, R. (1998) *The Corrosion of Character: The Personal Consequences of Work In The New Capitalism*. New York: W.W. Norton.

Shelley, R. (1993) *Culture Shock! Japan. A Guide to Customs and Etiquette*. Platypus Förlag.

Shikita, M. and S. Tsuchia (1993) *Crime and Criminal Policy in Japan*. Springer-Verlag.

Simmel, G. (1959) *Social Change in the Industrial revolution*. University of Chicago Press.

Singer, K. (1973) *Mirror, Sword and Jewel. A Study of Japanese Characteristics*. Croom Helm.

Skolnick, J. H. (1995) 'What Not to Do About Crime'. In *Criminology*, vol. 33, no. 1.

Skaarderud, F. (1998) *Uro: en reise i det moderne selvet*. Oslo: Aschehoug.

Slagstad, R. (1978) 'Det statskapitalistiske system'. In Slagstad (ed.) *Om Staten*. UniPax.

Smelser, N. J. (1967) 'Processes of Social Change'. In Smelser: *Sociology: An Introduction*. Wiley International Edition.

Smith, A. (1976) *The Theory of Moral Sentiments* (ed. by D. Rapael and A. Macfie). Clarendon Press.

Smith, R. J. (1983) *Japanese Society*. Cambridge University Press.

Steinhoff, P. G. (1993) 'Policing in Japan – A Study On Making Crime'. In *Law and Society Review*, no. 4.

Stevens, C. S. (1997) *On the Margins of Japanese Society. Volunteers and the Welfare of the Urban Underclass*. Routledge.

Sugimoto, Y. (1997) *An Introduction to Japanese Society*. Cambridge University Press.

Takahashi, K. (1991) *Structure of Submission to Authority in Japanese Society: The Interaction Between Benevolence and Obedience Under the Influence of Confucian Philosophy*. Japan Centre for Economic Research.

Tanaka, H. (ed.) (1976) *The Japanese Legal System*. University of Tokyo Press.

Taylor, I. (ed.) (1990) *The Social Effects of Free Market Policies*. Harvester Wheatsheaf.

Taylor, I. (ed.) (1998) *Crime and Political Economy*. Ashgate.

Taylor-Gooby (1997) 'In defense of Second-Best Theory: State, Class and Capital in Social Policy'. *Journal of Social Policy*, vol. 26, no 2.

The Daily Yomiuri, 15.08.2000.

The Daily Yomiuri, 28.08.2000.

Thornton, R. Y. and K. Endo (1992) *Preventing Crime in America and Japan*. M.E. Sharpe Inc.

Titmuss, R. H. (1974) *Social Policy. An introduction*. Allen & Unwin.

Triandis, H. C. (1994) *Culture and Social Behavior*. McGraw-Hill.

Triandis, H. C. (1995) *Individualism and Collectivism*. Westview Press.

Umehara, T. (1992) 'Ancient Japan Shows Postmodernism the Way'. *NPQ*, Spring.

US Federal Research Division (1994) *Japan. A Country Study* (ed. by R. Dolan and R. Worden).

van Wolferen, K. (1989) *The Enigma of Japanese Power*. Alfred Knopf.

Vogel, E. (1979) *Japan as no. 1. Lessons for America*. Harvard University Press.

von Wright, G. H. (1994) *Myten om fremskrittet*. Cappelen.

Wallerstein, A. (1995) *After Liberalism*. New York: New Press.

Watts, R. (1996a) 'John Braithwaite and Crime, Shame and Reintegration: Some Reflections on Theory and Criminology'. In *The Australian and New Zealand Journal of Criminology*, vol. 29, no. 2.

Watts, R. (1996b) 'Unemployment, the Underclass and Crime in Australia: A Critique'. In *The Australian and New Zealand Journal of Criminology*, vol. 29, no. 1.

Weber, M. (1964) *The Theory of Social and Economic Organization*. New York: The Free Press.

Westermann, T. D. and J. W. Burfeind (1991) *Crime and Justice in Two Societies*. Brooks/Cole.

White, M. (1987) 'The Virtue of Japanese Mothers: Cultural Definitions of Women's Lives'. In *Daedalus: Journal of the American Academy of Arts and Sciences*, no. 3.

White, M. (1992) 'Home Truths: Women and Social Change in Japan'. In *Daedalus: Journal of American Academy of Arts and Sciences*, no. 4.

White Paper on Crime 1998. Research and Training Institute. Ministry of Justice.

White Paper on Crime 1999. Research and Training Institute. Ministry of Justice.

White Paper on Crime 2000. Research and Training Institute. Ministry of Justice.

Wilkins, L. T. (1980) 'World Crime. To Measure or Not to Measure?' In G. R. Newman *Crime and Deviance. A Comparative Perspective*. Sage Publications.

Wirth, L. (1938) 'Urbanism as a Way of Life'. In *American Journal of Sociology*, vol. 44.

Wolf, R. A. and A. Wallace (1991) *Contemporary Sociological Theory. Continuing the Classical Tradition*. Prentice Hall.

Wrong, D. (1961) 'The Oversocialized Conception of Man in Modern Sociology', *American Sociological Review*. 26.

Wrong, D. (1994) *The Problem of Order*. The Free Press.

Yamazaki, M. (1984) 'Signs of a New Individualism'. In *Japan Echo*, vol. 11, no. 1.

Yomiuri Shimbun, 20.02.01.

Young, J. (1999) *The Exclusive Society*. Sage Publications.

Yoshida, T. (2000) 'Confession, Apology, Repentance, and Settlement out-of-court in the Japanese Criminal Justice System', *Conference paper.*

Ziehe, T. and H. Stubenrauch (1992) *Ny ungdom og usedvanlige læreprocesser.* Politisk revy.

Zoellner, L. (1992) *Fakta om barn i Japan.* Gyldendal.

Østerberg, D. (1988) *Metasociology. An Inquiry into the Origins and Validity of Social Thought.* Norwegian University Press.

Åm, E. (1981) *Japansk barnehage. Vindu mot en fremmed kultur.* Universitetsforlaget.

Index

Printed in the United States
134273LV00003B/12/A